NU SUN

NU SUN

ASIAN-AMERICAN
VOYAGES   500 B.C.

by

GUNNAR THOMPSON, Ph.D.

Pioneer Publishing Co.
Fresno, CA
1989

Library of Congress Catalog Card Number: 88-83728
ISBN 0-9621990-0-1

Library of Congress Cataloging-in-Publication Data:

Thompson, Gunnar   1946 -
Nu Sun.
Bibliography: p.
Includes index.

1. America--Discovery and exploration--Pre-Columbian; 2.
Indians--Foreign influences; 3. Indians--Maya;   4. China--
Antiquities; I. Title.

Printed in the United States of America

Published by Pioneer Publishing Co.
2350 E. Gettysburg Avenue
Fresno, CA 93726

for the sunshine poet

A Note of Special Thanks

Grateful appreciation is extended to the Asian Art Museum of San Francisco, the Kroeber Library at the University of California, the Honolulu Academy of Art, the Seattle Art Museum, the East Asia Museum of Stockholm, the Berlin Museum, the Museum of Anthropology in Mexico City, the British Museum, the Wisconsin Natural History Society Library, the University of Hawaii, the University of Washington, and the University of Wisconsin for sharing their manuscripts and collections. Without the previous efforts of countless scholars, whose work is gratefully acknowledged, the discovery of Nu Sun's voyage would have been impossible.

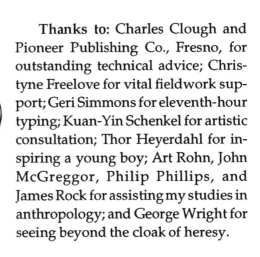

Thanks to: Charles Clough and Pioneer Publishing Co., Fresno, for outstanding technical advice; Christyne Freelove for vital fieldwork support; Geri Simmons for eleventh-hour typing; Kuan-Yin Schenkel for artistic consultation; Thor Heyerdahl for inspiring a young boy; Art Rohn, John McGreggor, Philip Phillips, and James Rock for assisting my studies in anthropology; and George Wright for seeing beyond the cloak of heresy.

Thanks to Joseph Satin; Bob and MaryAnn Ness, Kim, Shaine, and Elise; Thor Thompson; Lyn Tebrugge; Linda Martinez; Rick, Aud, and Susan Matland; Kathy Ryan; Jodi Lehman; Dave Berger; Sharon Chapman; Pat Teggatz; Nancy and Nicole Richard; Dave and Bonnie Dutton; Carol Bartholomew; Everett Stude; Doug and Lucinda Easterling; Ned and Mary Quistorff; Stefan, Margaretha, and Max Jonsson; Beth Starz; Joann Anton; Dave Clemmons; Susanne Bruyerre; Beth Feingold; Barb and Ken Langland; Scott Spencer; Dale Harris; Robert England; Toni Hammarlund; Jane Howard; Marjory Kennedy; Lanny Neider; Amanda Modorno; JD Bruinier; Marina Sanwanish; Coleen Trousdale; Wendy Wilson; Susan Lundgren; Patti Buhler; Bob Fraser; Rhude and Jenny Thompson; Tom and Nancy Word; Greg, Mike, and Claudia Greco; Monte Regier, Carole Moor, and Sam Alvarado for their generous support; and credit Florence and Roy for divine inspiration.

Contents

NOTE ON THE ILLUSTRATIONS: Drawings are by the author as derived from sources documented in the Appendix. Details of the originals have been simplified, where necessary, to make otherwise complex or cluttered designs more legible to the reader. The letter "A" is used to designate artifacts from East Asia, while "M" denotes artifacts found in Meso-America.

Preface

This is the true story of Asian voyages to America during the period from 500 B.C. to A.D. 900. Painstaking research has finally revealed a pattern of transoceanic migration and trade at levels previously regarded as impossible by leading scholars.

New evidence clearly shows that Asian explorers traveled to the New World more than two thousand years before Columbus. They sailed to the Pacific coast between Guatemala and Honduras, where they established a trading colony among the primitive Mayan tribes. At that time, the Mayans were in conflict with a more powerful society to the north called the "Olmecs." Indeed, the Olmecs used the Mayans as a source of slaves, tribute, and human sacrifice. The arrival of Asian explorers gave the Mayan people both the hope of gaining their freedom and the means to make it possible.

The new colony served as the foundation for the first great commercial alliance in the Americas--with trade routes spanning the Pacific Ocean to China and Indonesia. A host of Mayan tribes joined together into a confederacy that derived its artistic, religious, and political inspiration from the Asian colony. This was the beginning of an ancient civilization that endured for more than a thousand years.

Intriguing similarities between Asian and Meso-American artifacts have long encouraged speculation regarding trans-Pacific cultural contacts. However, prior theorists have failed to substantiate a valid claim with respect to the means of contact or the impact of Old-World cultures on the development of New-World civilization. *Nu Sun* is the first conclusive documentation of the fundamental and enduring role played by Asian merchants in the formulation of Mayan religion, astronomy, metal casting, architecture, writing, and commerce.

In the past, skeptics have questioned whether Asian explorers had the means of sailing across the ocean. *Nu Sun* proves that it was done.

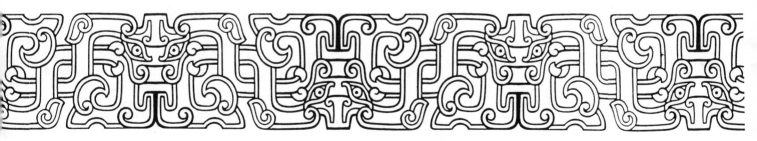

Merchant of the China Sea

Let the world know the secrets of the past.

From the shadows of time comes an amazing discovery: during the sixth century B.C., Asian merchants crossed the Pacific and established a colony in Central America. For decades, scholars and have sought to determine if native Americans could have developed civilization without assistance from the Old World. Now, thanks to an extensive research effort, it is clearly evident that the Mayan civilization was a direct consequence of Asian contact.

Trans-Pacific voyages were destined to occur--for it is the nature of our species to challenge the unknown. Even before the Asians had constructed ships capable of mastering the treacherous seas of the Pacific Ocean, there were gallant men eager to set out on the adventure of a lifetime. And when the ships were available, sailors and merchants began their journey towards the east.

They had no way of knowing they were following the pathway of prehistoric hunters who had migrated from Siberia to North America nearly twenty thousand years ago. At that time, there existed a land bridge, called Beringa, that stretched from one continent to the other. The existence of Beringa was the result of a dramatic change in the world's climate producing the great Pleistocene Ice Age. As glaciers grew to enormous proportions in the Arctic, the oceans receded from the shallow areas of Alaska and Siberia.

The climate was more temperate then, allowing the people we call the Paleo-Indians to follow migrating animals across the plains of Beringa. These primitive hunters were the inadvertent "discoverers" of North America--a land of virgin forests, smoking mountains, saber-toothed tigers, gigantic bears, mastodons, and salmon-filled streams. With the passing of millennia, their descendants increased in number as a consequence of the ample food supply and the absence of prior human inhabitants. The land was theirs, and they pushed steadily onward, staking claim to the southern territories, until they crossed the Isthmus of Panama and reached what is now South America. Then the climates of the world changed once more, and the great ice caps of the North and South Poles began to melt. The seas rose higher and higher, flooding across Beringa until the land bridge was no more. The passage to America was closed, and it would remain so until the inhabitants of the region devised ways of making ships that could withstand the rigors of ocean travel.

For many generations, travel within the New World was restricted by the climate and the primitive culture. Unlike Europe and Asia, there were no horses to carry the burden of man's ever increasing accumulation of possessions. Some people managed to construct large rafts using primitive stone tools, but these were awkward to sail, and often they were victims of the unpredictable winds and currents of the seas. A more versatile craft came into being sometime during the Neolithic Age. This ingenious vessel, called the kayak, was well suited for fishing and hunting small game, but it was not very useful for long-distance travel. Indeed, it could go only as far as the person inside could paddle. Kayaks were constructed from bent saplings and animal hides--making them light enough to transport for short distances on land, and easy enough to produce from natural materials. They were so effective as a means for food gathering and local travel, that they became the central feature of Northwest Coast American cultures--until the advent of the dugout canoe.

With kayaks and canoes, the indigenous peoples of America maintained trade relations with their neighbors, traveling from settlement to settlement and from island to island. In the far north, the Aleut Indians and the Eskimos traveled among the Aleutian islands, which stretch from Siberia to Alaska. It seems unlikely that many individuals traversed the entire distance between the continents, because most people lived short, arduous lives in villages and cultures that placed a high premium on the menfolks looking after their tribal responsibilities. Farther north, the inclement weather, high seas, and westerly currents were sufficient to deter weekend-warriors who fancied a trip to the far west. Nevertheless, as the ages passed and boat building technology improved, the hunters of the sea were bound to expand the distance of their travels. Some hardy outdoorsmen eventually made the crossing between the outer Aleutian Islands and Siberia. These travelers brought along legends from their homeland--tales of the mythical heroes that had sustained their tribesmen for many generations. They may have called their home The Land of The Raven--a name used by the natives of the Northwest American Coast to honor their spiritual ancestor and magical patron, or they may have called it The Land of The Great Bear--out of respect for the giant creatures of the forest. Regardless of its name, the stories they told about the magnificent cultures and lodges of the people of the Northwest Coast were sure to impress the people of Siberia.

By the sixth century B.C., Chinese traders occasionally visited the distant Siberian outposts as part of a commercial network of shipping lanes that stretched along the Asian coast from Japan to Indonesia. In Siberia, these gregarious merchants traded soybeans and millet for gold, ivory, and furs. They also brought iron tools--which were even more valuable to the inhabitants of the north than gold. It

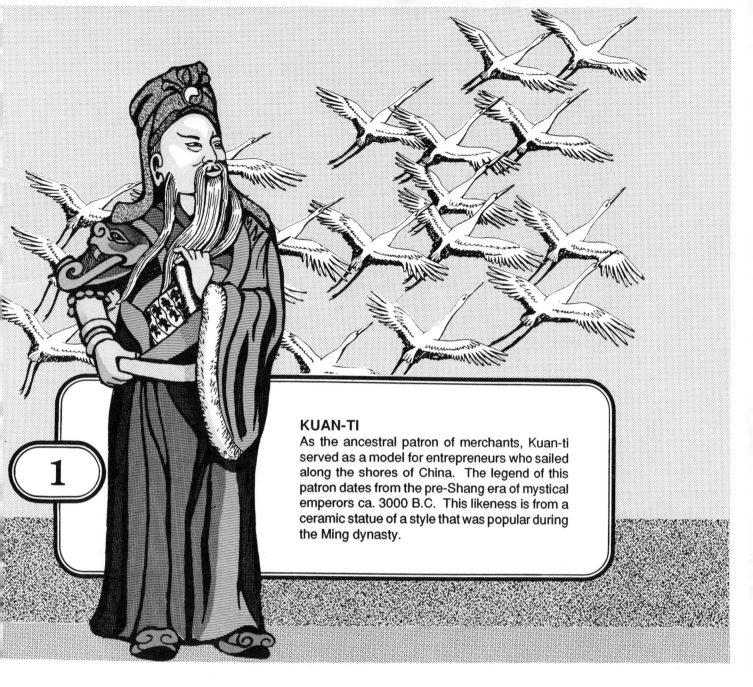

KUAN-TI
As the ancestral patron of merchants, Kuan-ti served as a model for entrepreneurs who sailed along the shores of China. The legend of this patron dates from the pre-Shang era of mystical emperors ca. 3000 B.C. This likeness is from a ceramic statue of a style that was popular during the Ming dynasty.

1

was the artistic qualities of gold which made it a prized medium for the manufacture of jewelry and export to the wealthy inhabitants of mainland China.

Surely, Asian merchants would have been intrigued by the sagas of Raven's Land--a mystical place that was known to the Chinese as the Isle of The Blest. They must have envisioned golden opportunities for trade with inhabitants of the fabled land as they sailed the long haul between China's outer islands and the Siberian settlements.

It has been the history of our species to transform inspiration into reality. This is a uniquely human enterprise that requires planning, contemplation, organization, and effort. It is not an arena for the foolhardy--or the timid. Skill is required to achieve success, and perseverance in the face of boredom and danger is equally important. Surely, there were more than a few Asian merchants who met these criteria. Precisely who they were is unknown, although the evidence suggests that the earliest merchant expedition to the Americas was predominantly Chinese in its cultural orientation.

The Chinese are regarded as the most likely promoters of such an expedition, due to their advanced technological achievements in shipbuilding and navigation, their involvement in long-distance commercial networks on the China Seas, and the semi-independent status of the merchant class which eagerly crossed the boundaries of nations. Furthermore, the preponderance of archaeological evidence from ancient Meso-America indicates that the earliest contacts were of Chinese derivation. Even so, the crews of merchant vessels were likely to include sailors from various ports comprising their routes of trade. Therefore, it seems likely that a merchant expedition to America would have consisted of a broad spectrum of Asian ethnic groups.

The starting point of the voyage may well have been Hokkaido--a large island to the north of Japan. Several factors suggest this location: it lies in a strategic position for launching an early spring expedition; it was a popular rendezvous for travelers bound for Siberia; and it was far enough from the imperial Chinese bureaucracy to escape the most dreaded imposition of governments: taxation!

A bay located somewhere along the western shore of the island probably served as the gathering place for a small fleet of oceangoing junks. The season was most likely early spring--after the hardest winter storms had spent themselves thrashing about over the ocean; the time of embarkation was probably early dawn. Indeed, that is when most fishermen, farmers, and entrepreneurs choose to begin their day's work, or undertake a long journey. Regardless of the exact date, or location, there must have been a spectacular vista along the horizon. According to the customs of the Orient, no ordinary day would have been adequate for such a momentous occasion. Either the dawn blazed forth in brilliant golden and azure hues, or the captains would choose to wait for a better day. That was the tradition of people who lived in harmony with the seasons, and amid the ageless beauty of the Orient they have lived that way for thousands of years.

The scene of departure is not difficult to imagine, as the coastal fishing villages and harbors of Japan have been the frequent subjects of landscape paintings on silk. These surreal images depict small villages nestled along fog-enshrouded mountains. In the growing twilight, a fleet of vessels may be seen huddled close to shore, as gentle waves swish against wooden hulls, and bare masts sway with the rhythm of the seas. Restless sailors stirred beneath the coarse blankets strewn along the decks, snoring and moaning as they resisted the encroaching daylight on the sanctuary of their dreams.

A solitary figure stood silently on the aft deck of the largest ship--his eyes gazing upon the disappearing constellation of Gemini. This was the admiral of the fleet--a captain of the ages--caught in communion with the heavens as he sought to grasp the meaning of his unfolding destiny. His wisdom was tempered by countless voyages, and it guided his thoughts as he stood beneath the fading night sky. His keen vision penetrated deeply the soul of nature--the fathomless wellspring of creative power that Asian mystics regard as the source of wisdom, fortitude, and compassion. From its heartbeat came the patterns of the earth, sky, and sea. They were the patterns that ruled the course of events and established the threshold between success and disaster.

From the stillness of a distant shore came the rushing flutter of a thousand wings. A flock of cranes rose skyward, their porcelain-white forms moving in graceful rhythm--like ballerinas dancing pirouettes before their king. Such an omen brought a smile to the sage. Nature had spoken. There could be no doubt that the forces of the cosmos were in proper balance, making the seas calm and the winds reliable for ocean travel. The time had arrived for departure to a land beyond dreams--a New World.

Unfortunately, we do not have an authentic portrait of the merchant admiral. Such a void in the historical record need not prevent us from drawing some assumptions about his appearance, however, as we can surmise much from what we know about the Oriental races and cultures. His features were probably much like those of his contemporaries which are portrayed in ceramic statues of the Ming dynasty (Figure 1). A robust countenance, flowing white beard, and subtle smile are not uncommon of the older Chinese, while silk and fur garments were traditional among the wealthy merchant class.

Regardless of his true appearance, it is important for us to have some image of the merchant admiral in mind, in order to help us appreciate the human aspect of his achievements. Indeed, it is a common practice in historical reconstruction to choose a model figure to represent an individual of historical importance. This has been the case with Jesus Christ, Christopher Columbus, Leif Ericsson, and many others for whom real-life portraits are not available.

Who was the leader of this epic Asian voyage?

The answer to that question may never be known. In the annals of Chinese history, the admiral's name has gone unrecorded. Considering the nature of ancient Chinese society, an omission of this magnitude is hardly surprising. There were numerous circumstances that would explain such an oversight by ancient historians. One obvious reason relates to the typical social standing of merchants in the early days of the empire. Even wealthy ship owners were generally regarded as servants of the establishment, rather than its masters. Consequently, it is unlikely that his activities would have warranted mention in chronicles that were reserved for members of the royal family.

It is unlikely that the merchant admiral was a famous philosopher like Confucius, or Lao-Tzu. Some merchants were wealthy enough to dabble in poetry, philosophy, and the arts, but a man destined to sail across the ocean would have been dedicated to the sailing profession, and not to the fine arts. Otherwise, he would not have had the time, the skills, or the perseverance to succeed in such a hazardous endeavor. Nevertheless, like most Asians of wealth and intelligence, he probably sought out the intellectual training that made him an exceptional strategist, humanist, and leader.

Another reason for the admiral's lack of notoriety is that international merchants often regarded themselves as being above the petty interests of provincial bureaucrats and warlords. They tended to go where they pleased without regard to the loyalties expected of royal subjects. Their ranks often included pirates, spies, and rebels--making them a potentially volatile force during times of social unrest. With such a reputation for non-conformity, and outright antisocial behavior, it is hardly surprising that local rulers took steps to limit their impact on the lower classes. At some port cities, the ruling tyrants forbade them from entering the marketplace, because their undisciplined behavior and cosmopolitan attitudes might encourage rebellion among the masses.

Although early capitalists sought to expand their operations into new territories, new markets invariably brought greater exposure to tax-hungry revenue agents. Consequently, publicity was avoided. The less the bureaucracy knew about a merchant's activities, the happier that merchant was likely to be. Indeed, the issue of excessive taxation was so prevalent and so irksome that merchants tried many devious ways to circumvent the tax codes. For example, if a tax was based on the girth of ships that passed by a city's port of entry, then merchants tended to use vessels that were long and narrow--even exceedingly narrow. Sometimes, these ships were so thin they were difficult to sail. However, if the tax was based on length, the vessels were sure to be short and squat--regardless of how unseaworthy the result.[1]

Even if the exploits of independent maritime explorers had been recorded during their lives, it is still possible that the knowledge may have been erased during subsequent generations. Rival warlords sometimes burned historical documents, and they had a tendency to revise official versions of history. This was done to reflect the temperament of successive dynasties, or to please a ruler who was dissatisfied with the way historians had treated his ancestors.

Major purges took place in 1111 B.C. and 213 B.C. They coincided with the rise of new dynasties and occurred on a national scale as soldiers stripped the libraries and official depositories bare of documents. Priceless journals and books, representing centuries of accumulated knowledge, were reduced to ashes in a matter of hours. The purge of 213 B.C. was particularly thorough. The new ruler, King Cheng of the Ch'in dynasty, was determined to eradicate the offensive memory of his predecessors. Not only did his henchmen burn the libraries, they also dealt severely with the librarians. Since the former bookkeepers and authors were regarded as a potential menace to the imperial dictatorship, Cheng had them buried alive, beheaded, or trampled under the hooves of his cavalry.[2] Needless to say, such atrocities have caused great inconvenience to scholars of ancient Chinese history, while the true story of Asian seafaring has been lost.

In order to rectify the erroneous impression that China lacked maritime explorers worthy of a place in our history books, we are called upon to give a name to the unsung hero of the first Chinese merchant voyage to America. The reason for doing so is that it would be difficult, if not impossible, for us to visualize the existence of an important figure of world history who is nameless. Therefore, we shall refer to the unknown admiral by the name of "Nu Sun."

This name is a translation for the ancient Asian symbols of *chi* and *hsing*--which stand for a star of good fortune. It is an appropriate designation for a daring merchant who lived in a society that was obsessed with omens, fortune telling, astrology, and alchemy. The title is of even greater significance considering the impact Chinese contacts had upon the native inhabitants of the Americas. Like a star of good fortune, Nu Sun and his followers became a beacon of hope for the Mayan Indians who were struggling under the tyranny of Olmec rulers. Indeed, it was a Dark Age in the New World until Nu Sun sailed from the Orient. His arrival marked the beginning of a renaissance that was to last for more than a thousand years. Indeed, this Asian voyage was the dawning of a new era in the growth of American culture.

In our journey through ancient history, we will board Nu Sun's ship, we will follow his path across the Pacific, and we will experience the native cultures he encountered on his incredible voyage. However, our departure for America must be delayed long enough to make adequate preparations. First, we must examine the origin and development of a Chinese art tradition that began nearly six thousand years ago. The reason for this examination is that it will provide the foundation we need for evaluating conclusive scientific evidence that Asian voyagers were responsible for the inspiration that led to the emergence of Mayan civilization. The art tradition, which was a product of Asian astrologers and mystics, is called The Omnibus Power Sign.

ANCIENT POWER SIGNS

Power signs can be identified by the importance of traditions, or by their placement in religious art. The Minoan double axe (1) is often held in the hands of a priest. This example is from a ceramic relief produced in Knossos, ca. 1000 B.C. A statue of Buddha (2) bears the *yin/yang* motif as a forehead emblem, while a Mayan religious leader (3) poses with the cosmic disk. Other examples shown here include the Egyptian *ankh* (4), the Christian cross (5), the *caduceus* (6), and the sacred tree of Rhodes (7).

Power Signs

Before the dawn of civilization, primitive societies realized that symbols have power. In the hands of a shaman, a magical object, such as the skull of a vanquished warrior, could strike terror in the minds of tribesmen. Even the symbol for a skull carved into a talisman or painted on the side of a robe evoked a similar response. It was this reliable response to magical symbols that enabled a few men to exercise control over the thoughts and actions of the tribe. The secrets of their power lay in the deep psychological bond that primitive societies maintained between ritual and reality. Indeed, for most simple-minded folk there was no reality beyond the mind-forged images of nature spirits and shamans.

The importance of power signs to our examination of Asian contacts with pre-civilized American societies is apparent from the fact that these ubiquitous motifs can be used to reveal patterns of cultural influence. Indeed, power signs are as important to archaeologists as fingerprints are to a detective. While it is true that some power signs are as common as the leaves on a tree, others have certain characteristics that enable the discerning eye to distinguish those that are diagnostic of a particular cultural heritage. Consequently, it will be worth a few moments of our time to consider what power signs are, how they come into being, and the ways they influence human behavior.

Among Stone-Age societies, power signs have many similarities and few differences. Circles commonly represent the sun, crescents the moon, while zigzag lines depict lightning--or serpents. Animal masks with horns often represent the qualities of powerful beasts in the environment, while shamans use horned head-dresses to indicate their magical supremacy over the spirits of animals. Because Paleolithic artists rely upon symbols which mimic the natural environment, they are of limited value as indicators of cultural contact. This limitation is due to the universality of their subject matter. That is, serpents, lightning storms, horned beasts, and celestial phenomena occur with regularity throughout the world.

9

Nevertheless, these rather simple motifs serve as the foundation for the emergence of more complex symbolism as societies progress towards civilization.

The advent of the Neolithic Age, with sedentary, farming societies, brings the establishment of a priestly class of specialists devoted to abstract nature spirits. Since their primary goal is to influence the weather in order to assure a bountiful harvest, the magical symbols they employ differ significantly from those used by hunting societies. In this stage of cultural evolution, symbols take on a greater level of complexity and uniqueness. Compound symbols derive from Paleolithic roots, combining circles, scroll shapes, zig-zag lines, and other shamanistic designs into intricate ceremonial artifacts. Rituals relate more to celestial events, like the equinoxes and solstices, which govern activities related to farming. When masks are used in rituals, they tend to be much more complex in design than those used by barbarian hunters, as they represent cosmological concepts of weather deities. Such deities combine attributes of humans, animals, and natural phenomena. Consequently, archaeologists have more effective criteria for determining cultural contact between Neolithic societies.

By the Bronze Age, many of the world's societies had established unique symbol complexes tailored to the specific needs of their cultures and the characteristics of their environments. Powerful rulers, priests, and historical events added further elaborations to the configuration of religious symbolism and ritual. And wherever major civilizations emerged, the effect of a strong, centralized theocracy was to standardize the ritual practices and symbols throughout the domain. Consequently, specific symbols came to be diagnostic of particular societies.

A few examples of Bronze-Age symbols are presented in Figure 2. These include the Minoan double axe, the Buddhist symbol for cosmic duality (*yin/yang*), the cosmic disk of Mexico, the Egyptian *ankh*, the Christian cross, the Greek *caduceus*, and the sacred tree of Rhodes. A common feature of religious power signs is their

SACRED BANNER
Banners representing earthly authority and heavenly power were carried in the processionals of royalty and high priests. This banner is from a 6th-century A.D. bas-relief carving in a Chinese tomb. It includes four scroll motifs, which represent germinating plants, or creative forces, in each of the four quadrants of the earth.

portrayal in the hands of priests, or their placement at the front of temples. They are also used to decorate religious objects, such as scepters, talismans, and monuments. Another common characteristic is that they tend to be used in a fairly consistent manner by adherents of the faith for an extended period of time. The *ankh*, for example, has been used as a symbol of life force for over five thousand years. The cosmic disk has an equally long heritage, while the Buddhist duality symbol is of more recent derivation. The oldest Asian archaeological evidence of this motif dates to the tenth century B.C.

Power signs frequently represent concepts of an ultimate heavenly power. In this regard, they are sometimes used interchangeably with more realistic portrayals of supreme beings. For example, the Christian Savior can be represented graphically as the figure of Jesus nailed to a cross, or symbolically as a cross embellished by a crown of thorns. This use of composite symbolism is a common feature of Bronze-Age societies and later civilizations. It gives symbolism the interpretive value of fingerprints, because the degree of complexity serves to differentiate one religious heritage from another even when the motifs look quite similar. For example, a crown of thorns serves to identify the Christian cross as a symbol of atonement and everlasting life, while the Egyptians used a simple cross as a fertility symbol associated with the rebirth of spring and the yearly flooding of the Nile River.

Ancient civilizations were isolated from one another by geographical barriers which restricted the impact of external influences. Consequently, they tended to develop fairly unique religious beliefs and symbols to represent those beliefs. However, as societies came into contact through trade or conquest, there was an opportunity for sharing both religious ideas and symbols. Wherever this occurred, we find a corresponding change in the assortment of symbols and artifacts in the archaeological record of the area. The resulting migration of symbols is particularly

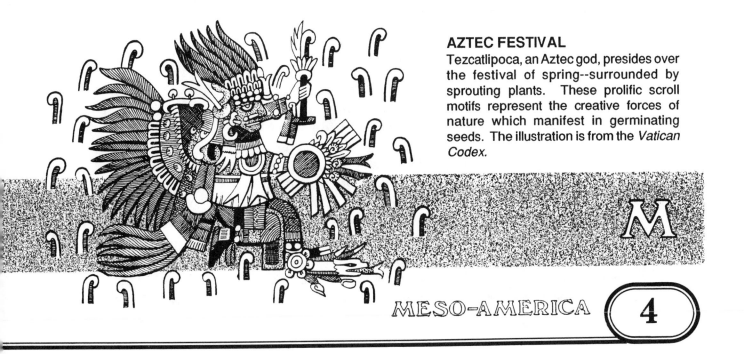

AZTEC FESTIVAL
Tezcatlipoca, an Aztec god, presides over the festival of spring--surrounded by sprouting plants. These prolific scroll motifs represent the creative forces of nature which manifest in germinating seeds. The illustration is from the *Vatican Codex.*

MESO-AMERICA   4

SCROLL MOTIFS FROM ASIA & MESO-AMERICA

Any collection of artifacts from East Asia and Meso-America is bound to contain some striking similarities. Asian motifs include: (A1) the *yin/yang*, (A2) a Ming cosmic egg, (A3) the conch of Buddha, (A4) the *varja* scepter, (A5) the Shang immortal owl, (A6) the Chinese longevity symbol, (A7) a Han Chinese deity, and (A8) a esoteric Buddhist skull with life-force scrolls. Asian

useful as an indicator of cultural transmission. For example, we can trace the expansion of Hindu influence into southeast Asia by examining the progressive spread of Hindu idols into Malaysia, Java, and Sumatra.

Close geographical proximity, however, does not always result in neighboring groups adopting each other's religious symbolism. Until the Han dynasty encouraged the adoption of Buddhist symbols (ca. 200 B.C.), there were few similarities between the art of the Chinese and the cultures of the Indian subcontinent, even though trade took place several centuries earlier.[1] This restriction of the spread of symbols among peoples who are engaging in trade is a consequence of cultural conservatism. That is, the religious traditions of a civilization are usually strong enough to resist the transference of belief systems and symbolism, unless some unusual event occurs--such as the conversion of a king, or the successful conquest of a neighboring country.

Religious symbolism spreads most readily when a more powerful culture engages in trade with peripheral societies that have not yet established strong, centralized theocracies. This type of situation is what occurred on the outskirts of the Chinese empire during the first millennium B.C., and it also occurred as Asian

MESO-AMERICA

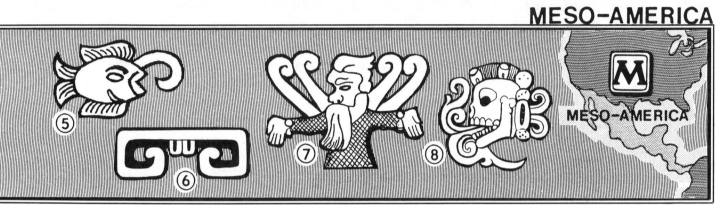

scrolls generally represent spiritual qualities, such as cosmic duality, holiness, cosmic origins of the universe, heavenly flight (or transcendence), consciousness, immortality, spiritual power, the breath of the soul, and infinity. Scholars have interpreted only three of the Meso-American examples: M2 is described as a feather; M6 is a winged man; and M7 is a skull with speech scrolls.

merchants traveled to North and Central America. Indeed, the tendency of primitive societies to adopt the religious symbolism of more powerful trading partners makes it possible for us to trace the path of Nu Sun's voyage.

Two examples of similar motifs found in China and ancient Mexico are presented in Figures 3 and 4. The scroll motif used in the Buddhist burial banner was a traditional motif associated with farming cultures in Asia. Originally, the plant-form scroll was a Neolithic motif that represented germinating seeds. By placing a scroll in each of four quadrants--which represent the four corners of the earth--the Buddhists sought to portray the universal spirit of creativity that came as a blessing of their religious movement. A similar function is indicated for the Mexican motifs which surround an image of the Aztec deity, Tezcatlipoca. In this composition, the scroll motifs portray germinating seeds--an event which follows the spring planting. Consequently, the message of a fruitful season at the hands of a beneficent deity is indicated.

Is it merely coincidental that both Buddhists and Aztecs chose similar scroll motifs to represent the concept of a bountiful earth? Or does the similar usage constitute evidence of trans-Pacific contact between Asia and Meso- America?

Strong arguments have been put forth supporting both interpretations. The likelihood of coincidence is supported by the universality of simple scroll shapes. Scrolls are common throughout the world in the forms of plants, clouds, seashells, and serpents. Therefore, it is hardly surprising that scroll motifs comprise part of the religious symbolism of almost all primitive societies. However, among more advanced cultures, such as the Celts, Danes, and Greeks, scroll motifs were fabricated into highly ornate forms which were often more decorative than symbolic. Likewise, Arabian societies have developed elaborate scrollwork designs, called arabesques, to decorate mosques, religious paraphernalia, and sacred texts. Because most historical cultures utilize highly specific styles and traditional designs, accurate identification of their cultural heritage is a rather simple matter.

Furthermore, most societies conform to the practice of *finite representation*--whereby a single motif represents a specific thing or idea. Although scrolls are common in the world's art, the interpretations of the motifs are usually quite specific from one culture to the next. Greek scrolls typically portray water, or the tree of life, as do the symbols of most Mediterranean and Mesopotamian cultures. The traditions of East Asia and Meso-America, however, deviate sharply from those typical elsewhere. East Asia generally refers to the land area comprising China, Malaysia, Indonesia, Japan, Korea, and the Philippines, while Meso-America refers to the area between Central Mexico and Panama. Among the Chou Chinese and the Mayan Indians, scroll symbols were used in great abundance to represent a multitude of religious concepts. Indeed, the usage of scroll forms is so prevalent as to render accurate interpretation a difficult process. Often, the particular meaning of scroll forms in these two cultures is impossible to ascertain--without an in-depth examination of the associated context of other motifs.

If there were abundant examples in the world's art of societies using symbols without regard to tradition and without regard to the rule of finite representation, then the occurrence of two cultures using scroll motifs in such a manner would not seem important. But that is not the case. The use of symbols is highly traditional, because societies rely upon culture to dictate their emotional affinities and cognative value.

Some examples of magic scrolls from East Asia and Meso-America are presented in Figure 5. Excavations in both areas have produced abundant examples of scroll-covered artifacts, giving the impression that vast scroll traditions are endemic phenomena. The accuracy of that impression will be tested in forthcoming chapters.

As can be ascertained from the illustration, the outward similarity of Asian and Meso-American designs is striking. Nevertheless, these individual specimens are practically meaningless as evidence for trans-Pacific cultural diffusion. About the only thing that can be said with certainty is that scrolls in both places seem to refer to a variety of religious concepts including the power of flight, the duality of cosmic forces, and the regenerative power of nature.

Since the usage of scrolls in these two cultural contexts departs from the customary rule of finite representation, we have reason to suspect that both societies made use of a highly unique power sign--an *omnibus* power sign.[2] This highly improbable occurrence begs the obvious question: Was there a relationship between

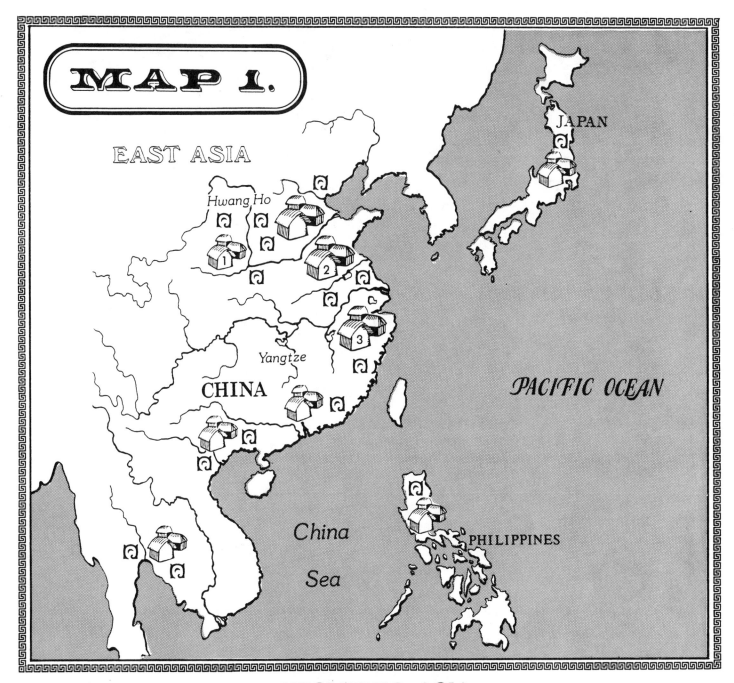

NEOLITHIC ASIA

Stone artifacts from the Neolithic Period (4000-1500 B.C.) indicate the presence of a growing population throughout East Asia. The greatest concentration appears to have been along the Hwang Ho and Yangtze River valleys in China. Ceramic decorations from this period show frequent use of scroll forms.

KEY

- Neolithic villages of 5-10,000

- Distribution of magic scroll designs

- Inscribed writing prior to 2400 B.C.
    1. Lo-tu, Lin t'ung
    2. Ning-Yang
    3. Shanghai

NEOLITHIC CERAMICS
Pottery vessels from East Asia show a long history of scroll-shaped power signs dating from the Neolithic Age. These examples include a burial jar from the Philippines (left rear, ca. 890 B.C.); jars from the Yangshao culture, Kansu, China (center and right rear, ca. 2500 B.C.); and ornamental vases from Ban Chieng, Thailand (front, ca. 4000 B.C.).

these two cultures that resulted in the use of similar omnibus power signs in both areas?

The answer to that question will require a thorough, scientific examination of the development of magic scroll traditions in both areas. We shall begin our investigation with East Asia--where the earliest evidence of magic scrolls is present in artifacts dating to the Late Neolithic Age, ca. 4000 to 3000 B.C.

Neolithic Origins

The distribution of artifacts using magic scrolls extends from mainland China to Indonesia and the Philippines (Map 1). The motifs on these artifacts seem to have four major themes: life force, nature spirits, magical horns, and cosmic forces. These themes correspond to the beliefs and environmental experiences of people who lived between 4000 to 1500 B.C.[3]

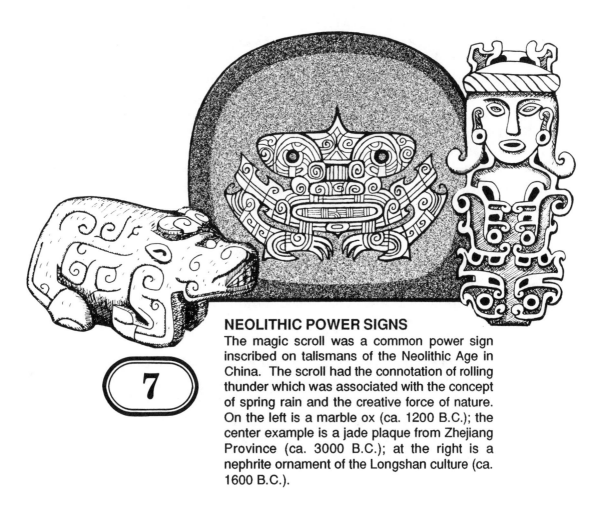

NEOLITHIC POWER SIGNS
The magic scroll was a common power sign inscribed on talismans of the Neolithic Age in China. The scroll had the connotation of rolling thunder which was associated with the concept of spring rain and the creative force of nature. On the left is a marble ox (ca. 1200 B.C.); the center example is a jade plaque from Zhejiang Province (ca. 3000 B.C.); at the right is a nephrite ornament of the Longshan culture (ca. 1600 B.C.).

It was a perilous time to be alive. People relied upon nature to provide food and shelter, with the consequence that much of their religious practice involved the appeasement of nature spirits whom they believed were in control of their destiny. Indeed, the invisible forces of nature often struck them with savage and unpredictable tragedy.

Along the major rivers, thousands of people lived in shallow caves dug into cliffs high above the water. These dark habitations provided shelter from the elements, however, unpredictable earthquakes could transform cave homes into mass graves. Hundreds of thousands perished amid such disasters. Even buildings located away from cliffs were not immune from catastrophe. Small wooden huts situated along the flood plains could be swept away if the monsoons were particularly severe or if there was an early thaw in the mountains to the west. Years of relatively mild weather would delude the farmers into a false sense of security drawing them nearer toward the water's edge and their tragic fate.

When people died, traditions prescribed the manner of burial and the appropriate rituals to assure the deceased a safe passage to heaven. Ceramic vessels were often used as offerings--thereby preserving a record of religious practices and motifs for discovery by future archaeologists. East Asian burial pots are frequently decorated with scroll or spiral motifs (Figure 6). Oriental scholars usually refer to these motifs as "stylized plant forms." However, their usage in a religious context, and their similarity to later religious symbols, indicates that they were actually being used as power signs. Their meanings can be inferred from the interpretation of contemporary motifs which serve as burial markers depicting the Hindu tree of life.[4] Similar motifs, called the *koru*, are used in Polynesia as part of the intricate scrollwork carved into caves and ceremonial artifacts. They are regarded as representations for magic and the regenerative forces of nature.[5] We are led to the conclusion that the primary religious function of the archaic scroll symbols in Asia is to represent the ability of natural forces to restore life--i.e., to confer immortality.

Another common power sign of the Late Neolithic is referred to as the *lei-wen*, or "thunder pattern." It can be seen on stone carvings of nature spirits such as those in Figure 7. The scroll-shaped motif is associated with fertility, and it occurs on objects throughout Chinese history--beginning as early as 3600 B.C. Modern artisans employ the motif as a symbol of good fortune on jade carvings. This usage provides us with evidence of a particular power sign tradition lasting nearly six thousand years.

Other kinds of power signs were used during Neolithic times besides scroll motifs and spirals. The most awe-inspiring symbol may well have been the shaman's horned headdress (Figure 8). Ancient artifacts provide evidence that the horns were regarded as a manifestation of nature's creative power. Each spring, the horned animals of the forest could be observed scraping their new horns against trees to remove the skin covering. At about the same time, trees produced new leaves. Later in the year, elk and rams engaged in combat using their powerful horns to win mates for the rutting season. The implicit power of horns in the yearly

SHAMAN'S HORNS

8

During the Neolithic, the shaman's horns were regarded as a symbol of magical power associated with nature, life, and rebirth. Many of these pagan symbols survived into the Bronze Age in rural areas of China. Examples include (1) a Chinese wooden tomb guardian, ca. 400 B.C., (2) a seated shaman of the Harappan civilization of India, ca. 2300 B.C., (3) a jade mask from China, (4) a figure from a Harappan seal, and (5) a Chinese jade figurine, ca. 500 B.C.

HEAD SCROLLS

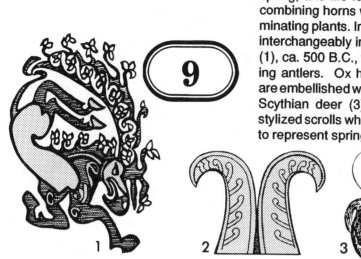

The association of horns and scrolls with nature, spring, and life force resulted in a hybrid motif combining horns with scrolls, or horns with germinating plants. Indeed, these motifs were used interchangeably in East Asia. A Siberian tattoo (1), ca. 500 B.C., features a moose with flowering antlers. Ox horns from the Philippines (2) are embellished with plant-form scrolls, while the Scythian deer (3) shows a typical pattern of stylized scrolls which are used in place of antlers to represent spring, or life force.

revival of life was readily apparent, which explains why powdered animal horns came to be regarded as a potent aphrodisiac.

During the Late Neolithic, the lives of farmers and hunters were closely interwoven with the patterns of the seasons. Winter was particularly harsh due to the bitter cold and cramped living conditions in riverside caves. Boredom and claustrophobia were as plentiful as food was scarce. Consequently, spring was a time of rejoicing accompanied by important religious ceremonies. These were commonly led by a tribal shaman whose horned headdress represented his magical power and spiritual authority.

Spring was also a time of sacrifice!

According to Neolithic religious beliefs, human lives were needed to placate the voracious nature spirits. This belief was particularly strong when the spirit's anger was manifest in raging floods. In those threatening moments, it was the responsibility of the shamans to select a suitable sacrifice. According to the customs of these pagan tribes, the most suitable offering was usually an attractive young woman. Her destiny was to become the bride of the angered spirit and thereby restore tranquillity to the river.

It seems reasonable to assume that most of those selected for sacrifice went willingly when called upon to die. People raised in a tradition of obedience to their elders and blind submission to shamanistic authority are not likely to resist a custom they deeply believe to be true. Consequently, at the shaman's command, villagers gathered for the sacrificial rite. They stood along the bluffs overlooking a swollen stream, just as their ancestors had done for countless centuries before them. They were confident that the magic would work, even as they witnessed the girl being thrown to her death. After all, there was empirical evidence to support their faith: every year, the flood waters miraculously receded *after* the sacrifice was made. If the river spirits were ever slow to respond, it was a simple matter to make another sacrifice. Sooner or later, the shamans were bound to get results!

It wasn't until the end of the Chou dynasty, nearly two thousand years later, that a statesman would gain renown for challenging the infallibility of shamanistic authority. The folklore of China recounts an incident in the life of Hsi-men Pao, who was both an enlightened scholar and a provincial governor. Pao confronted a group of shamans near the Yellow River as they were about to sacrifice a young girl. Being a peaceful man, Pao first appealed for compassion using the words of an accomplished poet. This had no effect on the stalwart shamans: they were adamant in their obedience to superstitious beliefs.

When they refused Pao's polite logic, he decided to implement a different strategy: inspirational leadership. If the ancient ritual required a sacrifice, Pao reasoned, it was his authority as governor to decide what it should be. To the dismay of all, he directed his escort--which amounted to a considerable number of soldiers--to seize the reluctant shamans and throw *them* into the river.

Bewildered peasants looked on with a mixture of fear and relief: would the temperamental river spirits accept such an offering of pious old men?

Nature had the last laugh! According to the chronicles, the Yellow River receded much earlier that spring than ever before in the history of the province! But it was a bleak year for shamans: recruitment fell sharply, donations declined, and adherents of the pagan faith departed in haste for the distant mountains--far away from Pao's jurisdiction.

Figure 9 depicts some of the magic horns used for shamanistic cults. Of particular note are the designs which combine horns, or antlers, with scrolls. These scroll motifs represent plants or germinating seeds, and they constitute the earliest association between horns and magic scrolls, or life-force symbols. These life-force symbols eventually served as the model for the Asian Omnibus Power Sign. Before that could happen, however, the archaic culture had to undergo a transformation from pagan beliefs to a scientific way of thinking. It was a transformation that wasn't long in coming, and it was brought about by the ancient practice of astrology.

Among the earliest shamans, astrology was a magical art that determined the appropriate sacrifices and rituals involving the sun, moon, and stars. Eventually, the growing preoccupation with the heavens and the telling of fortunes became the basis for scientific study. As growing villages became more dependent on agriculture, it was inevitable that people would direct their attention toward the night sky. In the long run, this fascination for astral bodies was to prove man's salvation from the ignorance of his past. But before that could happen, there would be centuries of patient study and recording of events as the heavens worked their mysterious magic on the simmering intellect of humanity.

There were practical reasons to study the stars: aside from the fact that astral bodies were mysterious by their very nature, even the most simple minded farmer was aware that the position of the sun was somehow related to the return of spring and the appropriate times for planting and harvest. Royal astrologers were even more aware of the implicit relationship between the movement of planets and the seasons because they kept detailed records on strips of bamboo.[5]

At some unknown moment in the depths of Chinese antiquity, there arose a belief that the existence of mankind was somehow involved in a delicate balance between cosmic forces. The existence of an invisible cosmic law, later referred to as *Tao*, was apparent from the movements of heavenly bodies which followed a reliable pattern or sequence.[6] These patterns were reflected in the seasonal changes of nature. It was an astonishing discovery that seemed to imply the omnipotence of cosmic forces over nature spirits.

This conceptual breakthrough was of particular importance to the rulers of emerging kingdoms along the Yellow River, because it provided them with a way to expand their empire. Presumably, if events in the heavens could be foretold, which was accomplished with solar tables and comet charts, then it was equally possible for astrologers to predict the course of human events. As far as these ambitious rulers were concerned, the most important function of astrology was determining the best time for victory in battle.

Astrology, fortune-telling, writing, philosophy, and science all grew hand-in-hand with emerging civilizations. From the astrologers came star charts; from the fortune tellers came the use of symbols to represent ideas; and from the philosophers came the concept of a karmic or spiritual balance between the heavens and the earth.

Most primitive religions develop a view of nature that stresses a conflict between opposites, such as light versus dark, good versus evil, and life versus death. Chinese philosophers, on the other hand, viewed natural phenomena much differently. They conceived the idea that complementary forces governed the universe. From their perspective, night and day were not separate, because they were always merging into one another. Sunlight, therefore, was regarded as a process and not a state of being in contrast with darkness: even in the depths of night, the twinkling, star-speckled sky held the embryo of the noonday sun! In other words, there was only one sky. The sky of day and the sky of night were inseparable! Light and dark were also inseparable--they were simply different aspects of a singular phenomenon.

Sometime during the Late Neolithic, the concepts of *yin* (darkness) and *yang* (light) became apparent in the religious practices of the more sophisticated astrologers. The relationship of *yin* and *yang* was conceived of as the passage of a shadow from one side of a mountain to the other as the sun moves across the sky. Presumably, all of life's experiences, including death, could be explained as continuously repeating processes that were in tune with immutable natural laws. Astrology and divination, therefore, were regarded as keys to the understanding of these processes and predicting the future. It was an important advancement over the previous reliance on superstition, and it marked the beginning of the end for shamanistic religion in urban areas.

The importance of beliefs concerning cosmic forces in Chinese religion is apparent from stone carvings attributed to the Late Neolithic. Two of these are illustrated in Figure 10. The square-shaped objects, or *tsung*, represent the earth, while the jade *pi* disks represent the sun, or heaven. They are usually manufactured from jade--a stone which the Chinese have traditionally valued above gold as a magical substance of natural purity. It is a material that does not occur naturally in

China. The closest known source lies two thousand miles to the west--requiring an elaborate trade network to bring raw materials to the Hwang Ho Valley.[7] The surface of *pi* disks is frequently embellished with a pattern of raised whorls or hemispheres in a uniform pattern. These designs are often referred to as a "grain pattern," or a "tadpole pattern." Both tadpoles and germinating grain have a scroll shape that Asian mystics identified as symbolic of life force emerging into the physical realm. Therefore, these motifs actually represent the matrix of cosmic power that was believed to encompass the heavens. It was a transformational matrix of creative energy that could assume the shape of germinating plants, rain clouds, or dragons.

Of particular significance regarding jade representations of heaven and earth is the central hole. Artifacts manufactured during the Chou and Han dynasties (ca. 1000 B.C. to A.D. 200) use the hole or "void" as the symbolic pathway through which invisible cosmic forces gained access to the physical world of mortals. Another intriguing function of the hole is to represent the place occupied by the "pillar of the sun"--a Hindu concept that is reflected in the art of ancient Babylon. By placing the sun at the top of a pillar, the Hindus implied that the sun was held aloft by immutable natural laws, i.e., the pillar represented invisible cosmic power. Such a belief can only occur where the science of astronomy has replaced paganism as the driving force of a culture.

During the first two millennia B.C., these artifacts were undoubtedly of primary importance to the development of later Chinese philosophy regarding the relationship between the heavens and the earth. Religious objects, like the *pi* disk and *tsung*, enabled philosophers to communicate their abstract concepts and to preserve their esoteric beliefs for future generations. It would take centuries of cultural evolution

CEREMONIAL OBJECTS Carved jade objects were used in Neolithic ceremonies concerned with astronomy and astrology. The square-shaped *tsung*, or *zong* (left), dates from the 3rd millennium B.C. The hole in the center represents the pathway of invisible cosmic forces. Circular <u>pi</u> disks (right) were embellished with scroll-shaped motifs representing rain, thunder, clouds, and cosmic energy. The surface of scrolls (bottom) is often referred to as a "tadpole," or "grain pattern."

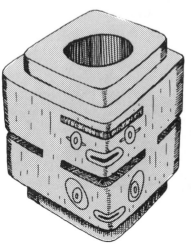

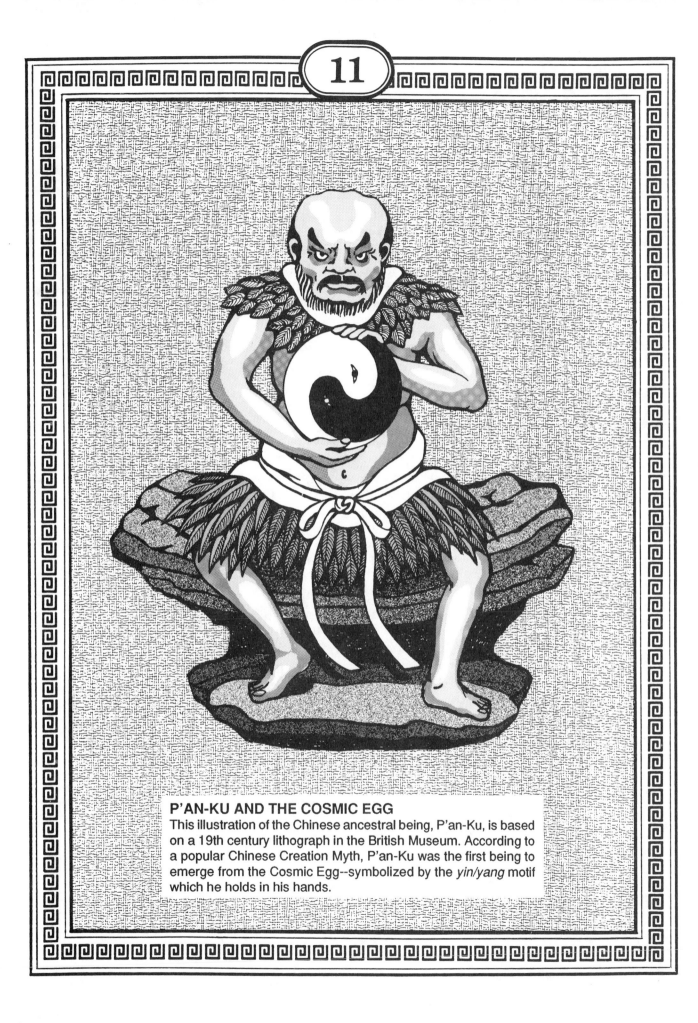

P'AN-KU AND THE COSMIC EGG
This illustration of the Chinese ancestral being, P'an-Ku, is based
on a 19th century lithograph in the British Museum. According to
a popular Chinese Creation Myth, P'an-Ku was the first being to
emerge from the Cosmic Egg--symbolized by the *yin/yang* motif
which he holds in his hands.

before writing would develop sufficiently to enable the adequate preservation of religious concepts using abstract symbols alone. Until then, these square and disk-shaped artifacts were the symbolic building blocks from which a later civilization would arise.

Early Dynasties and Magic Scrolls

Chinese legends attribute the emergence of civilization in East Asia to the Five Emperors--Fu-hsi, Shen-nung, Huang-ti, Yao, and Shun. They are credited with the introduction of government, social institutions, writing, carpentry tools, boat building, agricultural implements, medicinal herbs, domesticated plants and animals, silk production, and astronomy. They also established the lunar calendar which had a starting date of approximately 3000 B.C.[8] This date commemorates the reign of Emperor Huang-ti, who is acknowledged as the founder of Taoist philosophy.[9]

According to Chinese folklore, the symbol for cosmic duality and associated astrological charts emerged during the sovereignty of the legendary Five Emperors. The *yin/yang* symbol, which is also referred to as the *tai-chi*, or Great Monad, is portrayed in Figure 11. It rests in the hands of P'an Ku, who is characterized in some Chinese creation myths as the first human being. In some versions, it is his descendants, rather than those of Adam and Eve, who spread across the earth. In other versions, he is the creator of the heavens and earth, and he is portrayed holding the cosmic egg from which he emerged. Consequently, the motif is regarded as a symbol for the cosmic source of all creation. This identification of the cosmic duality symbol with myths of creation establishes the *yin/yang* as the preeminent power sign of the Orient.

Following the Five Emperors came Yu the Great--credited by legend with controlling the flooding of the Yellow River by organizing the people to construct a system of canals, dams, and reservoirs. Yu founded the first dynasty, the Hsia, and he divided the empire into nine provinces.[10] Traditions identify him as a great alchemist who knew the secret arts of the primal powers, i.e. astrology and alchemy.[11] According to legend, Huang-ti was the first to cast bronze cauldrons, but it was Yu who perfected the techniques of bronze manufacturing that later became a hallmark of the Shang dynasty. At present, there is no archaeological evidence attesting to the existence of these legendary emperors or their contributions to Chinese civilization. However, a bronze artifact has been recovered from a Thai archaeological site dating to the third millennium B.C., suggesting a more ancient time of origin for Asian bronze than has previously been accepted by historians.[12]

The role that mythical emperors had in the development of the Omnibus Power Sign is impossible to ascertain without archaeological evidence, and we have none available for our investigation. It is not until the seventeenth century B.C. that we find artifacts showing the continued evolution of this unique art tradition in Asia. That time horizon marks the beginning of the Shang dynasty.

The Dragon Kings

From the ancient past, the specter of Oriental dragons looms above the hills of the Hwang Ho River where archaeologists have recovered evidence of a well-developed, Bronze-Age civilization. Ruins of the Shang dynasty at An-Yang contained the earliest artifacts featuring the mythical beast which became the symbol of Chinese royalty for over three thousand years. The prevalence of this enigmatic power sign suggests that it was first introduced by an earlier dynasty--but no trace of their existence has yet been found.

The Shang dynasty (also referred to as the Yin) lasted from about 1751 to 1111 B.C. Legend suggests that the first ruler came to power in a popular uprising against a corrupt tyrant. It is a common theme repeated time and again in the history of the Chinese people. The Shang empire occupied the territory around the lower Hwang Ho Valley of northern China--as indicated by Map 2. The twelfth-century B.C. capital at An-Yang was a fortress city of more than 80,000 inhabitants.[1] This was the sixth capital in a land of feudal states that may have included a million or more subjects. Battles were common among the empire's lesser kings and warlords, while the extent of the ruler's sovereignty fluctuated with the fortunes of his armies and the strength of his own personality.[2] When the emperor was strong, the surrounding states were sources of tribute, slaves, and provisions for the capital.

It was an era of tremendous technological and artistic achievements. New inventions came into use as labor-saving devices, and new symbols were devised to represent the beliefs of a growing theocracy. During this time, scroll motifs (also called magic scrolls) gained increasing popularity for the representation of the supernatural qualities of plants, animals, and the weather.

Figure 12 is a composite illustration of some of the advances made by the Shang people over their Neolithic ancestors. In previous years, settlements moved as resources of wood and fertile land became scarce. With the arrival of the Shang dynasty, however, crowded urban centers provided a more stable way of life. The

SHANG CULTURAL MONTAGE, 1550--1030 B.C.
The period of the Shang dynasty was characterized by the rapid growth of urban centers consisting of 25-50,000 inhabitants. Cities were situated in accordance with astrological predictions, and streets were arranged on a north-south grid. Typical buildings (1) consisted of post and beam construction raised upon hardened earth platforms. Writing, in the form of thousands of pictographic characters (2), served the needs of magicians and merchants. Bronze casting was developed to a high art, with the casting of ornate

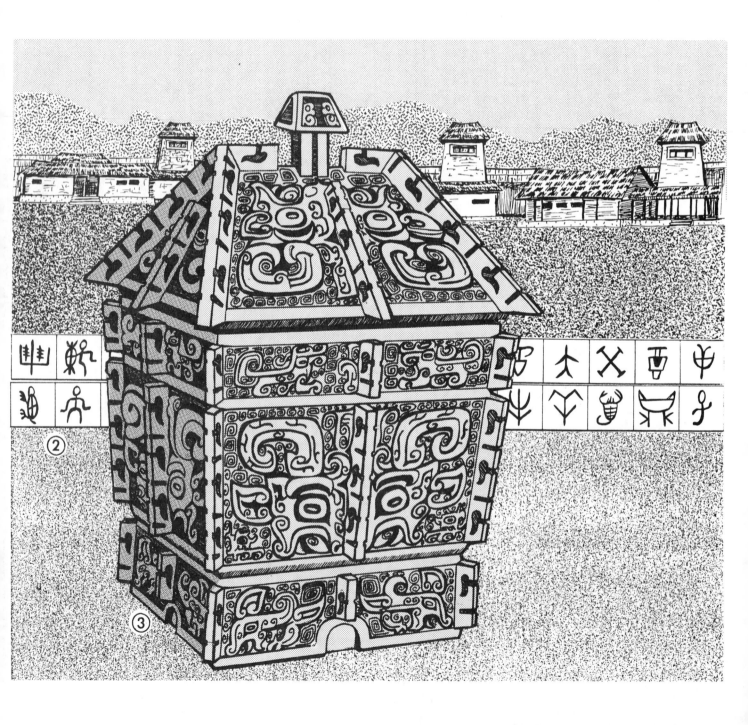

ceremonial vessels such as the *tsun* (3), which measures about two feet high. Giant bronze cauldrons weighed up to one ton. Jade objects, such as the *zong,* or *tsung* (4), and the nocturnal (5) were used in astrological ceremonies. Nocturnals were also used as an astronomical instrument for telling time and direction at night. Hence, they may have served as a navigational aid. Magicians, like Kiang Tze-ya (6) of the 12th century B.C., gained fame for making predictions using the *pa-kua* trigrams. The likeness of Tze-ya is from a 19th-century print.

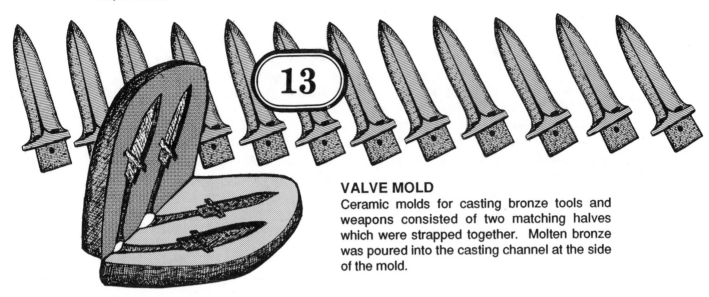

VALVE MOLD
Ceramic molds for casting bronze tools and weapons consisted of two matching halves which were strapped together. Molten bronze was poured into the casting channel at the side of the mold.

largest cities comprised nearly a hundred thousand residents, and they covered several square miles with buildings and streets carefully laid out in accordance with strict urban planning policies. Walled fortifications protected the one and two-story dwellings which were made of beam-and-thatch construction and situated on top of clay platforms.

Merchants were the mainstay of the city, bringing enormous quantities of fish, millet, wheat, and domesticated beef into markets from the outlying farms. Their close allies were the wagon smiths and shipbuilders who manufactured the carts and river junks needed for commerce, while tens of thousands of laborers worked the mines and foundries to produce metal tools.

Bronze was the primary product of Shang alchemists whose endless research and testing led to an increasingly more sophisticated craft. Two of the innovations from this period are presented in Figures 13 and 14. These are the valve mold, which enabled rapid production of tools and weapons; and the hollow crucible, which allowed artisans to maintain a high temperature in the molten bronze. The high temperature made it possible for the liquid metal to penetrate small spaces before

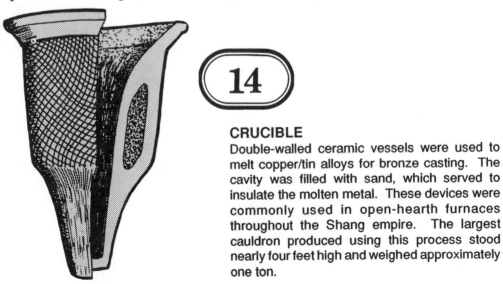

CRUCIBLE
Double-walled ceramic vessels were used to melt copper/tin alloys for bronze casting. The cavity was filled with sand, which served to insulate the molten metal. These devices were commonly used in open-hearth furnaces throughout the Shang empire. The largest cauldron produced using this process stood nearly four feet high and weighed approximately one ton.

SHANG EMPIRE

SHANG EMPIRE

Between 1500 and 1100 B.C., the Shang dynasty occupied an empire of provincial city-states along the lower Hwang Ho River valley. There were many independent city-states throughout the outlying region. All of these adopted the religious symbolism and customs of the Shang capital of An-Yang, which was the cultural hub of Southeast Asia.

KEY

An-Yang, Shang capital

Fortress cities of 50-100,000

Cities of 25-50,000

Cities of 10-25,000

Neolithic villages of 5-10,000

Omnibus Power Sign

EAST ASIA

15

COSMIC DUALITY

Shang art portrayed numerous religious concepts, including cosmic duality. Duality in nature is a common theme throughout the world, although Oriental beliefs stressed the union of duality as indicated by a single animal head with two bodies (above center, on a bronze *tsun* from Anhwei). Two dragons (left) were used to represent the forces of *yin* and *yang.* They flank the head of a human being, indicating the role of dual cosmic forces in human consciousness (from a bronze ca. 1300 B.C.). On the right is an example of a Shaman's horns embellished with symbols representing cosmic forces. Below is a 19th-century Tamishan wood carving, indicating that concepts regarding the union of dual cosmic forces had spread to the North America in prehistoric times. The diamond above the forehead is a diagnostic feature of Shang and Northwest Coast American Indian Art.

AMERICA

HORNED DRAGONS

Shang mystics elaborated on the horned dragon motifs derived from the late Neolithic religious art. Sometimes, the horns are embellished with flames, as in the upper left. Other dragon masks have more standardized horn shapes (lower left), while a few examples portray a headdress of flaming scrolls (right).

solidifying, thereby yielding a greater level of intricacy in the design. We often see only the finished product of Shang technology--a gleaming container like the *tsung* which was covered with intricate scroll motifs and dragons. Such vessels were destined to serve as sacrificial offerings at the burial of royalty.

This was a time when Taoist astrologers and other fortune tellers called "diviners," or *chenjen*, influenced the decisions of the ruling class.[3] Astrologers interpreted the movements of heavenly bodies and consulted the *I-Ching*, or *Book of Changes*, while diviners relied upon the way turtle bones cracked after being subjected to intense heat.[4] The bones were first inscribed with ideograms pertaining to alternate courses of action or future events. Presumably, cracked turtle bones could reveal the balance of cosmic forces related to the event, or they could betray the attitudes of ancestral spirits who might influence the future. Archaeologists recovered huge caches of cracked turtle bones from Shang ruins, attesting to the fact that the rulers had a great deal of faith in the diviner's art.

COSMIC HORNS

The association of horns with cosmic power, i.e., the forces of *yin* and *yang*, is indicated by the fact that Shang mystics portrayed dragons arising from the horns of shamans. This jade plaque depicts dragon horns above a shaman's head. Similar motifs occur with dragon masks and birds. At times, even the horns have the shape of stylized dragons.

HEAD SCROLLS
Numerous artifacts depicting humans and birds have crest or head scrolls in place of horns. These motifs probably represent life force, the soul, or consciousness as a power that animates life. This specimen is a jade ornament from the late Shang dynasty (ca. 1300 B.C.).

Veneration of ancestors (i.e., ancestor worship) was a primary focus of Shang ritual. It was manifest in yearly celebrations, sacrifices, and the burial of precious objects such as jade, or bronze cooking vessels with the deceased patron. Presumably, members of the royal family who left a bronze vessel in the burial chamber of a relative could expect some favorable intercession in the future by the departed person's earthly soul (*p'o*) or his intellectual counterpart (*hun*).[5]

The highest heavenly authority was called Shang-Ti. He was regarded as the most venerable tribal ancestor, and in his honor various rituals and sacrifices were required of subsequent generations. Royal priests determined the precise nature of these religious activities, and they also decided upon the number of sacrificial victims to be buried with a member of the royal household. In the case of a king, it was not unusual for several hundred men, women, and children to be executed on the day of burial.[6] Horses and dogs also accompanied the monarch on his heavenly journey, along with chariots, weapons, and food offerings. Since there was insufficient room in many of the burial chambers to accommodate large numbers of retainers, they were occasionally represented only by the presence of their decapitated heads.

The inscriptions on the turtle bones bear witness to a major contribution of the Shang government toward the advancement of Chinese civilization: standardization of the written language. Because the language was still evolving, and the growing population spoke a multitude of dialects, there was a tendency for each province to develop its own unique words, phrases, and written characters. However, by royal decree, all the emperor's subjects were required to use standard written symbols. By this time, there were more than two thousand characters (or ideograms) used for expressing the language. Standardization of written symbols enabled merchants and bureaucrats from distant provinces to communicate in writing, even though they spoke different dialects. Although some of the ideograms are no longer decipherable, many others are similar to those which are currently in use--allowing modern scholars to successfully interpret the ancient messages left on bronze castings and turtle bones.

So powerful was the movement toward standardization that art and religious expression throughout the empire also conformed to the high standards maintained by the cultural center at An-Yang. Among all the provinces, there emerged a consistent pattern of motifs that were characteristic of both the Shang philosophy and the Shang view of reality. At a practical level, the rulers accepted the concept of the immutability of natural law, because it was readily apparent in the accuracy of the astrologers' star charts and the alchemists' ability to produce incredible bronze castings.[7] In public, however, the kings resisted the philosophy of the alchemists. The human sacrifices continued--much to the horror of Taoist priests who argued against the archaic tradition.

The reason behind this apparent hypocrisy on the part of Shang rulers is that human sacrifices served the purpose of maintaining social order. This reflects an enduring paradox of Asian culture, i.e., the co-existence of the enlightened teachings of Taoist philosophers with the superstitious beliefs of rural peasants and the urban poor.

There was no stopping the relentless progress of technology. Before its awesome power, all superstitions would eventually yield. The reason is inherently simple: technology was the key to military superiority, and the god of war was held in high esteem by the emperors and warlords of China. That is not to say that technology would not serve willingly as a prostitute for conquest. It has done so for many centuries. However, as technology increases, so does the accumulated knowledge of science. And superstition can not win against the growing marriage of science and technology.

It is hardly a coincidence that bronze became an effective material for crafting weapons during the Shang dynasty. As soon as the valve mold was invented, metal workers could produce weapons and tools in unprecedented numbers. Suddenly, archers had an unlimited supply of arrows, horsemen had unlimited supplies of lances and hatchets, while shipbuilders had all the tools they needed to make the emperor's boats. With such enormous resources available, the kingdom could expand as far and as fast as the emperor's armies could travel.

And while the emperor engaged in warfare and consulted the spirits of his ancestors, Taoist mystics and bronze artisans managed to introduce a new symbol

19

COSMIC TREE
The Cosmic Tree is also referred to as the Cosmic Power Sign, and is portrayed by an arrow or triangle between two scrolls. The triangle is thought to represent light energy, or the sun, which arises from the dual forces of *yin* and *yang* indicated by the scrolls. It is a common motif in ceramics and bronze vessels of the Shang and later dynasties.

into the art of the age. It was a horn-shaped motif that extended above the heads of human beings and emerged from animal masks--much like the horns that a shaman might wear to represent the rejuvenating power of spring. Indeed, the purpose of the symbol was to represent power, but it was a unique kind of power. It was the power of the Cosmic Spirit believed to be manifest in all creatures as a result of the interaction of the two primal forces of *yin* and *yang*.

Mystical horns and cosmic concepts are illustrated in Figure 15. The shaman's horns are embellished with zigzag lines and scrolls which are symbolic of cosmic forces. Scrolls on either side, and curving in opposite directions typically represent the complementary forces of *yin* and *yang*. This concept of cosmic power is further represented by human beings suspended between the jaws of two dragons, or by animals having a single head with two bodies--representing the union of dual forces. From this union of forces comes life, consciousness, and intelligence--according to Taoist philosophy.

The most avant-garde of the mystics believed that *yin* and *yang* were simply different aspects of a single, unified force that animated the cosmos and all living things. There was no heaven and no hell in their view of the world--only a wellspring of cosmic power from which human beings and animals emerged for a time and then returned. Although some Taoist writings reveal the concepts of a soul and an afterlife, the afterlife was simply regarded as the "before life" from which the soul momentarily emerged to walk upon the planet earth. It might have been a useful concept for a convention of astronomers, or physicists, like those of modern times who call such forces "magnetism," "gravity," and "atomic power." In 1100 B.C., however, such concepts were far too radical. The emperor wanted a religion that would keep his subjects in line and make his armies victorious. For that purpose, he needed ferocious dragons--not esoteric fantasies about a single unified force of nature.

So, the mystics and the artisans provided the necessary beasts with glaring eyes and sharp teeth. For several centuries, they experimented with designs for an animal that would express the qualities of fierceness and power that would please an emperor, with the consequence that dragons sometimes had the composite features of many animals. The dragon was an awesome beast to look upon, but folklore made it an amiable creature--more playful than malicious. Eventually, dragons were regarded as creatures of wisdom, although they were prone to occasional bouts of reckless flight through the air. These sudden outbursts, it was believed, resulted in thunderstorms. Dragons lived in fresh-water seas and could be summoned to do the bidding of a generous priest, or a wise king. They were invisible to ordinary mortals, yet their shapes might be seen in water currents or swirling clouds. Magicians used mirrors and incense to betray the presence of these benevolent beasts, and everyone assumed that when the spring rains arrived, playful dragons were present in the clouds.

A few of the horned dragons of the Shang mystics are portrayed in Figure 16. These are images taken from bronze ceremonial vessels used for royal burial, and they are representative of hundreds of similar bronzes cast by Shang artisans. The ear-like motifs or horn-shaped symbols above the dragon heads vary from smooth inverted U-shapes to miniature dragons (as in Figure 17). Sometimes, the motifs are actually shaped like horns--but even then, the symbolic association is primarily with the creative forces of nature. In the context of Shang mortuary art, a simple "horn" is not what it appears to be. There is always a magical purpose underlying its use, because it has the religious function of a power sign.

In these ceremonial designs, the thunder pattern is abundant.[8] The consecutive spirals are thought to represent cumulus rain clouds which move through the air accompanied by thunder and lightning. Their deeper meaning involves the creative power of spring, fertility, good omens, and long life. For an agricultural people, all of these are interrelated concepts. Dragon motifs appear with a background matrix of spiral motifs which usually cover the entire remaining surface of the artifact. Here, the dragon is primarily regarded as a bringer of good fortune--the ultimate omen of a rich harvest.

Ultimately, the dragon is a symbol of the power of cosmic transformation. This popular concept is frequently encountered in Chinese parables about a lowly carp that transforms itself into a dragonfish, and then grows into a powerful spiritual being through perseverance and determination. Hence, even the carp is regarded as the embodiment of a powerful being on the verge of fulfillment.

The Shang emperor got his dragons, but he also got something else in the bargain: the Cosmic Horn. The earliest examples were simply a pair of horns portrayed above the head of a human or animal. Next, the power sign was embellished with other magic symbols. Then, it became a pattern of dragons, and finally it was reduced to a pattern of stylized scrolls emanating from the head or body (Figure 18). In this particular usage, the scroll-shaped motif can be regarded as a life-force crest. Its primary purpose is to portray the power of conscious will. At times, the symbol is smooth and may contain the effigy of another animal. At other times, the symbol may have a dualistic aspect (representing *yin* and *yang*). One variation of this theme is the flaming scroll seen earlier with the horned dragons. These motifs assume greater importance, later on, as we trace the progressive development of the Asian Omnibus Power Sign and its introduction into the ancient cultures of Meso-America.

As the power sign progressed from representing a horn to becoming a stylized scroll, the Shang mystics must have realized that they had invented a highly versatile motif that was capable of expressing the essence of their esoteric beliefs. Just as the creative forces of nature seemed to emerge in the form of growing clouds and plants, the scroll shape could be expanded from a single point into a bouquet of plant forms, or a cloud-like composition. It was a perfect symbol to represent the sprouting of leaves from the sacred tree (Figure 19).

Furthermore, they believed that the universe was a boiling cauldron of cosmic forces, and scrolls could be used to represent such a chaotic matrix. This meaning was commonly expressed with a matrix of transformational scrolls that had the appearance of tadpoles, germinating seeds, or clouds. As was the case during the Late Neolithic, the matrix was used to cover the surface of *pi* disks, and it filled the backgrounds of many other artifacts (Figure 20).

Toward the end of the Shang dynasty, urban philosophers began to challenge

RITUAL BRONZE ELEPHANT

This bronze statue stands about 8 inches high. It is covered with magical symbols, including dragons, the sun, and the cosmic serpent. The background of scrolls represents a matrix of cosmic energy that fills the universe.

20

the authority and beliefs of rural shamans. The die was cast and the mold prepared for a new vision to sweep across the land. Not only were the bronze cauldrons a result of man's mastery of technology, they were the primary vehicle for expressing the new religion of universal cosmic power. That was the important role played by symbols in this semiliterate society. The power signs actually had power--a very real power to spark the imagination and to transform the way people thought about their existence. It was a power that could be used either to control, or to liberate the minds of men.

The mystics conceived a new type of spiritual leader to replace the archaic shaman (Figure 21). He was not a ruler of pathetic peasants; instead, he was a

21

COSMIC SHAMAN
During the later part of the Shang dynasty, scroll forms replaced horns as a symbol of the cosmic forces of *yin* and *yang*. This indicates a shift in emphasis from pagan ritual to a philosophy based upon astrology, astronomy, and the concept of cosmic forces playing central roles in the life of mortals. This example is from a bronze drum.

teacher among equals. He was a *cosmic* shaman whose form encompassed all supernatural phenomena, and whose role it was to reveal the secrets of the universe. He was the shaman of technology--a Promethean figure who could bestow the powers of the heavens upon mankind.

The magic scroll was not yet the Omnibus Power Sign. That evolutionary leap would occur under the auspices of the Chou dynasty. Nevertheless, the magic scroll had become the premier Asian power sign, and it was well on its way to achieving a unique status among the world's religious motifs. In an era when the value of a symbol was usually determined by its singular meaning, magic scrolls were already being used to represent a whole host of related concepts. Soon, they would come to represent everything that had a spiritual or mystical quality in Asian art.

Time was running out for the Shang rulers. In the hinterlands, the Chou tribe was gaining power. Led by a chieftain who pledged to end the barbaric sacrifices of the orthodox Shang priesthood, growing numbers of warriors were training for combat. Propagandists also were preparing the way. According to rebellious Chou chroniclers, the king was a brutal tyrant who wallowed in debauchery--thereby dishonoring the sacred role of centralized government. With growing anticipation, the Chou leader consulted his diviners and astrologers. When the omens were favorable, he launched the attack.

Was it pure chance that the emperor was caught unprepared? Or was there cunning and deception behind the ominous message of the oracle bones?

History is elusive so far back in time. But one thing is certain: the rebels were victorious. And they were exceedingly thorough. A few years after the battle, a traveler visited An-Yang where the tyrant's palace had once stood. The meadows revealed no trace of the great Shang dynasty. As far as the eye could see, there was only millet grass bending in the wind.

ASIAN CEREMONIAL RIVERCRAFT
ca. 400 B.C. - 400 A.D.
Inscriptions like this one appear on bronze drums of the Dong-Son culture. They are believed to represent a vessel with a ceremonial purpose, however, the abstract nature of the composition makes any interpretation very precarious without additional information.

Symbols of a New Order

The destruction of An-Yang was only the first episode of a purge that ravaged the empire. Chou warriors rushed from city to city torching administrative records and chronicles in a ruthless effort to eradicate the literature, philosophy, and history of the previous dynasty. With the passing of generations, the very existence of the Shang state became shrouded in legend. For many, even the legends seemed unbelieveable. It was not until excavations of the buried An-Yang ruins in the 1920's produced irrefutable proof, that modern scholars were willing to concede that the Shang dynasty had ever existed.

Although none of the books written by Shang authors survived the purge, huge caches of oracle bones and inscriptions on bronze ceremonial vessels endured the passage of time. They reveal a much different version of the last Shang ruler than was propagated by the Chou Ministry of Education. The oracle inscriptions tell of a monarch who was held in high regard by the residents of the capital. Indeed, Ti-hsin risked his throne to protect the eastern provinces from invading barbarians. His palace guard at An-Yang was weakened considerably when he dispatched the main army to bolster the defense of the eastern cities.[1] It was hardly a coincidence that Chou generals chose the emperor's moment of weakness to attack. Inscriptions on Chou oracle bones reveal that spies were closely monitoring the movement of the Shang armies. Chou generals were well aware of the emperor's vulnerability, and they did not hesitate to exploit this moment for conquest.

The reign of the Chou emperors was a time of national expansion and commercial growth which spread from the northern provinces toward the south.[2] Eventually, the Chou empire encompassed an area nearly double that of the previous dynasty, as indicated by Map 3. In the span of nine centuries, from 1111 to 220 B.C., Chou rulers added thousands of square miles to the empire, while the population rose from a few million inhabitants to fourteen million.[3] By the middle of the Chou dynasty, there were more than a hundred provinces--each controlled by a warlord,

22

CHOU CULTURAL MONTAGE ca. 600 B.C.
The 6th-century Chinese had a highly developed state bureaucracy which administered to a population of thirty million inhabitants. Fortified cities (1) of 100,000 to one-half million residents were situated along the Hwang Ho and Yangtze Rivers and along the coast. Provincial monarchs battled with huge armies using bronze pikes (2) and swords, although the primary weapon was the steel-tipped arrow. Bronze was used extensively for casting ceremonial

vessels like the square-sided *tsun* (3) which were buried with nobles as an offering to ancestral spirits. Horse-drawn chariots (4) and wagons provided an effective means of transportation. These vehicles were depicted in Han dynasty bas-relief carvings. Jade *pi* disks (5), like those of the Neolithic Age, continued in use as part of a society oriented towards astrology and geomancy. Noble rulers, like the 8th-century B.C. King Wu, presided amidst the splendors of vast palatial estates. The King's image (6) is from a 4th-century A.D. painting.

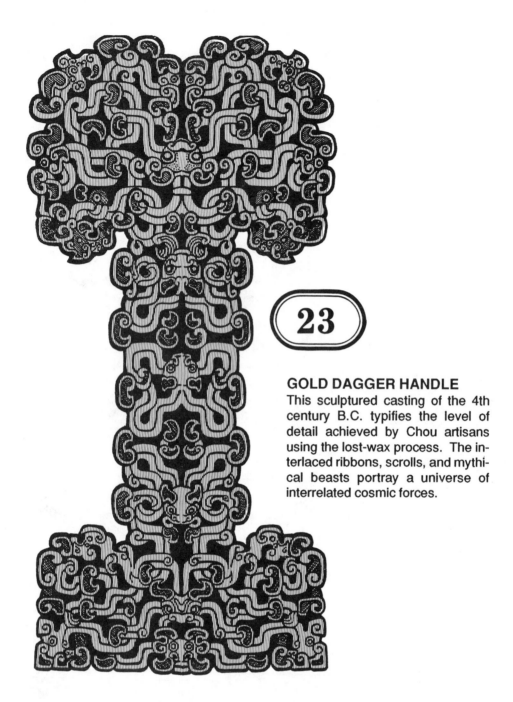

23

GOLD DAGGER HANDLE
This sculptured casting of the 4th century B.C. typifies the level of detail achieved by Chou artisans using the lost-wax process. The interlaced ribbons, scrolls, and mythical beasts portray a universe of interrelated cosmic forces.

or lesser king, and dominated by a fortified capital city. Warfare among the feudal provinces was virtually continuous, and merchants were hard pressed to resupply provincial armies. It was an exciting era for those who enjoyed the thrill of battle and the uncertainty of political intrigue.

In spite of the difficult times, philosophy, science, and the arts prospered. Figure 22 presents a cultural montage of mid-Chou art and architecture showing some of the incredible achievements of the dynasty. Fortifications with moats protected urban centers from marauding barbarians. In winter, these walled cities also provided temporary lodging for hordes of peasants who worked in the surrounding

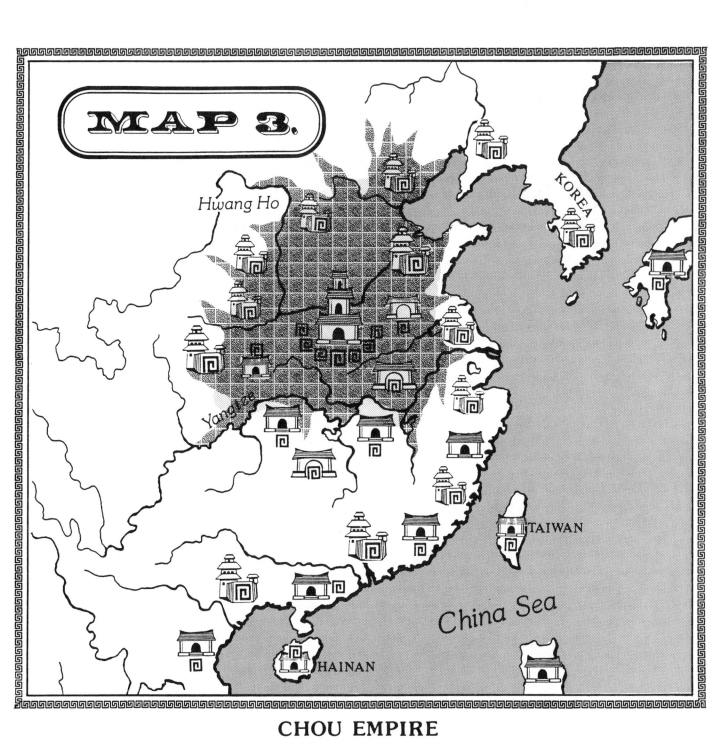

CHOU EMPIRE

Imperial conquests between 1100 and 700 B.C. expanded the empire to the south and west, including annexation of the central Yangtze River valley. Population grew rapidly, as did the number of fortress cities (a few of which are indicated on the map). The Omnibus Power Sign spread throughout the region along with the state bureaucracy.

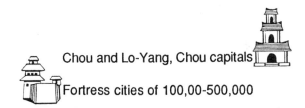

Chou and Lo-Yang, Chou capitals

Fortress cities of 100,00-500,000

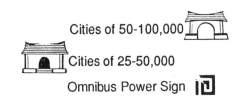

Cities of 50-100,000

Cities of 25-50,000

Omnibus Power Sign

CERAMIC TILES

These semicircular tiles were used to decorate the borders of tile roofs. They are embellished with power signs representing the creative forces of nature.

24

countryside. Millet and soybean farming constituted the primary sources of food, while ample supplies of fish, poultry, dogs, and wild animals provided variation to the diet.

It was an era of prodigious technological achievement, as farmers devised sophisticated methods of irrigation, crop rotation, fertilization, and breeding.[5] Metallurgy advanced at a rapid pace as alchemists experimented with new metals and casting techniques. By the seventh century B.C., iron casting came into use for the mass production of farming implements and tools.[6] There was another use for iron: the manufacture of weapons. Iron added to the mystique of battle by providing superior weapons that were cheaper and easier to manufacture. In a relatively short time, craftsmen were able to produce arrow points, axe blades, and swords in sufficient quantities to supply armies numbering in the hundreds of thousands. Warfare on a massive scale became the favorite pastime of kings--just as it had in the earlier civilizations of dynastic Egypt and Persia.

In spite of the public contempt Chou rulers held towards their predecessors, the artisans of the new empire chose to continue the artistic and philosophical traditions of the Shang dynasty. Consequently, Shang motifs and art styles continued in popularity as decorations for ceremonial bronze castings. However, Chou designs are often more elaborate than those of the Shang period. This stylistic commitment endured for the next nine centuries and led to the greatest elaboration of magic scrolls in religious art anywhere in the world. An example of the highly complex scrollwork is the sword hilt illustrated in Figure 23. It was produced by an innovative technique called "lost wax casting."

New products fueled the growing economy. Sun-baked, and later kiln-baked, bricks replaced mud and thatch as major building materials. Ceramic roof tiles gave Chinese architecture the distinctive orange and green patterns that still characterize pagodas and the homes of the wealthy. Tiles used to end the bottom row often carried the monogram of the proprietor, while magic scrolls were used as symbols of fertility and good fortune (Figure 24). Multistoried buildings towered over the smaller structures of previous years (Figure 25), while carts pulled by oxen brought increasing quantities of building materials from the distant forests. Silk was produced in enormous quantities to meet the local demand, and it was exported along the Silk Road to Persia and the Indus Valley. By the seventh century B.C., merchants from as far west as the Mediterranean visited Chinese ports.[7]

The growing demand for ritual objects and weapons resulted in a corresponding growth of mining and foundry work. Shipbuilding, road construction, horse training, and wagon repair emerged as thriving industries. Meanwhile, shopkeepers

IMPERIAL PALACE, 3RD CENTURY B.C.
Palatial architecture from the 6th century B.C. included spacious buildings up to seven stories high supported by beams, rafters, and columns. Walls consisted of sun-dried bricks and wood, and roofs were covered with ceramic tiles.

and local merchants occupied extensive market districts located within the walled cities. Like civilizations everywhere, China developed a state bureaucracy which set standards of conduct in every conceivable aspect of human endeavor, including business relationships. These were regulated by guilds. The increasingly more complex affairs of the monarch also came under the scrutiny of theologians and military leaders. Under the Chou government, urban religious leaders eradicated the archaic practice of human sacrifice--with the singular exception of a monarch's funeral.

The monarch continued to serve as the primary religious leader. He presided at major public rituals including the spring fertility rites which were held on giant ceremonial mounds (Figure 26). These stately pageants had a greater purpose than merely appeasing venerable ancestor spirits. Their primary social function was to

26 CHINESE PYRAMIDS ca. 600 B.C.
Excavations have identified the remains of ceremonial mounds from the Chou dynasty at Yang-tzu-shan, Szechwan province. It measures 140 meters long and 14 meters high. It was small by comparison to the Lishan tumulus of the 3rd century B.C., which rivals in size the great pyramids at Cheops, Egypt, and at Teotihuacan, Mexico.

preserve the traditional belief of the public in the divine sanction of the monarchy. By the fifth century B.C., religious practices among the ruling class were largely secondary to the more dominant bureaucratic relationships that governed day-to-day behavior.

Furthermore, monarchs found their own freedom and authority constrained by bureaucratic codes and tempered by tradition. Management of a growing empire required the services of numerous people, and the emperors found themselves surrounded by a flock of administrators, court followers, mystics, diviners, generals, and priests. Lesser kings and provincial warlords also found their actions being scrutinized more and more by vocal public figures who didn't always agree with their leaders. Nevertheless, Chou leaders fostered a benevolent attitude toward criticism and diversity of thought which resulted in a renaissance of philosophy and the arts. Successive monarchs allowed the intrusion of cadres of trained bureaucrats into their princely domains, leading to greater power--but less autonomy. They simultaneously encouraged the development of a state-centered moral philosophy advocated by Confucius, as well as the spiritual contemplation favored by the growing Taoist movement.

CHOU PHILOSOPHERS
This illustration from a Ming dynasty silk painting portrays Chinese philosophers contemplating the *yin/yang*. The origin of the symbol is attributed to the Mythical Emperors, ca. 3000 B.C., who are credited with introducing many of the attributes of civilization that give the Chinese their unique heritage.

Under the leadership of Lao Tzu, the Taoists emerged as a leading force in Chinese cultural development and philosophy during the sixth century B.C.[8] The enduring contribution of Taoists to the Chinese way of life was commemorated by tapestries produced during later dynasties (Figure 27). It was due to Taoist influence on alchemy and religion that the *yin/yang* symbol became a central motif in bronze casting between 1000 and 500 B.C. (Figure 28). Because of their influence and the standardization of motifs mandated by Chou leaders at Lo-Yang, dragon masks became prevalent throughout the empire.

The dragon mask, or *taotie*, was a versatile motif that met both the needs of the emperor and the needs of the mystics. The Taoists viewed God as a manifestation of cosmic power that permeated the universe. This cosmic force could appear in many forms, although its ultimate nature was one of formless energy. Therefore, the use of an abstract mask surmounted by innumerable scrolls was a suitable way to portray the infinite creative power of the supreme cosmic being.

These symbols from Chou dynasty bronze castings indicate the presence of a symbol that was a dominant theme in Chinese philosophy. The example at the far left (ca. 1000 B.C.) shows the motif as a composite of two encircling dragons with eyes and mouths. Eyes were retained in later stylized motifs of the Ming dynasty. The example on the near left shows the most common form of the *yin/yang* as two encircled scrolls. Consequently, dragons and scrolls were regarded as transformational motifs that could be used interchangeably in religious art.

PI DISK ca. 400 B.C.
This nephrite (jade) carving is one of many produced by Chou artisans. In addition to the surface pattern of germinating grain scrolls that was a tradition inherited from previous dynasties, dragons and scrolls are shown emerging from the disk as a representation of cosmic energy.

29

DRAGON MASKS

30

These bronze castings show two of the numerous mask designs that are common on Chou artifacts. Variously referred to as the *t'ao-t'ieh*, or "glutton" motif, the chinless dragon depicts a spiritual being that is composed of pure energy. Abundant use of scroll-shaped power signs indicates a transformational power to assume different shapes or to disappear entirely.

By using a mask to represent the supreme being, Taoist mystics were indulging in an act of deception: the same symbol that seemed to portray fierceness to the king's warriors was also the guidepost for a novice in his quest for spiritual growth.[9] Priests regarded the mask as an example of the illusion of an external god, and they used it to direct the attention of novices toward an awareness of the essential holy experience called *enlightenment*. The quest for enlightenment lead to unusual "paths" and unusual risks. So it was that some mystics achieved notoriety by drinking exotic potions, eating hallucinogenic plants, and engaging in exotic behavior as they sought to experience a fleeting moment of cosmic glory. As it turned out, some of these potions were poisonous--leading to death or permanent brain injury and seizures.

Followers of Confucius regarded the mystical Taoists as misguided charlatans. According to their doctrine of righteous behavior, the soul's journey to heaven was the reward given mortals for living a virtuous life. This doctrine also specified the principles of behavior necessary for maintaining a smoothly running bureaucracy. Confucius believed that mortal life was virtually independent of divine intervention, thus he stressed the importance of maintaining appropriate interpersonal relationships over a concern for supernatural phenomena. He expressed this belief by saying "Man is near, while Heaven is far away." Nevertheless, he also recognized the importance of ritual and tradition in controlling the behavior of the masses. Consequently, he encouraged the emperor to engage in frequent displays of pomp and pageantry for the sole purpose of maintaining the mystique a divinely-sanctioned monarchy. While urban bureaucrats found the path of virtuous action sufficient for their sophisticated temperament, the spiritual beliefs of the urban poor and rural peasants became a composite of pagan and mystical practices. It was the beliefs of the mystics, however, that were manifest in the art of the age.

A few of the artifacts designed by Chou craftsmen are presented in Figures 29 through 34. New scroll forms gained popularity for the representation of cosmic

OMNIBUS POWER SIGN (VARIATIONS)

These Chou artifacts portray some of the many symbolic uses made of scrolls. Above left is the sacred tree, or Cosmic Power Sign (1), emerging from the mouth of an earth monster. It is followed by two jade disks with dragons (2 and 3). The stylized scrolls represent the cosmos as a matrix of cosmic forces. Other designs portray bird wings (4 and 7), or the power of flight. Scrolls are also used as appendages to human heads (5) indicating life force and consciousness. Body scrolls (6) indicate life force, while antler scrolls are associated with the life-giving power of springtime. Usage of scrolls to represent multiple concepts indicate the presence of an omnibus power sign.

32 **TWO VIEWS OF HEAVEN**

Han dynasty mortuary carvings portray contemporary beliefs regarding the after life. The bas-relief on the left shows the mask god, or supreme being, as a symbol for universal cosmic energy. From the being's jawless mouth emerges the universe of cosmic energy as represented by the disk and dragons, while ethereal birds and animal spirits swirl about in clouds of cosmic power. It represents a Taoist impression of the harmonic forces of nature. The example on the right is more in tune with the Confucian philosophy of heaven as a smoothly running spiritual bureaucracy. At the top is the ancestral patron, Shang-Ti, while below are sequential levels of angels, spirits, and mortals doing their appropriate tasks and paperwork in accordance with the rules of honorable behavior.

33 THE COSMIC MATRIX

A universe of cosmic forces is indicated by this surface of interlaced scrolls from a Chou bronze vessel. The scroll background was popular during the Shang dynasty and received even greater emphasis and elaboration among Chou artisans.

34

SUPREME BEING (MASK GOD)
This portrayal on a jade vase of the Chou dynasty represents the supreme being as a formless source of cosmic energy and consciousness. Scrolls represent cosmic energy, which emerges from the being in the same manner that vines emerge from the ground, or clouds emerge mysteriously amidst the sky.

forces (i.e., *yin* and *yang*), which were rendered alternatively by two opposed or intertwined dragons. Magic scrolls were portrayed emerging from the heads of animals and human beings to represent consciousness and life force, while a host of miniature dragons and scrolled serpents represented other spiritual powers associated with humans and mythical animals.

Artists followed the Shang tradition of using magic scrolls to represent the sacred tree (Figure 31). However, they added a new variation by having the base of the tree emerge from the mouth of an earth deity--or "earth monster," as it is sometimes referred to by western authors. Scroll motifs continued in use to represent the clouds of heaven. Additionally, they were employed to represent sexual potency, rain water flowing from the mouth of the cosmic being, the breath of life, and the power of flight.

The uniqueness of Chou symbolism and beliefs is apparent when we examine the typical manner in which other dynasties portrayed the power of flight (Figure 35). Among the Shang, flight was regarded as a power of the cosmic serpent (lightning), and it was portrayed as a serpent and feathers. Many centuries later, during the first century A.D., Han dynasty artisans made use of flowing ribbons, or "flying scarves," which Hellenistic traditions regarded as a representation of heavenly wind.

Chou artisans, on the other hand, typically used scroll motifs to represent the concept of "magical flight." This unique concept explains why Chinese dragons seldom have wings--unlike their European counterparts which are characterized by wings suitable for giant eagles, or pterodactyls. The Asian tradition of using magic scrolls, or cloud scrolls, along with dragon motifs derives from the belief that dragons don't actually have to fly like birds. Instead, they are presumed to have magical powers that enable them to float through the air as effortlessly as a fish swims through water. Consequently, during the Chou dynasty, dragons were

35

HISTORY OF FLIGHT SYMBOLS IN ASIA

Early Shang symbols associated flight with the celestial serpent which was incorporated into wings (1). Chou artisans relied primarily on magic scrolls to portray the flight of dragons (2). Flight scrolls of Han dynasty deities (3) used a half-scroll/half ribbon motif as Helenistic influence spread north from India with the Buddhist religion. The main Helenistic (Greek) symbol for heavenly flight was the flowing scarf or ribbon (4) which became prevalent in China and Japan (5) by the 4th Century A.D. Nevertheless, the archaic flight scrolls endured in remote Tibet (6) and artists of 5th-Century China tried to compromise in the design of wings on monumental horse sculptures (7).

typically portrayed with scrolls emanating from their backs, or legs, to represent this supernatural ability.

Since Taoist philosophy contends that everything derives from cosmic forces--*everything* can be represented by magic scrolls. This belief and its artistic expression constitute an incredible development in the history of art, since the Taoists disregarded the rule of finite representation. In fact, it is often impossible to know what the Taoist symbols represent without examining their use in the context of a broad range of other motifs. It is this broader context which can be used, judiciously, to infer the symbolic function of the scrolls themselves. Nevertheless, the motifs can still have double or triple meanings--since the Taoists regarded cosmic forces as transformational or interchangeable entities.

This broad usage of magic scrolls provides substantial evidence that the Chinese mystics of the first millennium B.C. established a very unusual artistic tradition: the Asian Omnibus Power Sign. However, it probably wasn't the first. As we shall see, there is some evidence that Chinese cultures preceding the Shang used a bracket-shaped motif in a similar fashion. Be that as it may, the Omnibus Power Sign constitutes the primary scientific evidence for Asian trans-Pacific voyages to America during the time of the Chou dynasty.

It is by tracing the spread of this unusual motif tradition in the archaeological records of East Asia and Meso-America that we are able to substantiate the validity of Nu Sun's voyage. However, before we examine the evidence for the exportation of the Omnibus Power Sign to the Americas, it is appropriate for us to consider the kind of naval technology available in China during the sixth century B.C. This will enable us to ascertain whether or not such a voyage was even feasible for merchant sailors from the Orient.

MORTUARY BANNER
This is the lower section of a Han dynasty banner which portrays contemporary religious symbols. Many of these are continuations of Neolithic themes, such as the *Pi* disk at center and the two dragons representing *Yin* and *Yang*. Others, such as the ribbons and owls show more recent Hindu-Buddist and Mediterranean influences.

Asian Sailing Traditions

For many scholars, the issue of whether or not Asians may have played a role in the development of New-World civilization begins and ends with a belief that trans-Pacific voyages were impossible. This belief stems from an assumption that Asians lacked adequate vessels to make the crossing until the fourth century A.D.[1]

Furthermore, there is an implicit assumption that Chinese scribes would have recorded details about any successful crossing in their royal chronicles. But we have already determined that ordinary merchants did not warrant mention in the chronicles, and they expressly avoided public disclosure of activities that might lead to greater taxation. While chronicles may have been reliable following the Han dynasty, earlier records were destroyed by purges as the title of emperor passed from one dynasty to the next.

An attempt by Kuno Knobl to sail a junk from Hong Kong to America in 1974 was unsuccessful, leading some skeptics to regard the failure as evidence that ancient Chinese lacked sufficient marine technology for making the journey. Knobl's vessel, the *Tai-Ki*, was built in accordance with the design of a model riverboat recovered from a Chinese tomb dating to the first century A.D. The boat sank in the mid-Pacific after being battered by hurricanes and attacked by ship-worms.

Does the loss of the *Tai-Ki* support the belief that the Chinese lacked adequate vessels for crossing the ocean? Or, does it support the theory that twentieth-century scholars don't know much about the navigational skills of ancient seafarers? The answer will become clear as we examine the evidence for Asian sailing traditions.

Although the evidence of ancient shipbuilding technology and ocean travel is scarce, it is far from nonexistent. Other scholars have given extensive treatment to the legends, linguistic evidence, artifacts, and historical accounts, so we will provide only a cursory review for those who are unfamiliar with the subject.

36

SACRED MUSHROOM MOTIF
A Chinese legend popular among Taoists between 500 and 200 B.C. held that the sacred food of Immortals, or *ling chih*, grew plentifully on a mysterious paradise across the Pacific Ocean. This legend was strong enough for the mushroom motif to become a popular feature in the arts of the Sung, Ming, and later dynasties. These examples include designs from a ceramic vase (1), ca. A.D. 1000, plate decorations (2 and 3), a Korean motif (4), and a 19th-century jade carving (5).

There are several Chinese legends regarding voyages to a mountainous paradise across the sea. This land, called the Isle of The Blest, was considered to be the habitation of immortals.[2] Hsu Fu is said to have made a voyage there during the third century B.C., for the primary purpose of obtaining a sacred plant called *ling-chih*, or "food of the gods." The sacred plant was actually a variety of hallucinogenic mushroom which was supposed to grow in abundance. By eating this plant, mortals were presumed to achieve immortality, or become enlightened. Consequently, Taoists and wealthy Chinese were anxious to obtain the magic mushrooms. According to the legend, Hsu Fu took along a large entourage of young men and women, but alas, he did not return. Was the Isle of The Blest actually America? On that subject, the scholars disagree. Some say it was Japan, others claim it was simply a figment of some mystic's imagination.

A Buddhist chronicle, the *Laing Shu*, recounts the overseas journey of five monks in the year A.D. 458 to a land called Fu Sang. Some scholars assume this land to be America. Others have scoffed at such a presumption, because the account describes the presence of horse-drawn carts. Since carts and horses were probably absent in the Americas until the Spanish conquest, the validity of the Fu Sang account is questionable--unless it actually refers to Japan. Nevertheless, such glaring discrepancies should not discredit the entire legend. They might simply constitute the innocent additions of later storytellers who hoped to make the legend seem more realistic by adding embellishments that were familiar to their audiences.

Whether or not there is any truth to the legends, they were popular enough throughout the Orient for later generations of artisans to pay them considerable attention (Figure 36). Furthermore, the lure of immortality would have provided ample incentive for Taoists and wealty merchants to explore distant lands, just as the Fountain of Youth legends brought Spanish explorers into the swamps of Florida during the sixteenth century.

Linguistic evidence is more authentic than legend, although it also is quite limited in what it reveals about the nature of ancient marine technology. Ample references in the bronze and bone inscriptions verify that advanced marine technology was available during the Shang dynasty (ca. 1500 B.C.). We know, for example, that the Chinese pictogram for "boat" was used during this period, as were the pictograms indicating "sail," and "caulking the seams of a boat" (Figure 37).[3] Caulking is a concern only when ships are constructed from planks, and planks are the primary component of wooden ships. As soon as a builder has the technical skills necessary for the manufacture of planks, the size of vessel he can construct is limited only by his imagination and the amount of wood he has to work with.

The inscriptions on Shang oracle bones further reveal that shipping was a common activity on the major rivers,[4] while vessels of considerable size were used in military campaigns of the sixth century B.C. According to the bone inscriptions, large seagoing junks enabled the transport of armies to distant provinces. The same vessels returned with thousands of prisoners.[5] Such descriptions tell us little about the nature of Chinese ships, although it is reasonable to assume that military campaigns would have involved some kind of specialized craft suitable for combat.

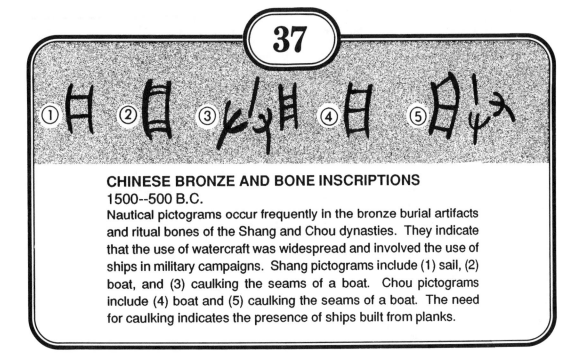

CHINESE BRONZE AND BONE INSCRIPTIONS
1500--500 B.C.
Nautical pictograms occur frequently in the bronze burial artifacts and ritual bones of the Shang and Chou dynasties. They indicate that the use of watercraft was widespread and involved the use of ships in military campaigns. Shang pictograms include (1) sail, (2) boat, and (3) caulking the seams of a boat. Chou pictograms include (4) boat and (5) caulking the seams of a boat. The need for caulking indicates the presence of ships built from planks.

38

CHINESE GALLEYS ca. 500--200 B.C.
These are the earliest known depictions of Asian watercraft. As was the case with many other cultures, the artists have sacrificed accuracy to focus upon the symbolic aspects of the design. Nevertheless, the position of the oarsmen and the warriors suggests the presence of a double-decked vessel.

Throughout the world, the rise of civilizations have been accompanied by characteristic patterns of technological development. Typically, advanced ship-building traditions emerge concurrently with the development of metal casting technology--as the materials, social organization, and scientific skills needed for metal casting are the same ingredients needed to produce sophisticated vessels.[6] In this regard, China was among the world's most advanced civilizations between 500 and 100 B.C., and it is likely that several major shipbuilding traditions were already in existence regardless of the scarcity of archaeological evidence.[7]

We can identify five major traditions in Asia. These include: double-decked galleys, catamarans (or boats with outriggers), sailing rafts, rivercraft, and ocean-going traders. We will focus our attention on galleys and oceangoing traders, since these are the most likely candidates for a merchant expedition across the ocean.

The earliest depictions of Chinese warships (Figure 38) come from bronze containers dating to the fourth century B.C. The designs are of double-decked galleys engaged in combat. Their precise dimensions are impossible to ascertain, because the artisans have sacrificed accuracy in naval architecture for the sake of showing the battle scene. We can surmise that the compositions show some kind of galley because the men on the lower level are drawing upon long oars rather than short paddles. Whether or not these vessels also included sails is impossible to determine, although sails were an integral part of imperial galleys during the Ming dynasty (ca. A.D. 1360-1600), and they are described in Shang writings of 1500 B.C.

Galleys were common throughout Indo-China from the eighth through the thirteenth centuries A.D. One type of vessel that engaged in commerce during this period is presented in Figure 39. The accurate detail of the Borobudur stone murals

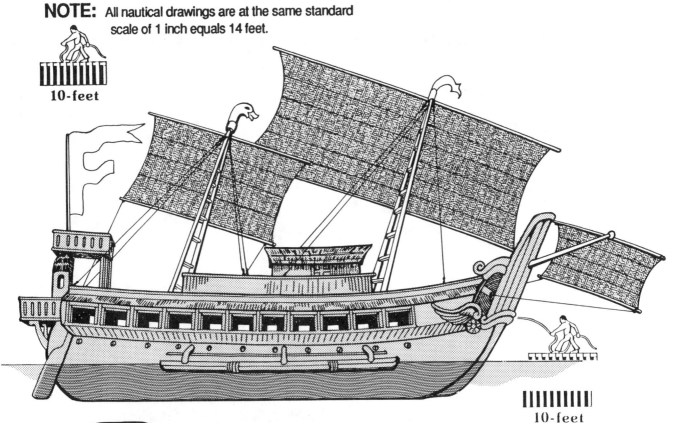

NOTE: All nautical drawings are at the same standard scale of 1 inch equals 14 feet.

10-feet

10-feet

(39)

JAVANESE GALLEY ca. A.D. 800--1300
This rendering of an 8th-century Indonesian vessel is from the highly detailed stone carvings of Borobudur. It featured two outriggers and mat sails. The ladder masts and side-mounted steering oars are characteristics that indicate an Egyptian source for shipbuilding technology. Length: about 80-100 feet.

is indicative of the highly-skilled stone carving tradition that came to Indonesia via India between the first and the eighth centuries A.D. The Java galley had ladder-style masts that seem reminiscent of Egyptian designs, as well as side-mounted steering oars that are suggestive of Mediterranean influence. The fact that galleys were still being used throughout Indo-China in the twentieth century indicates the presence of a naval tradition that has existed for at least 2,300 years in East Asia.

An even longer tradition is indicated for the most characteristic of Chinese vessels: the junk. A clay model of the common river junk dating to a time period between 100 B.C. and A.D. 200 was found in a tomb near Hong Kong (Figure 40). It has flat sides, a flat bottom, and flat prow which make it an excellent vessel in areas where a shallow draft is desirable. The primary means of propulsion was by a single reed-mat sail, or else it was towed by laborers and horses as they marched along the shore. During the Ming dynasty, vessels of this type were a common feature of paintings on silk. These paintings constitute our primary source of information regarding their design. Nevertheless, it is apparent from the dating of the clay model that there is a span of more than a thousand years for which we have virtually no evidence of their existence. The fact that similar vessels are still in use

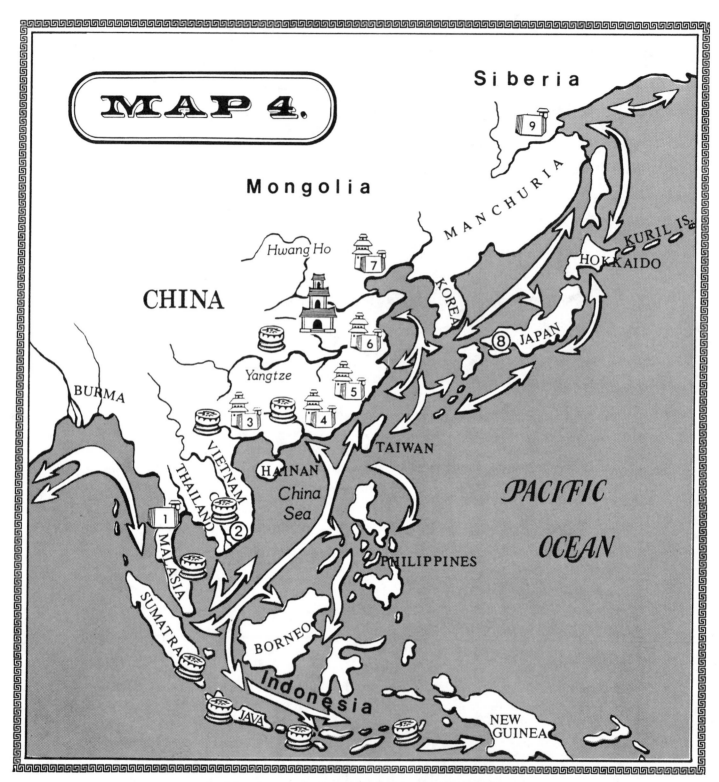

ASIAN MARITIME COMMERCE

on Chinese waters clearly demonstrates that the tradition is at least two thousand years old, while the bone inscriptions suggest that junks were present on Chinese rivers nearly four thousand years ago. Regardless of their antiquity, such vessels were not suitable for ocean travel due to their awkwardness and limited capacity for sail. Consequently, Asian shipbuilders adapted the design of junks to make them more seaworthy for long-distance commerce on the China Sea. The result was the oceangoing trader.

The ocean trader was characterized by a curved bottom hull, sternpost rudder, and up to four sails of reed matting. They also had water-tight compartments below decks and oil lamps for night lighting. The beginning date for the oceangoing junk tradition is another subject of controversy, although it seems reasonable to assume that suitable craft were in existence by the time Asian merchants were engaging in trade networks that stretched from Siberia to Indonesia (Map 4).

The primary evidence for merchant activity between 700 and 100 B.C. is the progressively larger geographical distribution of a diagnostic group of artifacts and motifs called the Dongson culture. By 700 B.C., painted pottery of the Dongson culture was present in Hong Kong--a port city that was already distinguished for its seafaring.[8] The Dongson ceramic style has a characteristic interlocking scroll pattern (Figure 41) which enables archaeologists to trace both the expanding limits of the culture, as well as the growing trade routes between China and outlying areas. Dongson bronze drums have been found in North Vietnam dating to the fourth century B.C.[9], and they occur in southeast Indo-China dating from the fourth to the third century B.C. Map 4 indicates the distribution of Dongson bronze drums which spread throughout Indonesia by 100 B.C. The symbolism of the Dongson style is prevalent in Indonesia--reflecting the existence of widespread trade networks established in ancient times. In Sumatra, Dongson ceramics occur in association with the *naga* serpent and swastika, indicating the long reach of Chinese cultural influence prior to the first century A.D. At that time, a massive Hindu migration came into the area from India.[10]

MARITIME TRADE ca. 500--100 B.C.

The vast growth of Chinese populations and maritime technology made possible extensive trade between the mainland and independent island states. Vessels from Phoenicia, Rome, and Persia passed between Malaysia and Sumatra on their way to Cathay (ancient China). Merchants traveled as far as Siberia for gold, ivory, and furs in exchange for iron and grain. In the tropical islands of Indonesia, they traded bronze and grain for spices and exotic birds. Bronze drums spread along with this trade from southern China and Vietnam to the outer islands of Java and Timor by 100 B.C.

KEY

MAJOR PORTS
1. Bangkok
2. Chochin China delta
3. Hanoi
4. Hong Kong, Kwang Chow
5. Foochow
6. Shanghai, Hangchow
7. Tientsin
8. Koyoto, Osaka
9. Chumikan

 Bronze drums traded before 100 B.C.

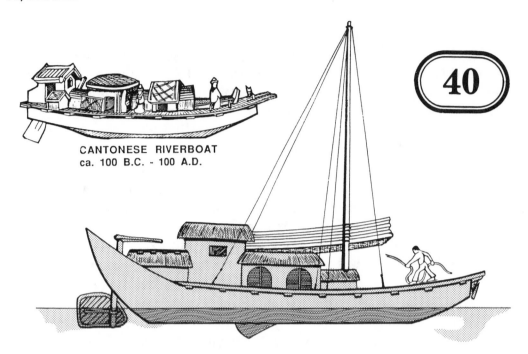

CANTONESE RIVERBOAT
ca. 100 B.C. - 100 A.D.

40

RIVER JUNKS ca. 1500 B.C. to the present
A long shipbuilding tradition is evident from these examples of
Chinese river junks. The Han dynasty model (inset) is from a
1st-century tomb, while the nautical drawing is from a Ming silk
painting of the 13th-century. Similar vessels are still used on Asian
rivers--indicating the great depth with which this ancient tradition
is ingrained in Chinese culture.

Records of early Chinese trade networks are virtually nonexistent as a consequence of the book burnings of the Ch'in dynasty in 223 B.C. Nevertheless, the
discovery of carved ivory pendants made from fossilized mammoth tusks in Chou
graves indicates the presence of trade contacts with Siberia by 500 B.C.[11] Although
land routes could have been used for the trade, the use of sea routes is also a
possibility. Recent excavations at Kwangchow, in the Peoples Republic, confirm the
emphasis given to trade on the high seas. By the third century B.C., shipyards had
the capacity for building merchant vessels as long as *eighty feet* and weighing up to
sixty tons.[12] The presence of such a facility shows that the Chinese were seriously
involved in shipping--in spite of the near void of historical and artistic evidence.

The annals of the Han dynasty (200 B.C. to A.D. 200) describe trade routes
stretching from India to Indonesia.[13] The *Han-Shu* (or Han history) indicates that
Wu Ti established a sea route to India involving the shipment of a cargo of silks and
gold weighing many tons. These were shipped to a town near Madras in the year
140 B.C. In order to undertake such a voyage over several thousand miles on the
open sea, the vessel must have been from a tradition of seagoing junks as opposed
to the flat-bottomed variety of river junk. This historical account of long-distance
commerce gives support to the view that development of oceangoing vessels had

DONGSON MOTIFS
Characteristic motifs of a culture that began in southern China and Vietnam, between 800 and 400 B.C., enable archaeologists to trace the spread of Dongson culture and Chinese influence to the islands of Indonesia by 100 B.C.

taken place at least several centuries prior to the Madras connection. Indeed, the account seems to suggest that the vessel was part of a well-established technology. That would suggest an origin for oceangoing ships by the mid-first millennium B.C., or earlier.

An account by Wan Chen, titled *Strange Things of the South,* indicates that four-masted, oceangoing vessels were equipped with fore-and-aft lug sails by the second century A.D. Such vessels reportedly carried up to 700 people along with 260 tons of cargo.[14] The fore-and-aft lug sail with battens was better suited for sailing into the wind and was much more versatile than the square-rigging typical of Mediterranean ship designs. Chen's account of sailing techniques is a clear indication that the Chinese had a fully developed ocean sailing technology by this point in time--regardless of the fact that no artistic evidence exists to show what the vessels actually looked like.

The Chinese were not alone. Before the first century A.D., merchants from the subcontinent of India were also sailing to Siberia seeking gold. However, competi-

INDO-CHINESE VESSELS ca. A.D. 200--1200
Murals and rock carvings in East Asia depict sailing ships involved in ancient commerce between India, Indonesia, and China. They include Hindu trading vessels (1--ca. A.D. 200, 2--ca. A.D. 600) and a Cambodian junk (3--ca. A.D. 1200).

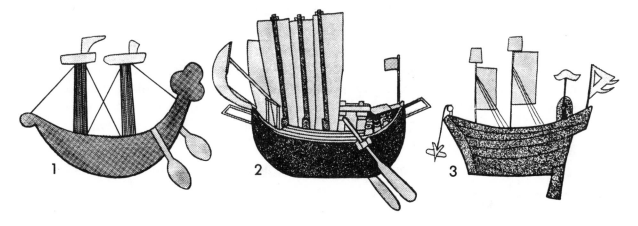

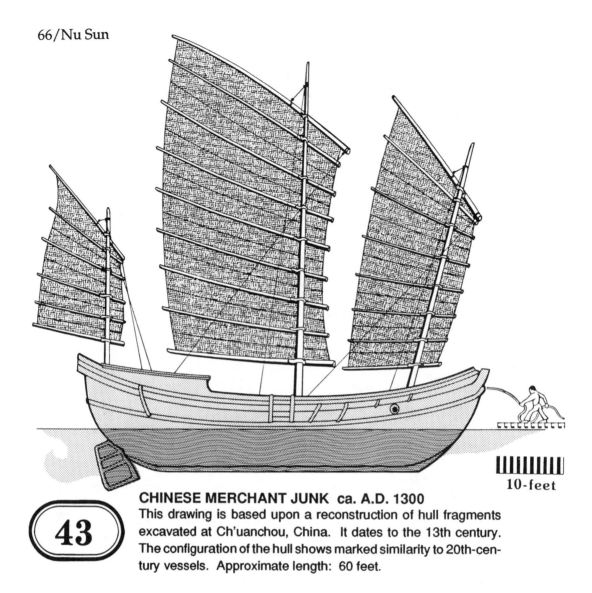

CHINESE MERCHANT JUNK ca. A.D. 1300
This drawing is based upon a reconstruction of hull fragments
excavated at Ch'uanchou, China. It dates to the 13th century.
The configuration of the hull shows marked similarity to 20th-century vessels. Approximate length: 60 feet.

43

10-feet

tion with the Chinese soon became too much of a risk for the Calcutta merchants, and they turned their attention toward Indonesia as an alternative source for precious metal.[15] They found it in abundance among the islands know as *Suvarnabhumi*--The Land of Gold. There is some speculation that these islands were actually a way station in a slave-for-gold trade with Meso-America.

This was not the earliest maritime venture from the subcontinent. Hindu books dating to the fifth century B.C., the *Puranas* and *Jatakas*, describe epic sea voyages reaching as far as Malaysia and Indonesia.[16] So it appears, after all, that the Far East was alive with shipping activity long before the Europeans began their conquest of the Orient.

During this same period, an atlas published by the Roman astronomer, mathematician and geographer, Ptolemy, indicates that his countrymen had extensive knowledge of the South China Sea.[17] The world was on the move! Sailors were traveling thousands of miles to distant lands--and Columbus would not be born for another thirteen centuries!

Several murals found outside of China depict large pre-Columbian vessels

SOUTH CHINA TRADING JUNK ca. A.D. 1800
Vessels of this design have been common on the South China Sea since the early 1800's. Use of cloth sails may be a feature adopted from Western sources, although the basic characteristics of lug sails, stern rudder, and curved hull constructed around bulkheads probably dates to 500 B.C., or earlier. Approximate length: 70 feet (as shown) to 200 feet.

(Figure 42). Most of these were probably more seaworthy than river junks, and they could easily have made a voyage to the New World across the Pacific. The vessels show a curious blending of Asian and Mediterranean design features--which is not surprising considering that they occur in India and Cambodia where Mediterranean influence was substantial.[18] The vessels are similar to ships depicted in the murals of Borobudur, and they would have been in service at a time when Indo-Chinese voyages to America were taking place (i.e., during the second to ninth centuries A.D.).

The most suitable vessel for Nu Sun's expedition was the curved-bottom junk or ocean trader. Such vessels are frequently portrayed in the paintings of the Sung and Ming dynasties, although the earliest archaeological evidence comes from the remains of a thirteenth-century vessel excavated near Ch'uanchou (Figure 43). It is

45

IMPERIAL CRUISER, A.D. 1200 - 1500
The Giant Junk, or *Pechili* junk, sailed in fleets of more than sixty ships from China to Africa in 1431. Estimates of the size of these vessels range from 200 feet (as shown) to nearly 600 feet.

10-feet

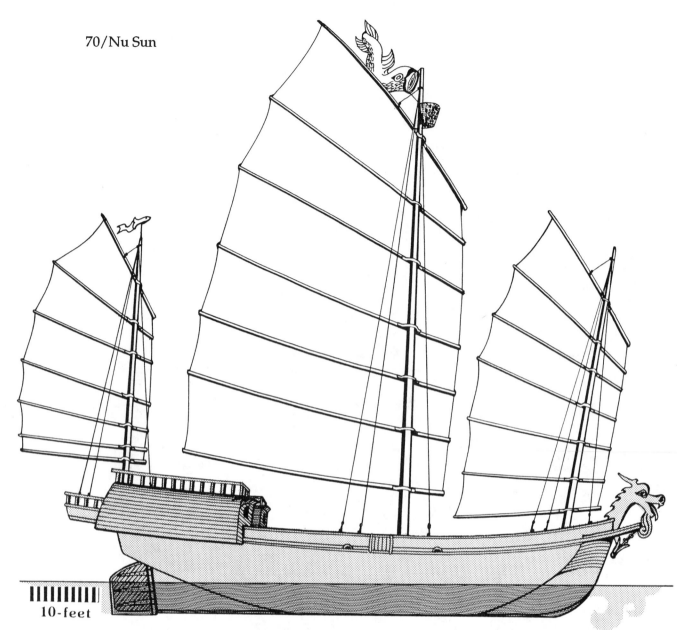

NU SUN'S SHIP ca. 550 B.C.

46

This is an artist's conception of the design of Nu Sun's expeditionary vessels, which sailed from China to Meso-America ca. 500 B.C. The vessel was probably an adaptation of an existing ship design that was ancestral to the Canton seagoing junk. Cloth sails may have been an early design feature borrowed from Phoenician merchants. Approximate length: 70-80 feet.

10-feet

a sixty-footer, with three masts and a stern rudder. It is similar in design to fleets of oceangoing junks from Canton and the South China Sea that plied Asian waters in recent centuries. By the late nineteenth century, some of them had reached *two hundred* feet in length. Similar vessels of this tradition are still in service in the outlying regions of Hong Kong.

An oceangoing junk similar to the Canton Trader (Figure 44) is the ideal candidate for a long-distance voyage of discovery. Vessels of this basic design were

EAST ASIA

THE VULTURE WING
During the Shang and Chou dynasties, wings were typically portrayed using scroll shapes, particularly when the wings were associated with serpents. During the late Chow (ca. 500 B.C.), however, a unique specimen (right) was found to have elongated wings that are similar to the characteristic vulture wings of Egypt (left) and Phoenicia (center).

probably in use as early as 1000 B.C.--at a time when Chinese trade routes seem to have begun a concerted expansion into southeast Asia.

One further example of the genius of Asian shipbuilders deserves our attention. It is surely one of the most bizarre vessels ever constructed by man: it is the Giant Junk of the Yuan dynasty (Figure 45). This two-hundred foot vessel is similar to giant ships depicted on silk paintings and described in chronicles of the Yuan and Ming dynasties between A.D. 1260 and 1600. In 1405, Admiral Cheng Ho led an expedition of sixty of these vessels, including 28,000 men and horses, on a twenty-two thousand mile voyage to Java, India, Persia, Mecca, Somaliland, and back to China.[19]

Although vessels of this variety occurred too late to have any impact on the design of Nu Sun's ships, they do provide us with some clues regarding the ingenuity of Chinese shipbuilders. Ultimately, the issue of what kind of ship Nu Sun used requires an educated guess, and we are in a better position to make an educated guess if we truly understand the nature of developing civilizations, the impact of bronze on shipbuilding technology, and the inventiveness of shipbuilders in a particular part of the world.

Nu Sun's Ship -- The Dragon

As the basis for designing an expeditionary vessel, Nu Sun selected a ship he was familiar with: the Canton seagoing trader. With its curved bottom and large size (50-60 feet), it had ample cargo capacity for a long-distance voyage. Nu Sun's vessel, however, was a bit longer than the average merchant junk--perhaps twenty feet longer. It was by no means a giant ship--being only slightly longer than the caravels of Columbus. However, a few extra feet provided vital storage capacity for the long voyage, and there was room for a larger crew. From his trips between Siberia and Sumatra, Nu Sun knew the hazards of long-distance travel: some men would become too ill to do their jobs, while others might die. There had to be reserves to take their places.

He also knew the importance of sailing with a companion vessel that could provide assistance in the event of attack by pirates, or an accidental beaching on a sand bar. Consequently, he built at least two vessels to his demanding specifications, and he arranged for several industrious colleagues to accompany him in their own junks. As a merchant of considerable wealth and connections, he had the resources required for building ships and mounting a successful expedition to the Isle of The Blest. However, being an enterprising capitalist, he demanded substantial investments from colleagues who stood to benefit from his venture.

In order to avoid the clutches of the empire's tax collectors, Nu Sun chose a site far from the empire to build his innovative ships--perhaps Canton or Hainan. It is equally possible that they were built even farther from the empire--perhaps, as far away as Cambodia, Korea, or Indonesia. But that is a matter of no great concern to us--considering the comparatively greater magnitude of the voyage itself.

An artist's conception of Nu Sun's flagship is presented in Figure 46. Most ships of his day probably had only two masts. However, Nu Sun's ship had three--partly because adding twenty feet of length to the hull provided room for an additional mast, and particularly because the admiral wanted the extra speed and security an additional mast could provide. The tiller, which controlled an adjustable rudder, was surrounded by a deckhouse at the stern. In high winds or stormy seas, the helmsmen could control the ship without fear of being washed overboard. Also, in case of attack, the men at the helm were not vulnerable to arrows or spears, enabling them to maintain steerage and maneuverability throughout the battle. Finally, an aft deck behind the deckhouse supported rigging for the aft sail, while providing a convenient toilet for the crew.

The most unique aspect of Nu Sun's vessel were the sails, which were made of muslin instead of matting. Perhaps the idea occurred to the admiral as a result of

CHINA   CHINA   PHOENICIA

48

ALIEN OWLS IN CHINA
During the Shang and Chou dynasties, owls (left) are typically portrayed from a profile view, and the wings often have scroll forms incorporated into the design. However, by the Han dynasty (ca. 200 B.C.), a new style of owl is sometimes seen in mortuary carvings and banners (center). The new design is suspiciously similar to the Aegean/Phoenician owl of the 5th century B.C.

CHINESE DRAGON BOAT
This woodblock print shows a dragon boat of the Ming period, ca. A.D. 1300. It is equipped with a sail and rockets. The side-mounted steering oar was occasionally used alone or in addition to the more popular rudder suspended below the stern.

49

contact with a Phoenician trader in Java; or perhaps he got the idea from watching someone's sheets dangling from a clothesline. At any rate, he used the cloth primarily because it was easier to stow in a bad storm, and it was quicker to hoist because of its lighter weight. A seasoned traveler like Nu Sun was cognizant of such minute details before departing on a long voyage to uncharted lands. And because of his attention to detail, the voyage was destined to be successful.

Two alien art motifs occurred in China during the time of Nu Sun's voyage, and they may shed some light on the issue of Phoenician contacts. On the other hand, they may simply be some of the extraneous clues that are part of another puzzle entirely. They are presented in Figures 47 and 48, depicting serpent and owl motifs of Asian and Mediterranean origins. The peculiar feature of the winged serpent is the wings. The highly elongated and pointed wing is a fairly common motif throughout the Middle East. It also occurs in Greek and Roman mythology in the form of the *caduceus* (i.e., intertwined serpents on a staff). In Egypt, the serpent gods and the sun disk appear with wings--but they are very unusual wings in terms of prehistoric art. They are long and slender--like the wings of vultures. Only one example of this kind of winged serpent occurs in the art of the Chou dynasty, and there are no other known examples from other time periods. It is apparent, therefore, that we are dealing with something that has no traditional basis in Chinese art. Since the art of most primitive societies and emerging civilizations tends to manifest certain traditional themes, we are led to suspect the possibility of an intrusion from a foreign culture.

The same is true with regard to the owl motif. Usually, the ancient Chinese portrayed the owl from a side view. The quarter-side view, however, is a trait most commonly identified with Classical Greece of the sixth century B.C. The importance of these artifacts is that they provide additional evidence that Chinese merchants had contact with Mediterranean cultures--a further indication that Nu Sun was in a position to benefit from the latest advances in Phoenician marine technology. Indeed, Phoenician visits are regarded as a possible source for the introduction of canvas sails among the Chinese.[20]

At the bow of Nu Sun's vessel was the detachable head of a dragon. Such figureheads were not unusual in the Orient. Indeed, it seems likely that the Chinese have celebrated the Dragon's Holiday since the time of the legendary emperors. Traditionally, a parade of ships with such figureheads assembled each spring in the main harbors and river towns--because the dragon was their symbol for the creative forces of nature which inhabited rivers, lakes, and the sea (Figure 49). Nu Sun's trading vessels had carried similar effigies on an earlier voyages to Siberia, and the skipper had noticed how the local people suddenly paid him more respect. He guessed wisely that such an ominous figurehead would be an advantage in foreign lands. It would also be a good omen to those of his crew who were superstitious.

The fitting out of Nu Sun's vessels was completed with a coating of whitewash and painted trim including the *yin/yang* symbol on the aft deck railing. The whitewash, made from a combination of lime and wood oil, was not for aesthetic purposes. These were two ingredients that Asian shipbuilders traditionally used to withstand the devastating attacks of barnacles and shipworms.[21] The cloth sails also received a dunking in a preservative made of water and mangrove bark which protected them from insects and mildew.[22] The final act of the master builders was the christening ceremony--involving the sacrifice of a game cock whose blood was sprinkled on the bows and deck to protect the ships from harm at sea.

The Asians were still not ready for the voyage to America. Sea trials followed the launching in order to acquaint the crews with the sailing characteristics of the new vessels. When the captains were satisfied that the seamen had mastered their duties, they set sail toward Hokkaido, Japan--the staging area for their great adventure. And along the way, they added to the stores of grain and trading goods they needed for the markets they hoped to find in the New World.

Voyage to The Rising Sun

Hokkaido was the logical place for Nu Sun's fleet to spend the winter. By late summer, hurricanes ravaged the seas of Asia, making it difficult, if not impossible, to cross the North Pacific before freezing rain and gale-force winds made such a venture suicidal. Regardless of what Nu Sun's contemporaries may have thought, he was not a lunatic. The skipper was as cautious as he was daring: it was simply his *timing* that made the difference.

So the crews of Nu Sun's ships and those of his compatriots had several months to make final preparations for their voyage and to experience their final days of shore life before spending many months at sea. During that time, they enjoyed the hospitality offered by the Ainu--a tribe of pale-skinned natives who were Hokkaido's primary residents.

The Ainu were a courageous people who hunted and fished in the Sea of Japan as far north as the Straits of Tartar bordering on the Siberian Sea. Their culture was midway between Chinese and Eskimo--judging from the way their artifacts and customs compare with bordering ethnic groups. In many ways, they were similar to the Northwest Coast American Indian tribes.[1] Certainly, their totemic clans, rituals, and artifacts indicate that they had much in common. Ainu communal houses were warm--having sod roofs and thick walls made of logs. These were clustered in small groups near farming and fishing areas. Villages numbered only a few score inhabitants, but a feast or celebration brought together hundreds of people from related clans.

Nu Sun's men saw the Ainu wearing their distinctive ceremonial robes covered with a blend of symbols indicating their mixed cultural heritage. The robes of their descendants (Figure 50) are probably little different from those of the ancestors. Scrolls and chevrons join together in compositions that are distinctly Oriental--yet they also reflect similar traditions of other cultures like the Haida of Queen Charlotte's Island who also used chevrons and bracket-shaped power signs in their ceremonial costumes.

50

AINU CEREMONIAL ROBE
This traditional robe of the 19th century shows magic scrolls used to represent the head, eyes, and mouth of the supreme being. This style reflects 13th-century motifs from Indo-China and Indonesia. Similar chevron motifs, or brackets, are found in the arts of the Northwest Coast American Indians.

51

JAVANESE KALA HEAD
This stone sculpture from a Javanese Temple at Chandi Singasari is indicative of the Omnibus Power Sign tradition in the 13th century A.D. The scrolled eyes and chinless mouth are unique features of the ancient religious ceremonial complex.

52 AINU CEREMONIAL OBJECTS
Ainu artifacts of the 19th through the early 20th centuries exhibit
the Omnibus Power Sign along with other traditional Asian motifs,
including brackets, wave patterns, and coins. The Ainu were
highly skilled carvers of wood, bone, and ivory.

The most notable aspect of the Ainu robe is the use of the scroll-shaped eye. This feature is most prevalent in the art of Southeast Asia (Figure 51). The importance of scrolls in other Ainu artifacts, as indicated by Figure 52, is an indication of the close contact which existed between the Chinese and the island people of Japan. Whether this was a consequence of trade relationships or migration is uncertain without extensive research. Nevertheless, northern Japan was remote enough from China for its people to maintain a distinctive art style. Archaic motifs, like the chevron and bracket, survived among the Ainu long after Chinese artists on the mainland replaced bracket motifs with magic scrolls.

By early May, Nu Sun's fleet headed north towards Siberia. Their first destination was Chumikan--a trading center for gold and ivory. The most probable route of their journey is presented in Map 5. It seems likely that the merchants traded with the inhabitants of each successive port in an effort to increase their profits and to obtain goods that would be of value to people living in the east. Meanwhile, Nu Sun made detailed observations of the sun and stars in order to create a nautical chart for future use. During the hours of darkness, he determined the time and his position using a nocturnal and a calibrated dial.[2] He may have recorded this information on bark paper or bamboo, but most likely, he painted on silk using the twenty symbols of his astrological mirror to correlate the position of the stars with his position at sea.

After a voyage of nearly a thousand miles, the merchant fleet arrived at Chumikan, Siberia. The three-week trip up the eastern coast of Sakhalin Island probably left many of those on board wondering if they would ever be warm again.

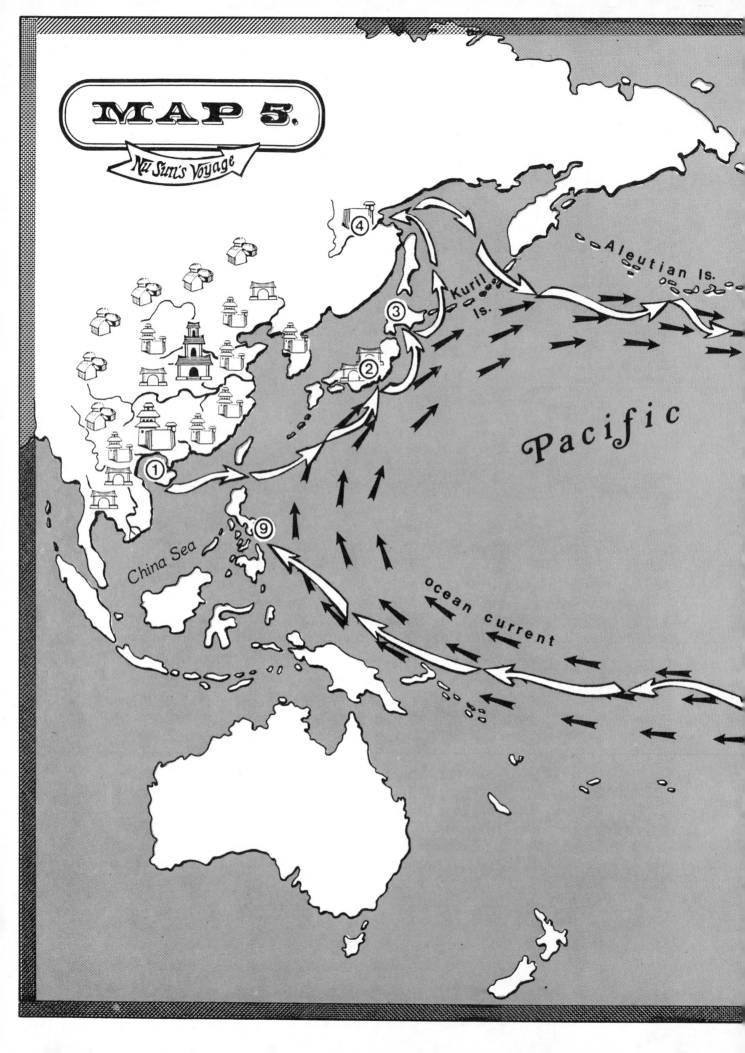

MAP 5.

Nū Sun's Voyage

Aleutian Is.

Kuril Is.

Pacific

China Sea

ocean current

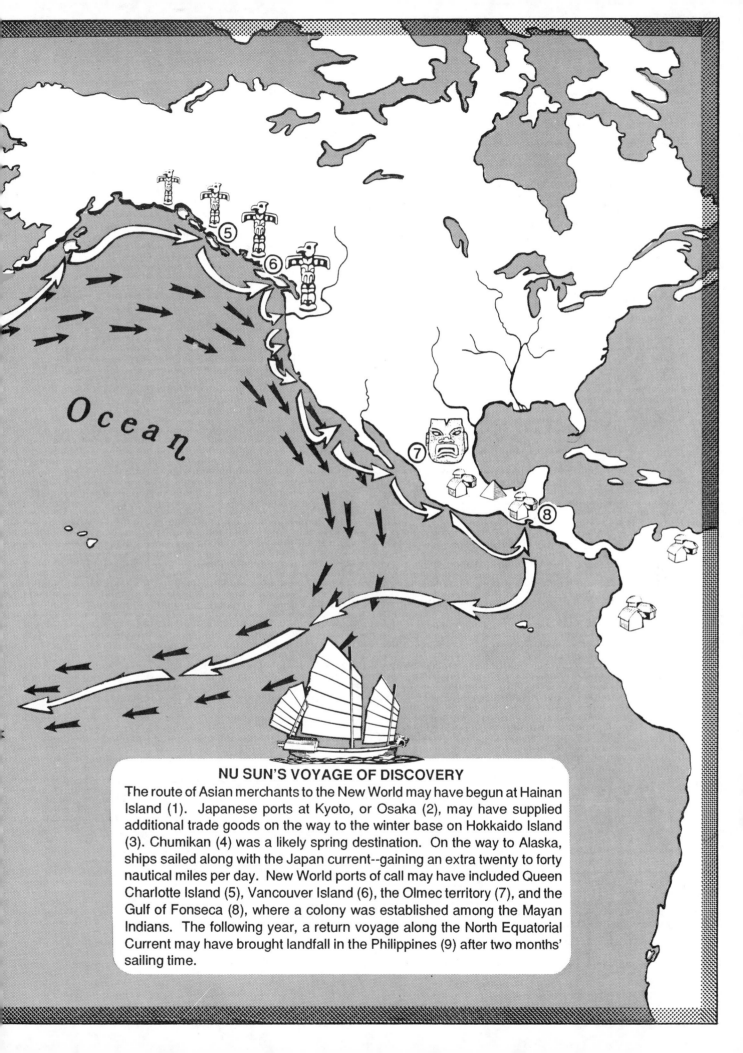

NU SUN'S VOYAGE OF DISCOVERY
The route of Asian merchants to the New World may have begun at Hainan Island (1). Japanese ports at Kyoto, or Osaka (2), may have supplied additional trade goods on the way to the winter base on Hokkaido Island (3). Chumikan (4) was a likely spring destination. On the way to Alaska, ships sailed along with the Japan current--gaining an extra twenty to forty nautical miles per day. New World ports of call may have included Queen Charlotte Island (5), Vancouver Island (6), the Olmec territory (7), and the Gulf of Fonseca (8), where a colony was established among the Mayan Indians. The following year, a return voyage along the North Equatorial Current may have brought landfall in the Philippines (9) after two months' sailing time.

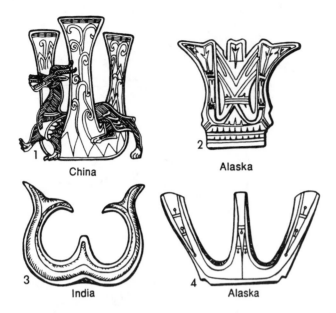

China

Alaska

India

Alaska

POWER SIGN TRIDENTS

Similar portrayals of tridents in ancient artifacts from China, India, and Alaska suggest the presence of significant cultural contact by the 1st century A.D. The Chinese dragon-trident is from a 3rd century sculpture; the Buddhist trident (lower left) is from the 1st-century temple at Sanchi, India; and the two Eskimo tridents (upper and lower right) are from the Punuk culture of Alaska, ca. A.D. 1000.

Even in the spring, cool inland breezes streamed down from the icy north. Regardless of the inhospitable temperature, however, the settlement was a popular trading center, and the merchants from the south traded iron tools and grain for gold, ivory, and furs.[3]

Meanwhile, Nu Sun had an even more important task to accomplish: he had to find a guide who could lead them past the Kuril Islands to the Bering Sea. There were no maps of these dangerous waters, but there were men in Siberia who traded with Aleutian natives. And among these rugged inhabitants of the Arctic, there were a few gifted navigators who could find their way even in a fog-hidden sea.

The stay in Siberia was brief. Nu Sun and the other merchants were anxious to press on with the journey. There was no way of telling how long it would take to cross the great ocean and return home. Consequently, they all knew it was important to leave as soon as possible to make the best use of their time--and the good weather.

The climate grew much colder as they passed the Kamchatka Peninsula and sailed on a north-by-northeast heading. At some point along the way, their Siberian guide directed them toward a small bay in one of the western Aleutian Islands. It was at this unlikely rendezvous that they encountered their first Aleut natives. Even at such a desolate place, Nu Sun and his mystic associate, the Taoist from Shanghai, recognized the telltale signs of Asian immigrants who had passed this way many centuries before. Nu Sun wasn't surprised. The frequent battles and religious disputes on the mainland had a reputation for causing the sudden departure of large populations. And the flimsy sailing craft of earlier generations would have been adequate for a one-way voyage toward the east. One thing was certain: the passing immigrants had left their mark on the native island cultures, even if the culture bearers hadn't settled in the desolate north.

ASIA

AMERICA

54 **LIFE FORCE MASKS**
Similar ritual masks from Asia and Alaska show magic scrolls used to represent the breath of the soul and life force arising from the head. These examples include a 4th-century bronze from China, and two ancient Aleut burial masks from Shumagin Island, Alaska.

Aleut talismans were replicas of religious objects prevalent in the steppes of Russia and in Southeast Asia (Figure 53). Even their burial masks (Figure 54) use motifs that were popular in China between 1000 and 500 B.C.

As the fleet proceeded eastward and stopped to trade among the island settlements, Nu Sun's followers noticed the first signs of trade goods from the Haida Indians of British Columbia. As far as the islanders were concerned, their point of origin was a warm and distant paradise known by its totemic traditions as the Land of the Raven. This reputed "paradise" became the fleet's first New World destination. Among the anxious merchants of Asia, there was hope of finding a booming market for their wares.

A succession of local guides led the way from one island to the next until they reached Alaska. Then, an Eskimo who was familiar with the western coast of North America took them down the inland sea that skirts the continental shore. Each time they parted company with a native guide, the captain showed his gratitude with gifts of ivory--huge Siberian mammoth tusks the likes of which they had never seen before--and iron tools.

One thing is certain: iron tools have been found in ancient Eskimo archaeological sites.[4] Only China had an iron producing industry of sufficient antiquity to produce the iron tools found so far to the north.

Throughout their journey, the voyagers encountered fantastic vistas: the northern lights darting across the Arctic Circle at night, vast glaciers, and towering, snow-capped peaks. At times, the seas became fierce cauldrons of enormous waves, but shallow waters near the Aleutian Islands and favorable summer weather

55

HAIDA VILLAGE
QUEEN CHARLOTTE ISLAND, B.C.

This reconstruction of a Haida fishing village is based on photographs taken between 1880 and 1910. It represents a level of artistic development and architecture which a stone-age society could have developed by the 5th century B.C. Lodges housed extended families and were constructed with planks made by splitting huge trees. Dugout canoes of sixty to eighty feet in length carried one hundred men. They were capable of sailing on the ocean. During times of warfare, villagers were moved to remote fortifications.

NORTHWEST COAST INDIAN MOTIFS
Examples from 19th-century Kwakiutl and Haida art show the diverse use made of the bracket, or U-shaped motif. These include beaver teeth, the rays of the sun, bird feathers, whale fins, and beaver ears. As is the case with similar Asian motifs which have been mistaken for ears, the Indian symbols always

allowed for reasonably smooth sailing for most of the journey. It was a three-thousand mile trek from Siberia to the Northwest American coast.

Icebergs were a problem during the evening hours when visibility was low. To reduce the hazard, Nu Sun's ships either dropped their drag anchors in a coastal haven and waited for daylight, or they sailed farther out to sea. Since they traveled at a relatively slow pace, striking an iceberg or a reef would not have been a catastrophe for these Oriental vessels. Each ship had twelve or more water-tight bulkheads--providing sufficient protection from sinking under most circumstances. Minor scrapes were repaired at sea, since the crews included men who were skilled shipwrights.

They landed at Sitka and the Queen Charlotte Islands--each time hoping to find an urban center with bustling markets like the ones they were use to in Southeast Asia. But the markets were small, and the natives urged them to go farther south where the largest villages were located. Gradually, they sailed southward to Vancouver Island. Somewhere along the way, Nu Sun ordered the dragon heads to be mounted on the foreposts. It was an awesome experience for the natives to see "real" sea-monsters cruise into the harbor. There must have been some surprises on both sides when this unusual confrontation took place. Certainly, the Asian sailors were astonished to see the colorful totem poles, dugout canoes, and lodges of the Haida Indians (Figure 55).

Although none of the ancient Haida structures have survived, it seems reasonable to assume that they were not much different from those encountered by European explorers during the eighteenth and nineteenth centuries. Indeed, the

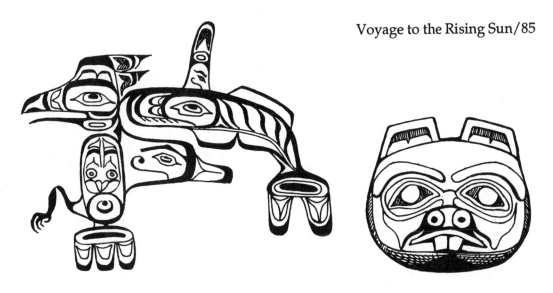

denote a spiritual quality of cosmic power. The beaver carved
on a totem pole is not the local aquatic resident and dam builder.
Instead, it represents a mythical being who played a central role
in the folklore of a clan. Consequently, even when the bracket
motif takes the place of an ear, it has the symbolic function of
representing spirituality, i.e., it constitutes a power sign.

very stability of contemporary art styles and designs suggest that the basic traditions
have continued virtually unchanged for a considerable period of time. Had the
situation been any different, i.e., if the artistic traditions of the Haida not been based
on many prior centuries of development, they would not have been so resistant to
change during the historical period of colonization.[5] The only significant change
in native art during the modern era was probably a greater ease of construction with
the increased availability of iron tools. But even that impact may not be as recent
as we might suspect.[6] Historical accounts indicate that the battered remains of
Japanese vessels occasionally washed up along the shores of North America long
before the time of European exploration in the 1800's. Any survivors to reach
Raven's Land presumably were enslaved, while the iron was stripped from the ships
and used for tools.[7] Asian vessels were carrying iron implements as early as the
seventh century B.C., so it is possible that the Indians knew of iron even before Nu
Sun's voyage.

Nevertheless, Nu Sun's arrival was a cathartic event for the locals. A few women
and children ran away in fright, while the braves and some undaunted matrons
stared respectfully at the sea serpents sailing out from the mist. Meanwhile, the
native guide acted as a friendly interpreter--explaining that holy men from the west
had come to visit the Raven's children. The Taoist magician dazzled the natives by
producing his little bag of tricks--including the metal fish that moved on the end of
a string and the mirror that flashed the sun's light into their eyes.

Some historians believe that the Chinese used magnetized iron in the form of a
compass prior to 1500 B.C.[8] Legends from that era refer to an instrument called a

SORCERER'S TOTEM
This design from a Northwest Coast Indian robe shows the complex usage made of the bracket motif. There are a total of thirty symbols used in various patterns to represent a multitude of cosmic or spiritual powers. It dates to the late 19th century and is probably indicative of symbolic traditions more than a thousand years old.

"south-pointing chariot" which enabled a great general to find his way through the fog. The device may have employed either a compass or a set of gears. Even so, the mariner's compass may not have been in common use by Chinese seamen until after the ninth century A.D. Whether or not it was available to Nu Sun is a matter for speculation. Certainly, he was observant enough to take advantage of any useful devices that were available. However, a compass is virtually useless without a map, nor is it essential for navigation--particularly when local guides are employed in sequential forays into unknown territory. Nevertheless, the meticulous captain carefully charted their course as the fleet proceeded down the Pacific Coast. Later trips would be much easier as a result of Nu Sun's charts and the recorded wisdom of his guides.[9] Indeed, his most enduring contribution was the kind of accurate recording that enables civilization to move forward along the chartered pathways of its explorers.

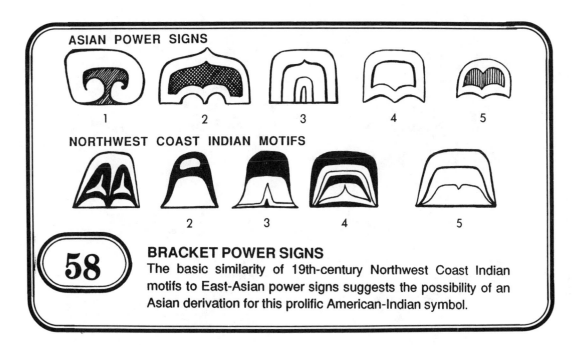

ASIAN POWER SIGNS

1   2   3   4   5

NORTHWEST COAST INDIAN MOTIFS

2   3   4   5

58

BRACKET POWER SIGNS
The basic similarity of 19th-century Northwest Coast Indian motifs to East-Asian power signs suggests the possibility of an Asian derivation for this prolific American-Indian symbol.

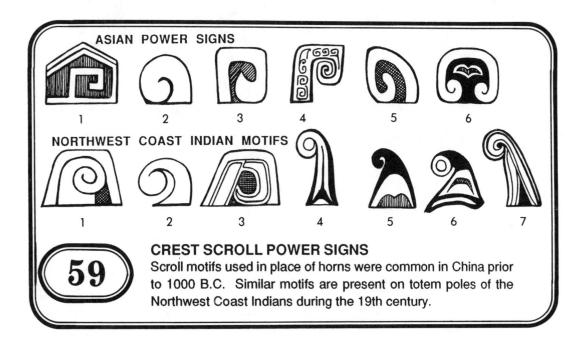

ASIAN POWER SIGNS

1   2   3   4   5   6

NORTHWEST COAST INDIAN MOTIFS

1   2   3   4   5   6   7

59

CREST SCROLL POWER SIGNS
Scroll motifs used in place of horns were common in China prior to 1000 B.C. Similar motifs are present on totem poles of the Northwest Coast Indians during the 19th century.

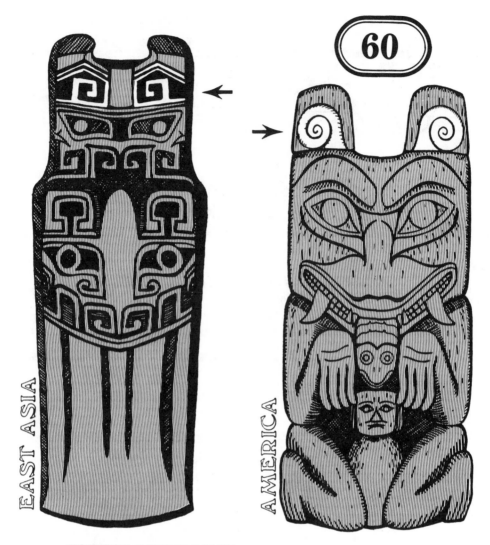

TOTEMIC POWER SIGNS
Scroll-shaped motifs on a Shang ceremonial axe (left) are similar to Northwest Coast Indian totemic power signs (right). The squatting bear totem is a traditional Haida design from Prince of Wales Island, B.C.

Without paper (or silk) to draw upon and a language to communicate useful information, Nu Sun's voyage would have been irrelevant in the opening of the New World to future Asian travelers. However, we can be sure that the merchant admiral left detailed records of wind directions, sea currents, and landmarks, because the evidence shows that his route was used often during the following centuries.

One of the first things to strike the curiosity of the Asian visitors to Raven's Land was the unusual art style the Indians used on their totem poles, canoes, bark clothing, and tattoos. A few examples of nineteenth century designs are presented in Figure 56. The Taoists among Nu Sun's crew may have recognized the characteristic U-shaped power signs, or brackets, used by the native shamans. After all, their form and function was quite similar to bracket motifs used in China as late as the Chou dynasty (ca. 500 B.C.). Furthermore, the bracket had been a popular motif among the Neolithic and later Shang peoples--before the scroll motif became the Asian Omnibus Power Sign, and before all other Chinese power signs dwindled in frequency.

The bracket symbols have many characteristics in common with the Omnibus Power Sign. The most significant is that they are used in every conceivable manner--as eyes, feathers, horns, whale fins, and the rays of the sun. Another similarity is that they were used profusely in ceremonial artifacts, such as the sorcerer's robe in Figure 57. This illustration shows only a portion of a single robe that had in excess of forty-eight bracket power signs on one side. In addition to these symbols, there were eighteen "ovoid" power signs and several other motifs of lesser frequency. Power signs of the Pacific Northwest are similar to those of Asia in the way they were used to cover an object, however, that characteristic is hardly indicative of cultural contact. What is more important is the intriguing similarity of forms and functions the power signs manifest on numerous artifacts.

Selections of bracket motifs and scroll-shaped crests are presented in Figures 58 and 59. Asian specimens include power signs from the Shang and Chou dynasties, as well as historic Ainu carvings. All of the Northwest Coast items date from the nineteenth century A.D. We can not be certain of the configuration of more ancient American Indian symbolism due to the fact that their primary medium of expression was wood--and wood decays rapidly in the moist Pacific Northwest. Nevertheless, it seems apparent that the function served by Indian power signs is fairly consistent with similar Asian motifs. The placement patterns of scroll forms is virtually identical. This placement is demonstrated by Figure 60. We are fairly safe in concluding that scroll-shaped crest symbols in both Asia and the Northwest represent spiritual power.

In general, the similarity of Northwest Coast Indian power signs to early

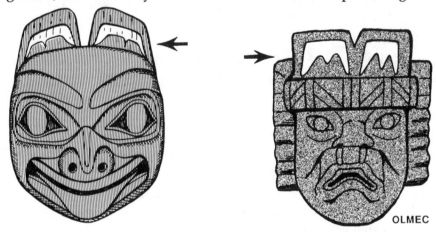

OLMEC

POWER SIGN ANTIQUITY
The probable age of Northwest Coast Indian bracket motifs like those on the 19th-century Haida mask (left) is suggested by the presence of similar motifs in the Olmec culture dating to the San Lorenzo B cultural phase (1050-950 B.C.). The Olmec example (right) is from a stone statue which was hollowed out in the back. This feature is reminiscent of the Northwest Coast Indian practice of hollowing out the backs of totem poles to prevent cracking.

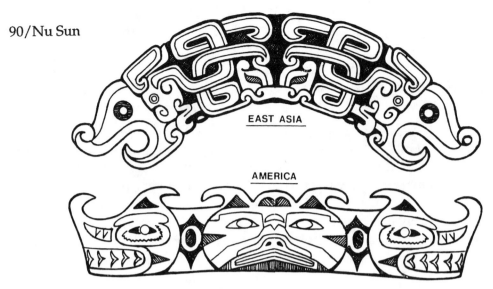

EAST ASIA

AMERICA

KALAMAKARA/SISIUTL TALISMANS
Similar talismans are found in ancient China ca 500 B.C. (top) and in historic Northwest Coast Indian collections from the 19th century (bottom). Both examples clearly show two curled-nose dragons emerging from the central head, which represents the supreme being as a union of dual cosmic forces.

C-horns of the Shang Chinese, as well as chevrons of the Ainu, suggest the possibility that these symbols are all derived from common ancestral designs. The most likely explanation for this phenomenon is that some of the Northwest Coast Indians may have migrated from Asia much more recently than was previously thought--perhaps as late as 2000 B.C. Bracket power signs were probably used in Raven's Land long before Nu Sun's voyage, and they were subsequently modified to suit the emerging style of folk art indigenous to the Pacific Northwest. Many of the native Indian symbols seem to reflect pre-Shang designs from Asia, while others, such as the scroll motifs, appear to be a more recent cultural overlay.

The approximate age of the bracket symbol in the New World is suggested by its occurrence on a stone monument in Mexico (Figure 61). Assuming that this motif was derived from the same wave of migration that established bracket symbols in the Pacific Northwest, the dating of the sculpture (ca. 1000 B.C.) indicates a minimum age for the migration. The earliest likely time period would correspond to when Neolithic Asians are believed to have developed the oceangoing rafts and dugout canoes, i.e., sometime after 5000 B.C.[10]

One other motif from the Northwest Coast Indians is suggestive of contact following 2000 B.C. This motif is known as the *kalamakara*, or cosmic being. In the Pacific Northwest, a virtually identical spiritual entity is called the *sisiutl*, or "soul catcher." Examples of these similar art forms are presented in Figures 62 and 63. The motif consists of a mask representing either the supreme being or a mythical creature. It includes two dragons or serpents emerging from the sides of the being's head. The concept is not uniquely East-Asian in derivation. Indeed, a Greek artifact from the fifth century B.C. shows a gorgon's head with two serpents emerging from

EAST ASIA

AMERICA

COSMIC BEING--THE MASK GOD

A principle feature of ancient Asian religion and the Taoist philosophy was a belief that all of existence, including the supreme cosmic being, derived from the interacting forces of *yin* and *yang*. In religious art, these forces are often portrayed as two dragons emerging from a bodiless head--the mask god, or supreme being. An example of this concept is a Han bronze mask (top) from the 1st century A.D. The concept was present as early as the Shang dynasty (ca. 1500 B.C.) and received its greatest elaboration in the art of Indo-China between A.D. 800 and 1500. Exactly when the concept reached the Northwest Coast Indians is unknown; however, it is frequently portrayed as the *sisiutl*, or "Soul Catcher" in 19th-century art (bottom).

the sides.[11]   What differentiates the Asian and Northwest Coast Indian motifs from others is the presence of scroll elements emerging from the mask god and serpent heads. Furthermore the motif has similar functions in both Asia and the Northwest Coast where it was carved into talismans or located around doorways as a spiritual guardian against evil. [12]

Because this symbol is not represented in ancient Chinese art prior to the Shang dynasty, it is possible that its counterpart in Northwest Coast Indian art represents an acquisition during the period following Nu Sun's voyage. But that is an issue for future investigation.

After spending several days learning about local traditions and trading iron tools for bark blankets, Nu Sun's men were ready to head south. Another guide took them as far as the Columbia River, while the crew and passengers again grew weary of shipboard life. Nevertheless, the captain raised their spirits with his conviction that some great center of commerce must lie just a few days' sail away. And so they pressed on.

From the Columbia, their next stop may have been Coos Bay--a place destined to foster a growing sense of disappointment. Fresh water was abundant--in the form of rain. Tasty shellfish added a welcome variety to their diet. But there were no large cities to offer the comforts of civilization. There were no potential trading partners to brighten their commercial horizons--just the dismal rain beating down upon their souls.

Again, they sailed from the placid inland waters to the offshore current where another guide took them to the Land of The Towering Trees--the Sequoias. They passed intriguing seascapes and unusual marine life, but their search for lucrative markets seemed futile. It was a stunning setback as they traveled from one majestic wilderness to the next, and it must have shattered Nu Sun's dreams. Wherever they stopped, be it San Francisco Bay, or the Cape of San Lucas, they were met by primitive men with stone tools. They had no bows and arrows, no ships, and no writing to speak of other than a few simple hieroglyphs. The reality of the situation was crystal clear: North America was still deeply embedded in the Stone Age.

Finally, they reached the Land of the Giant Heads and the western shore of what is now Mexico. Nu Sun's hopes grew brighter. Being a perennial optimist, he wondered if he would find a real civilization at last. They had traveled more than six thousand miles in three months, and they were all sick of beans and fish. Would this be the Promised Land--the land of their dreams?

Land of the Giant Heads

For the weary Asian travelers, arrival at the Land of The Giant Heads was a disheartening experience. There were no thriving port cities and no welcoming committees from the Chamber of Commerce. By all the standards of civilized China, Mexico's parched seacoast was extremely primitive. It was burdened with a barter economy, it lacked wheeled vehicles, and there were no horses or cattle. The political situation was even more discouraging: the scattered villages were all dominated by a totalitarian ruling class referred to by anthropologists as the "Olmecs."

Olmec territory extended across what is now Central Mexico from the Pacific Ocean to the Gulf of Mexico, and it extended as far south as El Salvador, where frontier markers have been found carved into stone cliffs.[1] The extent of the territory is indicated by Map 6. A tribute system maintained discipline, while a network of dirt paths provided routes for commerce and the mobilization of military forces. Fighting among rival clans was frequent, while rebellious tribes resisted the authority of Olmec surrogates in the outlying provinces.

Regardless of where Nu Sun's vessels approached shore, they caused a sensation among natives who were unaccustomed to visitors from abroad. As word of their arrival spread, the attitudes of the peasants turned from curiosity to fear as Olmec leaders dispatched their warriors to the coast. At some point, Nu Sun's Korean mercenaries confronted an Olmec war party barring their way to fresh-water streams. With superior weapons and tactics, the Asians won the skirmish, obtained the water they needed, and withdrew to the safety of their ships.

Scholars of Olmec culture often characterize the ancient Mexicans as bloodthirsty barbarians. According to their grisly scenarios, the Olmecs were prone to kill and eat any unlucky sailor who might have survived a Pacific crossing.[2] Of course, the assumption is generally made that such a crossing would have been accidental, and the impact on native culture insignificant. Nevertheless, the dis-

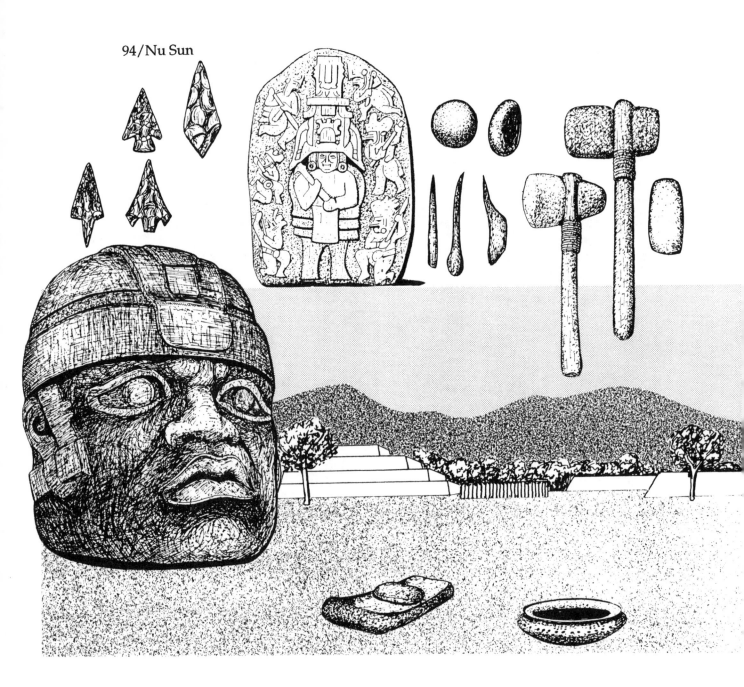

covery of charred and broken human bones at Olmec sites confirms that cannibalism was an integral part of their way of life.[3]

Regardless of their barbaric manners, the Olmec were not totally lacking in cultural achievements. Indeed, some of their artifacts are laudable, considering the limited technology they had to work with. Among these are colossal stone heads, measuring from five to ten feet high, carved out of basalt. The most beautiful specimens were produced at the ceremonial centers of San Lorenzo and La Venta along the Gulf Coast. Some cruder examples have been found near the Pacific, marking the distant borders of the Olmec territory.

An example of the giant heads is presented in Figure 64, along with a cultural montage typical of the period between 1000 and 700 B.C. It might be noted that the features of the stone head are distinctly Negroid. This is characteristic of numerous

OLMEC CULTURAL MONTAGE, 1200--700 B.C.

The Olmec society dominated much of Meso-America from ceremonial centers like La Venta, located near the Gulf Coast. Earthen pyramids up to forty feet high were the focus of ritual activity for an elite ruling class. Their tool assemblage consisted of bone and stone implements such as celts, axes, awls, and scrapers. *Manos* and *metates* were used for grinding corn. Several colossal stone heads with Negroid features have been found at La Venta and San Lorenzo. Small villages of one to ten thousand inhabitants were located near ceremonial centers. They consisted primarily of one-story wood and mud dwellings built on low earthen mounds. Dart points were used for spearing small game. Warriors used wood clubs, as well as the *atlatl*. Arrow points are missing from the archaeological record until A.D. 700 to 900.

sculptures found at San Lorenzo and La Venta, and it has sparked a controversy regarding the apparent arrival of African immigrants prior to the Spanish Conquest.[4]

Several major themes dominate Olmec art. The prevalence of warfare is evident in the numerous relief carvings of armed warriors (Figure 65). Their features conform to fairly standardized designs having large lips, earspools, thick thighs, and stumpy feet. And don't expect a smile from any of these somber-faced minions of the Dark Ages. Even the children, who are portrayed in simple relief carvings, do not seem to be enjoying their existence. Their characteristic frown is the most distinctive aspect of the culture--reflecting the human sacrifice and brutality used to maintain control over pathetic peasants.

Votive figurines reflect the second major theme of Olmec art, portraying a deity

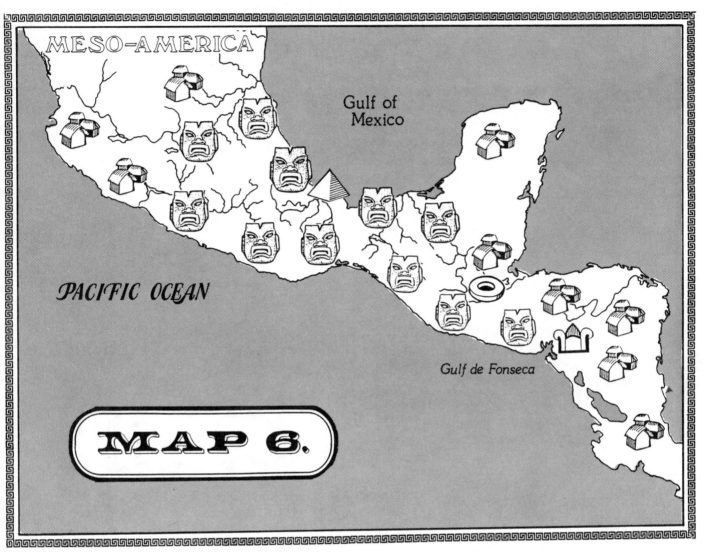

OLMEC NATION

THE OLMEC NATION

The focus of Olmec power was located in religious centers situated along the Gulf of Mexico coast. It was a land of small villages, numbering 1,000 to 10,000 inhabitants who lived in mud and thatch huts built upon clay platforms. Between 1500 and 500 B.C., the Neolithic Olmecs dominated the entire region, extracting tribute, slaves, and victims for human sacrifice from the outlying provinces. Towards the south, proto-Mayan tribes inhabited the region of the Yucatan Peninsula, and the area that comprises the modern-day nations of Guatemala, Honduras, El Salvador, and Nicaragua. This was the area that was most receptive to Asian voyagers.

KEY (6)

- Olmec territory and allied villages
- Olmec capital at La Venta
- Independent Neolithic villages
- Motagua jade source
- Possible site of Nu Sun's colony
- Omnibus Power Sign

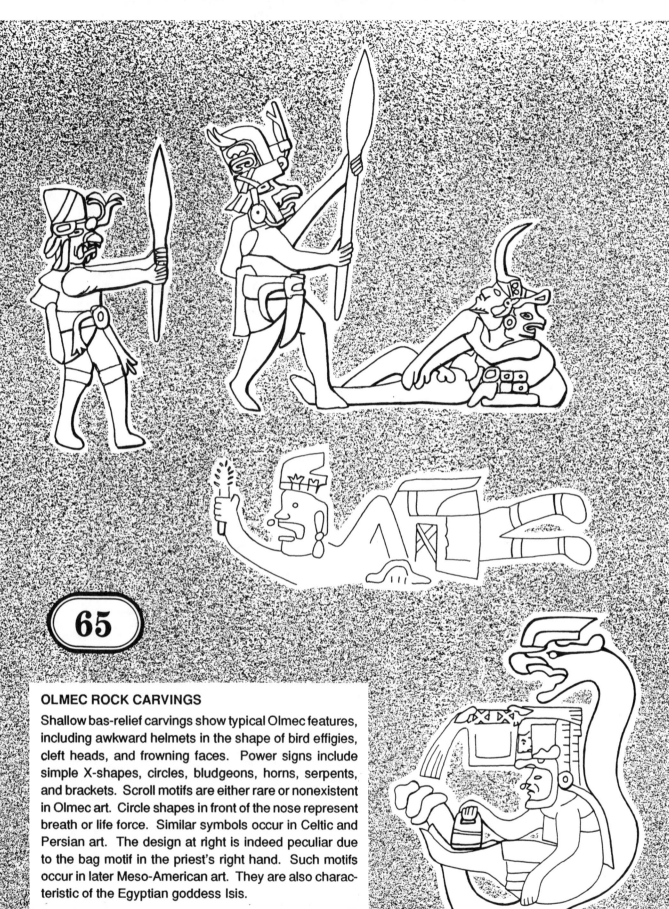

65

OLMEC ROCK CARVINGS

Shallow bas-relief carvings show typical Olmec features, including awkward helmets in the shape of bird effigies, cleft heads, and frowning faces. Power signs include simple X-shapes, circles, bludgeons, horns, serpents, and brackets. Scroll motifs are either rare or nonexistent in Olmec art. Circle shapes in front of the nose represent breath or life force. Similar symbols occur in Celtic and Persian art. The design at right is indeed peculiar due to the bag motif in the priest's right hand. Such motifs occur in later Meso-American art. They are also characteristic of the Egyptian goddess Isis.

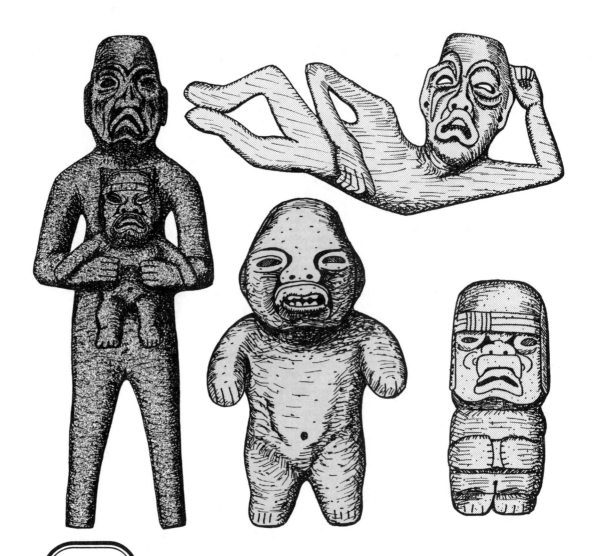

66 OLMEC FIGURINES

Jade figurines and votive axes (bottom right) typically show sloping foreheads. This feature has been interpreted as evidence of cranial deformation in childhood. A group of figurines similar to the one on the left were recorded at La Venta, and the center figure was excavated at Cerro de Las Mesas, thereby enabling verified dating to the 8th century B.C., or earlier. The recumbent Olmec on the upper right indicates the presence of a leisure class. Scroll motifs are characteristically absent from these artifacts.

67

OLMEC STONE MONUMENT, LA VENTA
Relief sculptures exhibit typical Olmec features such as the cleft
head and the bracket-shaped mouth. The designs are simple,
as might be expected where the artists were reliant on stone
tools. Scroll motifs are extremely rare in these compositions.

that combines human and presumably jaguar features (Figure 66). The figurines
were carved out of jade using a grinding process that is extremely difficult without
metal tools. These small sculptures are of particular note since they have fairly
uniform design. Olmec art does not show a great amount of variation, creativity,
or inventiveness throughout a period of time lasting more than seven centuries,
from 1200 to 500 B.C. This aspect of Olmec art argues in favor of a very rigid social
structure along with a conservative intellectual climate.

Figures 67 and 68 illustrate typical Olmec relief carvings. Besides featuring the
usual, frowning warriors, they tend to be simple in design and execution. This
simplicity is most likely attributable to the hardness of the medium and the difficulty
of crafting detailed designs, when the artist has only stone tools to work with. Relief
carvings tend to be very large: they are life-size in some cases, or even larger. They
exhibit a rather limited mix of power signs, including U-shapes, circles, triangles,
and brackets. The lack of magic scrolls is readily apparent. Olmec religious traditions feature other kinds of motifs, such as serpents, jaguars, plant forms, and
frowning faces--all of which occur in abundance in the archaeological record prior
to 500 B.C.

Similar patterns are seen in Olmec cave paintings (Figure 69). Although the
designs are often more elaborate than relief carvings, because of the relative ease in

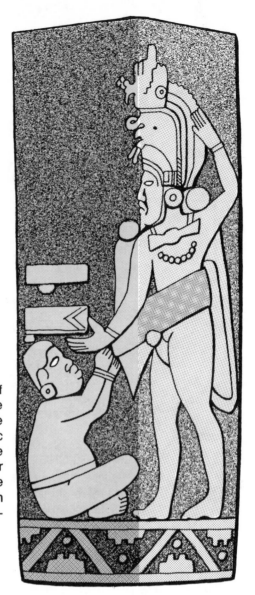

OLMEC STONE MONUMENT
This monument from Alvarado, Vera Cruz, is of simple design and carved in very low relief--due mainly to the stone tool technology used by the artists. In that respect, it is like most Olmec monuments. The standing figure is notable due to the presence of a beard. Since facial hair was rare among the indigenous population, the bearded warrior may represent a race of foreign visitors. Scroll motifs are absent in this composition.

using brushes and pigments, the artists rarely employed scrolls in these compositions. Instead, they chose the characteristic X-shapes, circles, triangles, animal masks, and brackets that are prevalent throughout Olmec culture. Some cave paintings produced during the period after Nu Sun's voyage do show a greater use of scrolls--as would be expected considering the overwhelming impact of new Asian culture in the area.

Scroll motifs are absent from Olmec ceremonial celts. These elongated pieces of stone were highly polished and then inscribed with a design. Celts recovered from the ruins of La Venta depict some unique motifs, along with the typical frowning face and brackets, however scrolls are not among them (Figure 70).

It is readily apparent from an examination of Olmec artifacts that scrolls do not constitute part of the basic religious symbolism. Indeed, of all the world's cultures, few are as deficient in the use of this versatile art form as were the Olmecs between the tenth century and the sixth century B.C. Were it not for the occasional use of "opposed volutes," as indicated by Figure 71, it would be reasonable to conclude that Olmec artists did not use magic scrolls at all. Certainly, they are virtually nonexistent in the archaeological record.[5]

69

Ceramic designs at both La Venta and San Lorenzo show a fairly characteristic pattern during both the San Lorenzo and Nacaste archaeological phases which span the time period from 1150 to 700 B.C. The high degree of similarity during this time suggests the presence of a centralized and rigid culture. Although simple scroll shapes in the form of inverted volutes do occur, their frequency is no greater than would be expected from any other stone-age culture. Instead, it is the frequent X-shapes, circles, and brackets which reflect the typical variety of power signs used in the Olmec religion. Of all of these, the bracket was the most important.

Bracket power signs are a distinguishing feature of much of Olmec art. They are found in stone sculptures such as the altar from Portero Nuevo, which is supported by two Atlantean midgets (Figure 72). The presence of such motifs as the only decoration on the altar is evidence of the importance of this motif in Olmec religious art.

The bracket is present in the head decorations of idols and figurines (Figure 73), while the bracket mouth is a common feature of Olmec religious art (Figure 74). Brackets form the circumference of the mouth opening in another monument from Olmec territory (Figure 75). In this composition, they apparently represent the sacred source of rain, wind, and cosmic power, i.e., the mouth of the supreme being. This usage of power signs to represent the method by which creative forces come into being through a sacred hole, or passageway, is fairly consistent throughout the world among ancient religions. The monument has been referred to as a representation of a "cave," but it actually corresponds to a concept of an invisible source of cosmic power. This concept was portrayed in three-dimensional form for the benefit of an illiterate public. It was a focal point for rituals in which priests acted out symbolic cosmic powers--just as they do in any religion, during any age.

As might be expected, an Olmec symbol for rain clouds also incorporates the bracket symbol (Figure 76). This motif has the connotation that rain emerges via cosmic power, or via the cosmic mouth which the bracket represents.

We have taken a very broad survey of Olmec art prior to the time of Nu Sun's voyage to gain some understanding of the religious foundation and types of motifs that were characteristic of the culture. A number of Olmec sites in Mexico have not yet been excavated, but we have artifacts from many others. Indeed, there is sufficient evidence to gauge the overall characteristics of the heartland of Olmec expression around San Lorenzo and La Venta. If any of the elements which comprise the Asian Omnibus Power Sign had been present, we would have found them. But we found none.

At this point, it would be useful to recall the level of cultural development that had already taken place in China by the sixth century B.C., and to reconsider the central role of magic

scrolls in Asian art. In China, there were numerous cities with populations in excess of a hundred thousand residents. The empire may have included some fifteen to thirty million inhabitants. China was an iron-age culture with large ships, extensive commerce, inland ship canals, and tens of thousands of wheeled vehicles drawn by horses and oxen. It had a standardized writing system, advanced astronomy, metal casting, the abacus, silk and cotton clothing, and a multitude of domesticated plants which provided ample food supplies for a steadily expanding population.

OLMEC JADE CELTS
Like the Chinese, the Olmec regarded jade as a material of extreme religious importance. It is also a very hard material that can be worked only with even harder crystalline substances such as garnet, or metal. Highly polished celts, like those portrayed below from La Venta, were used as ceremonial objects. Engravings feature typical Olmec motifs, including brackets, X-shapes, and the profiles of Olmec figures. Scroll forms are not present in any of these artifacts with a verified dating prior to 600 B.C.

70

71

**OLMEC
CERAMIC
DECORATIONS**

Decorations on potsherds found in layers of earth at La Venta and San Lorenzo indicate that decorative traditions were fairly consistent between 1200 B.C. and 700 B.C. Generally, the frequency of various motifs reflect their presence in other media, although scroll forms (left column) appear more frequently. Nevertheless, there are only two characteristic types: opposed volutes and the lazy-S. These scroll shapes are typical of primitive ceramic industries throughout the world, where they often represent water or fertility concepts. There are no significant similarities to Asian scroll forms of the same period, although the anchor shape in the left column appears vaguely like the Koru motif of aboriginal art of New Zealand. Symbols in the right column indicate a variety of bracket power signs seen frequently on other Olmec artifacts.

**NACASTE CULTURAL PHASE
900-700B.C.**

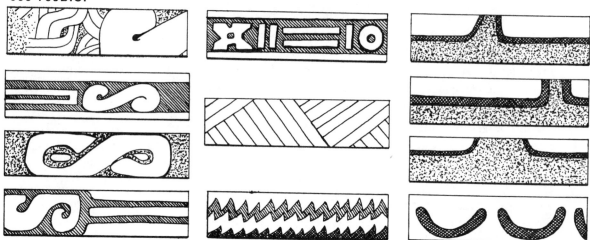

By contrast, Mexico was a land still struggling to emerge from its Paleolithic roots. The inhabitants lived in small villages--perhaps numbering only five thousand in the large ones.[6] They had one main ceremonial complex on the Gulf Coast, at La Venta, while a few secondary religious sites were located near San Lorenzo. La Venta had two medium-sized pyramids made of clay with several wooden buildings for priests and rulers, but it lacked the urban population required to qualify as a center of the arts and culture. The only indigenous tools were made of stone, with the consequence that artifacts recovered by archaeologists are of the most primitive execution and simple design. A few of these may even be the product of metal tools obtained from Mediterranean explorers. Granted, some Olmec art has enduring beauty. Nevertheless, it is extremely simplistic by comparison to the highly intricate bronze castings and jade carvings being produced in China during the same period of time.

There are ample reasons why the development of civilization in Mexico lagged

OLMEC ALTAR
A sculpture in the half-round from Portero Nuevo (near La Venta) shows the bracket power sign as the primary embellishment along the bottom edge of the altar.

more than a thousand years behind that of Asia. First, there was a chaotic settlement pattern in North and South America as Paleolithic hunters were followed by successive waves of displaced Asian immigrants. This situation did nothing to provide the stable population necessary for long-term cultural development. Stability of a large population center is a key ingredient needed for the evolution of language, writing, and the arts. And there has been no evidence found indicating the use of writing, calendars, metal casting, or the sequential numbering of years at either of the major Olmec sites.[7] These are typically regarded as the hallmarks of civilization, leading to the conclusion that Olmec society was still functioning at the barbarian stage of human cultural evolution.

Another reason for the retarded development of Meso-American culture was that domestication of food crops was late in getting started. Early hunters who

73

BRACKET HEADS

Olmec talismans and idols from as early as 1000 B.C. show a characteristic V-cleft in the center of the head. Examples 4 and 5 show a secondary bracket pattern superimposed on the headdress. These have been interpreted as rain motifs, although their similarity to bracket motifs of the Northwest Coast American Indians suggests alternative functions. They may represent heavenly power, the cosmic mouth, or the power of flight. The bracket theme was popular in China nearly five thousand years ago.

BRACKET-MOUTH POWER SIGN

As a representation of the source of rain and wind, the Olmec priests incorporated the bracket symbol into the mouths of deity figurines, idols, and talismans. The Olmec head shown here is from an engraving on a ceremonial jade dish found at Cerro de Las Mesas. The first two examples below are Northwest Coast Indian power signs. The remainder are Olmec deity mouths found on a variety of artifacts.

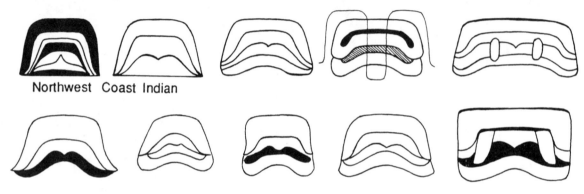

Northwest Coast Indian

BRACKET MOUTH MONUMENT

75

Olmec priests used the bracket power sign to surround the open mouth in this monument. The mouth area was chiseled into an opening that was large enough for a priest to pass through--thereby symbolizing the means by which creative forces, such as the wind and rain, passed from the spiritual realm into the physical world. The monument has also been interpreted as representing a cave, or "earth monster," which is conceivable--since any opening in the earth that released steam or cool air could be regarded as a mysterious source of wind. The brackets, however, represent spiritual power--just as they do in other Olmec talismans and idols.

crossed the Bering land bridge had an abundant food supply following the migrating herds of game animals. Consequently, there was little incentive for the kinds of proto-agricultural activities required for plant domestication.

New World societies were deficient in the rate of cultural development for one other important reason: they lacked draft animals. In the Old World, men developed symbiotic relationships with horses, and cattle--using these accommodating beasts to pull the load. That freed up time for men to exercise their intellectual capabilities, and it provided surplus resources that made it possible for a leisure class to grow. It was the indulgence of the leisure class in promoting conquest, producing consumer goods, encouraging the arts, and developing technology which fostered the rapid rate of progress that typified the Chinese and other Old-World civilizations. Such an impetus was lacking among New-World hunting societies. Be that as it may, there was an even greater reason why the New World lagged in cultural development: it lacked the challenging intellectual stimulus generated by meaningful contacts with other developing civilizations.

All of the Old-World cultures engaged in commerce and exploration at an early age. As they came into contact with one another, their own technologies and world views were challenged to improve. Those who failed to compete effectively were inundated by nations having superior military equipment. Consequently, the production of vessels for amphibious operations was at the forefront of the escalating arms race.

By 1000 B.C., numerous Old-World empires had sufficient maritime technology to sail across the oceans and return to their home ports virtually at will. Considering the natural tendency our species has for exploration, it is only reasonable to presume that numerous voyages took place across the Atlantic and the Pacific during the

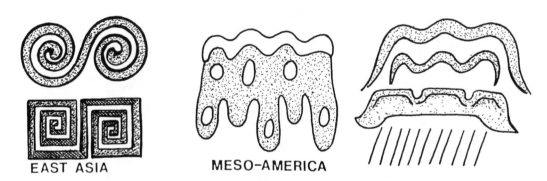

EAST ASIA   MESO-AMERICA

OLMEC RAIN CLOUDS
Two examples of Olmec rain-cloud motifs (center and right) are compared to Chinese motifs (left) of a similar time period, ca. 1000 to 500 B.C. Unlike the Chinese who typically used scrolls to represent rain, traditional Olmec rain-cloud motifs apparently did not incorporate scrolls. The typical bracket power sign was used in the center example from Chalcatzingo, Mexico.

period from 1000 B.C. to A.D. 500. The most skilled and daring captains probably succeeded in making the journey more than once. By the sixth century B.C., Phoenician sailing craft circumnavigated Africa--traveling a distance of fourteen thousand miles.[8] Greek *quinquiremes* of more than two hundred feet in length sailed the Mediterranean during the third century B.C., while fleets of Greek and Roman merchant vessels sailed to ports in Africa, Persia, and Asia.[9] From these voyages and the later exploits of Celtic and Norse adventurers emerged legends about Atlantis, the Isles of Brendan, and Vinland.

The primary issue in the development of civilization in the Americas is whether someone arrived at a critical point in time when the native people were receptive to external influence. If that were the case, then we would expect to find a significant shift in the art styles, motifs, and other cultural traits of the area where contact took place. We would expect to find evidence of trade or occupation, and we would expect strong similarities between donor and recipient cultures at the time of contact. As we shall see in the following chapter, all of these conditions were met by a strong influx of Asian culture into Meso-America at a time when the proto-Mayans were undergoing a transition from barbarian to civilized society. Therefore, we will be able to conclude that the major impetus for the emergence of Mayan civilization was Nu Sun's voyage.

Nu Sun arrived on time!

From Colony to Civilization

With hostile Olmecs controlling the shores of Mexico, there was no place for the Asian voyagers to go besides farther south. By now, they were getting desperate. Time was running short. Summer would be ending soon, and they had not yet found a safe haven for the colony they hoped to establish. Nor did they have anything of real value to show for their considerable investment. With the seasonal storms beginning to brew in the mid-Pacific, it was not the time to even think about risking the hazards of a return voyage to Asia. Consequently, they had no choice but to proceed with their search for a Meso-American homeland.

Obtaining fresh water was a recurring problem as the Asians sailed toward the tropics. When the mercenaries went ashore, they had to contend with small bands of Olmec warriors who were poorly armed. Their main weapons were *atlatls*, or spear throwers, and stones.[1] While they were effective at close range, they were no match for the Asian bow-and-arrow which was deadly accurate at a distance of more than two hundred yards--over twice the throwing distance of the hardiest Olmec warrior. The Asians also brought blowguns--which could be used from concealed positions to strike down Olmec sentries. The poisoned darts terrified the superstitious natives who imagined they were being attacked by ghosts.

Nu Sun did not fear the Olmecs--however, he respected their strength in numbers and the advantage of their defensive positions. The Asians could always prevail in minor skirmishes, but a pitched battle was a different matter entirely. Victory was dubious at best, while the losses in men and equipment could have crippled the entire expedition. An egotistical barbarian might have stormed into battle without thinking of the consequences, however, the Asian leaders were not egotistical barbarians. Indeed, they were men of Nu Sun's temperament. They were well versed in the Taoist philosophy which cautioned in favor of restraint and prudent action. Such men were not likely to risk the lives of their followers in a frivolous gesture of machismo.

TUXTLA STATUETTE

This phallic statuette was carved in stone and incised with some of the oldest known hieroglyphic writing from Meso-America. It is dated at the 2nd century A.D., or earlier. Note the presence of scroll motifs on the chest area and a stylized *yin/yang* motif near the base.

78

HIEROGLYPHIC WRITING

A comparison of glyphs from the Tuxtla statuette (right column) with contemporary Chinese characters of the Chou and Han dynasties (left column) establishes the close similarity between early Chinese writing and the earliest known writing from Meso-America. Similarities include the use of stylized *yin/yang* symbols, vertical alignment of characters, use of boxes to group related symbols, empty boxes used as place holders, dashed lines to represent numbers, and the presence of characters representing the elephant god, Ganesa. The last two show the use of couplets.

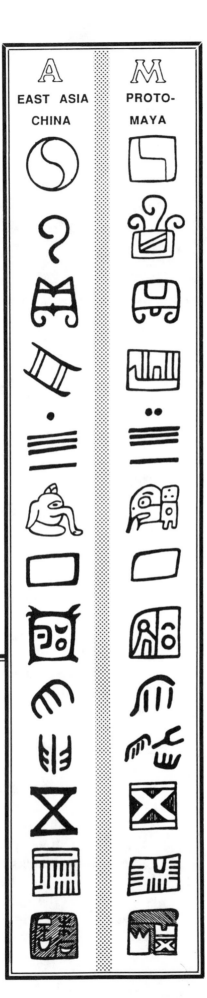

A
EAST ASIA
CHINA

M
PROTO-
MAYA

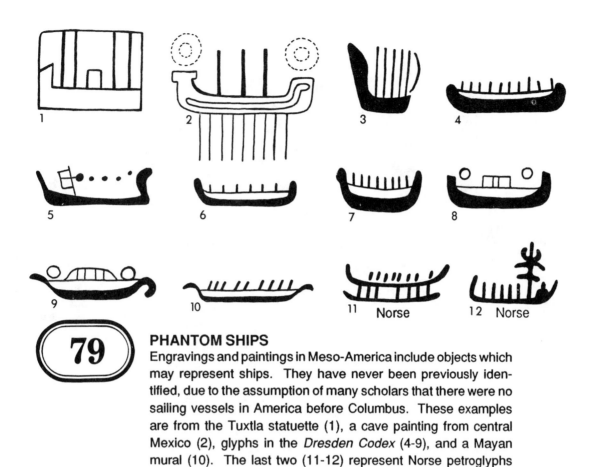

PHANTOM SHIPS

Engravings and paintings in Meso-America include objects which may represent ships. They have never been previously identified, due to the assumption of many scholars that there were no sailing vessels in America before Columbus. These examples are from the Tuxtla statuette (1), a cave painting from central Mexico (2), glyphs in the *Dresden Codex* (4-9), and a Mayan mural (10). The last two (11-12) represent Norse petroglyphs included for comparison.

Presumably, the Asian voyagers did not receive a hospitable reception until they passed beyond the southern boundary of Olmec territory--near the modern country of El Salvador. At this point along the coast, a large inlet reaches toward the shores of Honduras and Nicaragua. This inlet, called the Gulf of Fonseca, presents an ideal moorage for oceangoing vessels, while the nearby territory is ideally situated for a trading colony.

There are several important reasons which support the western Gulf area as the location for a colony: it was far enough from the Olmec heartland to protect it sufficiently from a sudden attack; it was located in a strategic position to dominate the coastal trade routes between Mexico and Panama; and it was at the center of abundant sources of trade goods that were suitable for Asian markets. These included exotic feathers, jadeite, gold, and hallucinogenic mushrooms.[2]

The Gulf of Fonseca is not far from where the earliest evidence of proto-Mayan tribes has been found. Furthermore, there is abundant archaeological evidence of trade and migration between East Asia and the Mayan region of Southern Mexico, Guatemala, and Honduras during a period of fourteen centuries. The nature of contact falls into two broad phases, indicating a major shift in the source of Asian contact. Between 500 B.C. and A.D. 200, the primary influx of new culture is distinctively Chinese in its cultural pedigree, and it will be referred to as the "Colonial Period."

The second phase of contact, lasting from ca. A.D. 200 to 900, is characterized

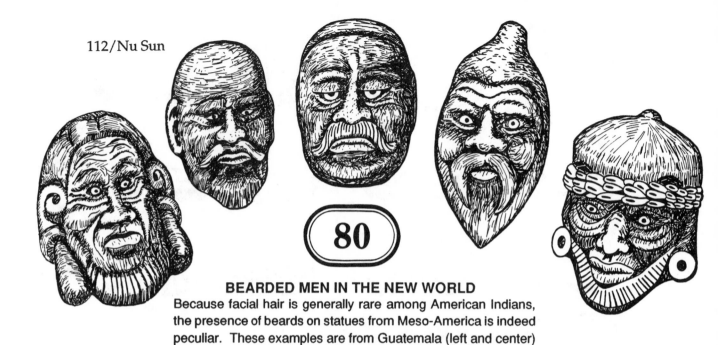

BEARDED MEN IN THE NEW WORLD

Because facial hair is generally rare among American Indians, the presence of beards on statues from Meso-America is indeed peculiar. These examples are from Guatemala (left and center) and Mexico. Dates range from the 6th century B.C. through the 5th century A.D. They are particularly common at Monte Alban. Some natives of high rank wore false beards--perhaps in commemoration of an ancestral figure of great prominence who came by ship from the Old World. The example on the right probably represents a false beard, while the others are most likely representations of authentic visitors from abroad.

by an influx of Indo-Chinese culture, along with cultivated plants that are indigenous to Southeast Asia.[3] Although Mayan culture had asserted its independence from Asia by developing hybrid art, architecture, and religious practices, Oriental traditions continued to leave their mark in the archaeological record, leading us to conclude that trans-Pacific commercial contacts persisted for nearly 700 years. This phase will be referred to as the "Commercial Period."

The Colonial Period

Few mysteries are more confounding than the sudden rise of Mayan civilization. In the space of a few centuries, an extensive network of metropolitan areas emerged from the tropical jungles near the Pacific shores of southern Mexico, Guatemala, and Honduras, as indicated in Map 7. These included Monte Alban, Izapa, and Kaminaljuyu, as well as the cosmopolitan city of Teotihuacan, Mexico, which was an incredible assemblage of bustling markets, palaces, and huge pyramids. So rapid was this assent to prominence that it reveals a most unusual phenomenon in the history of mankind: the native inhabitants of Meso-America sidestepped many centuries of cultural evolution. Not until modern times has there been such a quantum leap in cultural development anywhere in the world, and it has led many scholars to speculate on the possibility of Old-World contacts as an inspiration for the religion, social organization, and architecture of the area.

The surprising speed of cultural growth is equalled by the unlikely location of its origin: the tropical jungles of coastal Guatemala. This area presents a relatively

PHALLIC FIGURE

This stone monument carved in bas-relief shows some of the earliest magic scrolls used in Meso-America. It is from Kaminaljuyu, Guatemala, and dates to about 500 B.C. Scrolls represent life force and the breath of the soul.

SKY GOD

This bas-relief monument from Izapa, Mexico, shows a variety of scroll forms, including scroll-headed deities and holy fish. It was carved in high relief ca. 400 B.C.

MASK GOD

This ceramic vase is from Monte Alban, ca. 500 B.C. Scrolls emanating from the eyes, nose, mouth, and forehead represent spiritual power, wind, rain, and fertility. The figure has been identified as Itzamna--founding patron of Mayan civilization.

84

ASIA

CHALCATZINGO PETROGLYPH

This relief carving, known as "The King," has been assigned a date of origin ranging from 700 B.C. to 100 A.C. This broad range of dates reflects the difficulty of determining the age of rock carvings. Located in Morelos, Mexico, it is most similar to murals at Teotihuacan, ca. A.D. 300. The composition incorporates aspects of earlier, Olmec art, including the bracket mouth in which the priest is seated. However, the shape of the priest and the presence of scrolls suggest that a portion of the composition is of Mayan derivation. The scrolls are believed to represent rain clouds and wind. A Chinese symbol for rain clouds (right) is included for comparison.

85

WINGED FIGURE

This bas-relief monument from Izapa, Mexico, uses scrolls to represent wings, or heavenly status. Scrolls above the winged-man represent the cosmic opening, or mouth of heaven, from which blessings flow. The man arises from an alligator's mouth situated between the ends of a two-headed dragon ship. Wrist scrolls represent magical power. The monument dates to about 400 B.C.

BES Egyptian God

RAIMONDI MONOLITH
This gargantuan relief carving from Peru, ca. 200 B.C., represents a mingling of Asian and Mediterranean influences. The figure is reminiscent of the Egyptian dwarf god, Bes, who is associated with flowers and springtime. The highly ornate detail suggests that metal tools were used in its manufacture.

hostile climatic setting for rapid progress. In this respect, it is unlike any of the Old-World locations where civilizations emerged. There are no regional river systems to serve as the focal point for a gradual evolution of culture, such as occurred in Egypt around the Nile, or in Mesopotamia around the Tigris-Euphrates, or in India around the Indus, or in China around the Hwang-Ho. Nor did the coastal inhabitants have either the stability, or the large numbers of people that were typical elsewhere in the world where major civilizations arose. On the contrary, the various tribes which later formed the great Mayan civilization lived in isolated villages, and they spoke a variety of languages and dialects which made communication difficult--if not impossible.[4] Even today, the twenty-four different dialects of the Nahua language spoken by Mayan descendants are mutually unintelligible.

This remarkable situation leaves us with a perplexing problem: How could such a diverse population living in an environment that seems to foster isolation come together into a powerful military and commercial alliance?

EAST ASIA

IZAPAN FESTIVAL MONUMENT

This bas-relief stone carving from Izapa, Mexico (ca. 300-400 B.C.), depicts a mythological assemblage of folk heroes and deities. Fourteen of the symbols have direct counterparts in Asia, including: 1) the Taoist teacher with a pointed hat; 2) a Taoist pupil; 3) two fishes; 4) the

Three ingredients were required: 1) a common purpose; 2) hope for a better tomorrow; and 3) a common means of communication. Hatred of the Olmec warlords served as their common purpose; Nu Sun's magic and his fanatical Korean mercenaries provided inspiration; and use of Chinese pictograms enabled the scattered Mayan tribes to communicate with one another.

After wallowing in the backwaters of Olmec domination for several centuries, the proto-Mayan peoples had learned to detest the continuous drain of tribute, slaves, and human sacrifices that their overlords demanded. Consequently, they were anxious to welcome Asian visitors--just as Cortez found allies among the later inhabitants of the north who suffered under the tyranny of the Aztecs. It seems

serpent/turtle motif; 5) two fishes; 6) the rain cloud symbol; 7) a plumed bird with life-force scrolls; 8) a chinless deity with scroll eyes; 9) roaring tiger; 10) the parasol; 11) a sacred cieba tree; 12) the peaked scroll cloud; 13) the *yin/yang*; and 14) the cosmic power, or heaven motif. The similarity to Asian motifs (shown in the background) suggests a close affinity to Asian culture.

likely that the Asians approached the Mayans peacefully, while offering to exchange gifts and indicating their desire to trade for native products rather than attempting to steal what they wanted. The natives were fascinated by Asian weapons, such as the blowgun and bow, which the men in Nu Sun's command shared with their new allies.[5]

Meanwhile, the Taoist mystics amazed and entertained the inhabitants with an array of stunning devices, including magical mirrors, pipes for smoking herbs and opium, magnetic needles, iron knives, oil lamps, mercury, and dragon kites.[6] The apparent magic and military power of the visitors soon become a sensation in the area, drawing in curious natives from outlying villages, while the chiefs gathered to declare their homage to the gods from abroad. However, the Asians didn't want to rely too heavily on an erroneous impression that they were immortals, since their primary intention was to establish a trading colony. Sooner or later, the false pretense of immortality would be exposed, and that would be the end of their influence on the natives. However, the presence of a permanent settlement could produce valuable benefits for many seasons in the future, and that was precisely the kind of outcome an Asian sage like Nu Sun wanted to achieve.

So it was that the Asian colony served as the impetus for the formulation of the New World's first major commercial alliance: the Mayan Confederacy. It seems likely that a formal declaration, or treaty, brought together native tribes for the dual purposes of transoceanic commercial development and mutual defense. The Mayans took this opportunity to adopt Taoist customs restricting human sacrifice and establishing the primacy of the individual quest for enlightenment. Considering the Asian merchants' repugnance toward taxation, they included provisions for a merchant system that was exempt from state levies. It is hardly coincidental that a Chinese legend mentions a land across the sea where merchants paid no tax.[7]

Was it merely wishful thinking, or the true state of affairs in Mayan territory?

Ethnographic evidence indicates that Mayan merchants were exempt from tax, as we shall see in the next chapter. However, whether this was due to Asian influence or the brilliant foresight of Mayan forefathers is an issue for debate. Another legend stemming from the origin of the Confederacy deals with a mythical being called "Itzamna." This immortalized figure is regarded as an ancestral patron who taught the Mayan people how to write.[8]

MAYAN TEMPLE GUARDIAN

This bas-relief stone monument from Kaminaljuyu, Guatemala, shows the frequent use made of the *yin/yang* motif in Mayan art. The motifs are located on the headdress, behind the earspool, and on the belt insignia. The *yin/yang* knot (shown enlarged) represented the cohesive strength of cosmic power. It is one of the most frequently encountered motifs in all of ancient Meso-America.

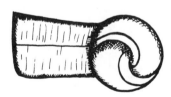

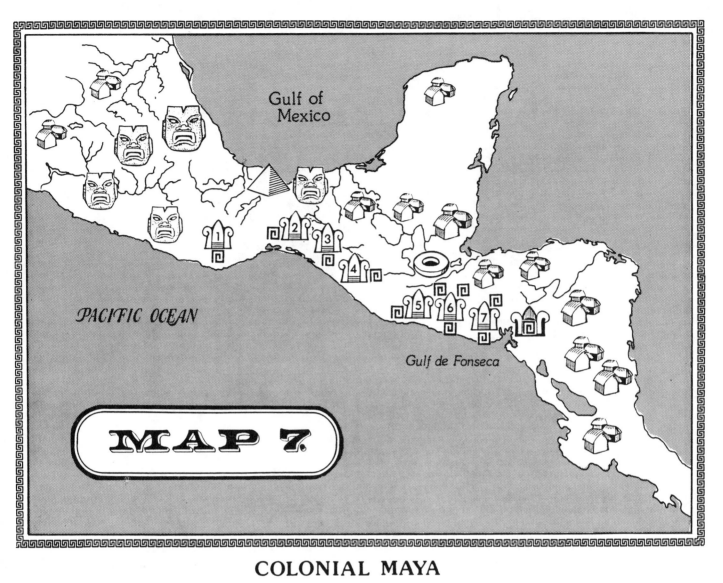

COLONIAL MAYA

COLONIAL MAYANS

Between 500 B.C. and A.D. 200, the Mayan Confederacy grew in power, pushing the Olmec tribes out of southern Mexico, Guatemala, Honduras, and El Salvador. During the first two centuries of this period, a new art style spread northward along the Pacific coast. Called the Izapan Style, it is characterized by abundant scroll forms, as well as elements of the Asian Omnibus Power Sign complex.

KEY (7)

-Olmec territory

 -Izapan style and ceremonial centers

 -Nu Sun's Colony

 -Neolithic villages 5-10,000 inhabitants

 -Omnibus Power Sign

IZAPAN SITES

1. Monte Alban	4. Izapa, El Jobo	7. Chalchuapa,
2. Mirador	5. Abaj Takalik	El Salvador
3. Chiapas de Corzo	6. El Baul, Kaminaljuyu	

MODIFIED ARTIFACTS

Jade carvings of unknown origin sometimes combine Olmecoid features, such as the bracket mouth and bracket head, with superficial scrolls. The objects are difficult to date with any accuracy, and the scrolls appear to be a secondary feature incised with metal tools--long after the original sculpture was completed. There are no known artifacts of this nature with a verified dating earlier than 500 B.C.

There is some evidence suggesting that early writing in the Confederacy was inspired by Asian contacts, although it would be ludicrous to suggest that Nu Sun introduced the *first* writing to New-World inhabitants. Indeed, all ancient peoples have learned to use primitive methods of written communication--such as drawing with sticks on the ground or using charcoal to write on stone. Since the earliest days of human antiquity, there have been commonly understood symbols. These are usually sufficient to engage in bartering or to express personal needs and fears. However, such primitive techniques are insufficient to compose poetry, to organize intertribal commerce, or to conduct intricate military operations. A more sophisticated form of written communication is necessary. This requires a standardized list of symbols, schools to train scribes, and suitable writing materials. Archaeological evidence indicates that the ancient Mayans, like the Chinese, used bark paper, although an Asian source for this cultural trait has not yet been proven.[9]

The ancient Mayans are generally credited with developing the earliest writing system in the New World.[10] However, even this quintessential attribute of civilization appears to have been derived from Asia. The precise characteristics of the earliest writing of the Confederacy are impossible to ascertain at the moment, because we have no way of knowing which of the many Oriental styles Nu Sun happened to use. Furthermore, there are no surviving copies of Mayan writing dating to the sixth century B.C. In fact, only four *codices*, or books, of the many hundreds written by Mayan scribes survived the sixteenth-century A.D. purge which was perpetrated by the Spanish Inquisition. Unfortunately, the remaining *codices* were produced after the collapse of the Confederacy in 900 A.D., making them unsuitable for comparison to more ancient Chinese documents. However, archaeologists have recovered a few stone artifacts with inscriptions that use earlier

Mayan hieroglyphs, and these are suitable for comparison. Some of the oldest available writing appears on the Tuxtla statuette (Figure 77). A portion of its second-century A.D. inscription is presented in Figure 78, along with some Asian examples dating to the Colonial period. The similarity is striking.

The earliest writing system was probably not a mere reproduction of Chinese. It was most likely a hybrid language suited primarily to the needs of local people with an emphasis on religious, commercial, and military matters. The important thing to realize is that the core language was probably standardized at the very beginning among tribes who were otherwise unable to communicate using a spoken language. For thousands of years, a similar situation has confronted Chinese inhabitants of different provinces. They are generally unable to communicate with one another except by using a common set of written symbols that have been periodically standardized by the reigning emperor.

The composition of hieroglyphic writing in both China and Meso-America appears to be fairly similar in overall design. The presence of parallel structural features is perhaps more significant than the occurrence of many similar characters in both writing systems. Indeed, most pictographic writing systems throughout the world have at least a few similar characters. For example, the sun frequently appears as a circle, the moon as a crescent, and people as stick figures. However, there are several less superficial commonalities between Chinese and proto-Mayan hieroglyphs that may indicate an ancestral linkage. Both the Mayan and Chinese systems used place holders, such as a zero or a blank box to indicate a place with nothing occupying it. Both systems used the concept of a couplet--in which two or more characters are linked together in the form of a noun/adjective combination. In this manner, the main subject character is modified by a secondary character

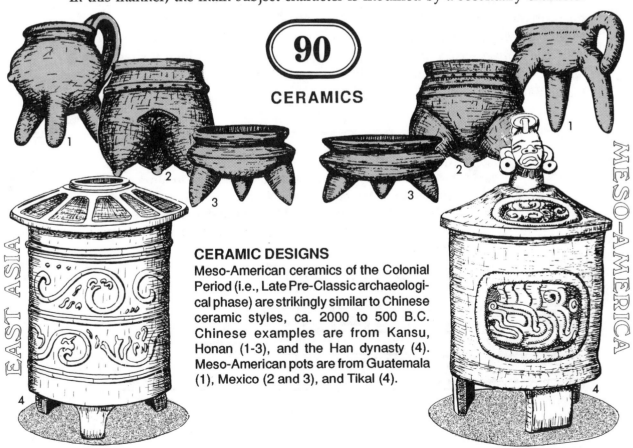

90

CERAMICS

EAST ASIA

MESO-AMERICA

CERAMIC DESIGNS
Meso-American ceramics of the Colonial Period (i.e., Late Pre-Classic archaeological phase) are strikingly similar to Chinese ceramic styles, ca. 2000 to 500 B.C. Chinese examples are from Kansu, Honan (1-3), and the Han dynasty (4). Meso-American pots are from Guatemala (1), Mexico (2 and 3), and Tikal (4).

placed beside it. Both systems at this point in time also made abundant use of elaborate pictures to supplement the more standardized pictograms. Eventually, the Chinese ideographic system became so extensive that pictures were no longer necessary to explain complex religious beliefs. The Mayan system never reached this level of development.

A suitable writing system with its associated communications network provides the underlying temporal continuity and functional cohesion of a civilization--hence the obsession of bureaucracies with keeping voluminous amounts of forms. Standardized ways of recording information, like customs, help to control behavior and maintain social order. That is the normal consequence of a well-organized civilization. However, it is most unusual for groups of jungle tribes, speaking different languages or dialects, to band together and devise a common written language entirely on their own. The fact that it was done early, by scattered Mayan tribes occupying an extensive area of land, bears testimony to the immense power of the colonial alliance. It is indicative of the strong faith the Mayans had in the wondrous power of the people from Asia. Indeed, this was a magical time among the coastal Indian villages, and much of that magic can still be sensed from the archaeological relics that have survived two thousand years of decay in the tropical climate.

Some of these relics have strange motifs which may indicate the presence of sailing ships long before the arrival of Columbus (Figure 79). Other artifacts depict bearded men with diverse racial characteristics (Figure 80). These ancient artifacts bear silent testimony to foreign visitors from the Old World, including Asia and the Mediterranean.

More substantial evidence of Asian colonization is to be found in the sudden shift that occurred in the pattern of motifs and art styles of Meso-America during the sixth century B.C. In a land where magic scrolls were virtually nonexistent prior to Nu Sun's voyage, they suddenly occurred in great abundance (Figures 81 through 86). The earliest scrolls have been found primarily in archaeological sites located along the Pacific Coast, including Izapa, in southern Mexico, and Kaminaljuyu, Guatemala.

CERAMIC DECORATIONS

The earliest "key pattern" ceramic decorations in Mexico and Guatemala (center) date to the Colonial period. They are similar to Chinese designs of 1000 B.C. (left) and to Greek ceramic decorations. The stepped-fret of Monte Alban (right) also dates to this period.

EAST ASIA   MESO-AMERICA

92

TEMPLE MOUND
One of the earliest stone temple mounds of the Mayan territory was located at Uaxactun, Guatemala. It was constructed in approximately 100 B.C. The structure is notable for its masked gods flanking the stairways and the magic scrolls emerging from their heads.

Many other Asian symbols can be traced to this same general location as early as the fifth century B.C., leading to the conclusion that this area is near the location of the first Asian colony. The archaeological record further indicates that the use of Asian symbols spread along with the growing Mayan Confederacy. Apparently, Nu Sun's colony quickly expanded its influence over the tribes in the coastal areas as the Confederacy grew in power.[11] This was the beginning of religious, artistic, and political influence that had a lasting impact on native cultural development.

Figure 87 shows a detailed festival scene carved on a stone monument found at Izapa. The monument is of interest to us because it contains fourteen symbols that are characteristic of Southeast Asia. The central element of the composition is the *cieba*, which was regarded as the sacred tree throughout the Orient.[12] Numerous examples of the Buddhist *cieba* are present in the archaeological record of India as far back as 100 B.C. Other Asian symbols on the monument include the two fishes (which represented matrimonial harmony in China), the serpent/turtle motif, the *yin/yang*, the thunderhead scroll, the parasol, the cone-shaped hat, and the chinless deity with scroll-shaped eyes. The composition appears to be a local design executed by native craftsmen in accordance with the requirements of Mayan religion. The symbols and religious themes, however, are anything but local. They are distinctly Asian in their cultural pedigree.

The religious themes of the early Maya, as portrayed on stone carvings, are highly divergent from those of the Olmec. The adoption of so many Asian symbols during the Early Colonial Period is clear evidence of the importance given to the Taoist mystics who were the religious leaders of Nu Sun's colony. This is probably the reason why the *yin/yang* symbol was adopted as one of the most important religious symbols of the Maya (Figure 88). It was used by the Maya for a thousand years, and later it was adopted by the Aztecs prior to the Spanish Conquest.

The Colonial Period was a time of unprecedented cultural development--a time when many Asian cultural traits were readily borrowed and adapted to local needs. Apparently, it made more sense to Mayan religious leaders to infuse their rapidly evolving culture with symbols that already had a long-standing tradition. Perhaps it was a way of giving their own religion validity. Even so, there was another factor to consider: the Taoists undoubtedly had sufficient accuracy in their astronomical predictions and use of magical paraphernalia to make it seem plausible that they were the Almighty's chosen representatives on earth.[13] Consequently, it was only logical for the Mayans to adopt Taoist symbolism and Asian religious practices.

As the Mayan Confederacy grew in power, raids against the Olmec provinces became more frequent.[14] These culminated in the invasion of the Olmec capital at La Venta and the collapse of the Olmec nation. Evidence of widespread destruction of Olmec religious monuments during this time period is well documented in the archaeological record. For that matter, so is the formulation of a "confederacy" of Mayan tribes whose capital may have been located at Monte Alban.[15] Nevertheless, Olmec art traditions persisted in some areas until the end of the Colonial Period. Apparently, some of the Olmec artisans incorporated symbols from the burgeoning civilization to the south as a way of augmenting their own archaic style. Between 550 B.C. and A.D. 200, magic scrolls were sometimes superimposed on typical Olmec designs (Figure 89). In this context, the new symbols appear to be lopsided--almost as though they were applied long after the original design was completed.

Why would Olmec artists borrow an alien art form?

COSMIC POWER SIGN

This symbol consists of a central flame element, triangle, or circle (for the sun), with two scrolls. The Asian examples (1 and 2) are from India, while the Meso-American examples (3 and 4) are stone carvings from Colonial Guatemala, ca. 500 B.C. In both places, the motif is closely associated with the sun. On the right is a cartouche, which the Mayans used to enclose the glyphs that represented the days of their calendar. Consequently, the symbol is associated with the passage of time among the Mayans.

EAST ASIA

MESO-AMERICA

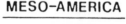

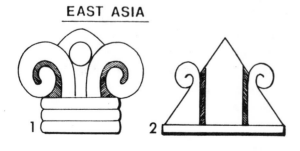

SEXUAL POTENCY
This bas-relief carving from Kaminaljuyu, Guatemala (M), marks the earliest New-World usage of the Cosmic Power Sign as a symbol for sexual potency. The tradition of using this fertility symbol in association with a phallus, or apron, persisted throughout the Mayan civilization. An example of the phallic symbol from India (A) is shown for comparison.

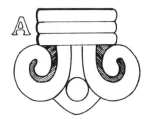

Perhaps it was an attempt to add extra power to the old talismans? Or, it may have been a vain effort to re-energize old gods who had lost their power. If it was, the experiment was a failure. The real power of the Mayans lay in their willingness to ally themselves with the immigrants and culture of East Asia.

The hybrid, or "Olmecoid," artifacts that incorporate scrolls have led some authors to assume that scroll motifs must have come from indigenous, i.e., Olmec, sources. However, the evidence sufficiently refutes this assumption. None of these unusual specimens have been found in a stratigraphic context dating earlier than 500 B.C. And sufficient research has been done on earlier Olmec sites to uncover any possible precursors to the complex of magic scrolls--but there are none.

As we have seen from our review of the evidence during the period from 900 to 500 B.C., scroll-work designs are virtually nonexistent on Olmec religious artifacts. Furthermore, when scrolls do appear in the sixth century B.C., a majority of the designs from Mayan territory have only peripheral artistic relationships to the Olmec style--i.e., they exhibit proto-Mayan themes that were foreign to the Olmec heartland. [16]

95

COLLAR INSIGNIA
Some proto-Mayan designs such as these deity figures carved into bones incorporate the Cosmic Power Sign as a collar insignia. The bones are from Chiapas, Guatemala, with a date of origin ca. A.D. 200, or earlier.

There are no developmental forms of magic scrolls in early Olmec art that would explain how a diverse scroll complex like the Mayan Omnibus Power Sign came into being. This fact leads to the conclusion that the Omnibus Power Sign complex did not emerge from native artistic traditions. However, the prior existence of an Asian Omnibus Power Sign of magic scrolls leads to the obvious realization that the motifs were imported en masse from across the Pacific. This is the only tenable conclusion, as it explains why the entire motif complex appears suddenly in the Mayan archaeological record at approximately 500 B.C. This further correlates to the origin of the scroll complex along the Pacific Coast of Guatemala, and southwestern Mexico. If the Olmecs had been instrumental in developing this unique art form, we would expect the earliest evidence of a magic scroll complex to occur in the Olmec heartland of Veracruz along the Gulf Coast--not in the far-flung provinces of the proto-Mayan tribes.

The highly intricate style apparent in the Guatemalan rock carvings suggests that metal tools were used in their production. Although it is technically possible to make such monuments using stone chipping and grinding techniques, we seldom find detailed sculptures of such colossal magnitude in Paleolithic cultures. Several modern archaeologists have experimented with using stone tools such as choppers in an attempt to fabricate similar monuments, but the results have not been supportive of the hypothesis that natives had an adequate lithic technology.[17] Even when they tried to carve comparatively soft materials, like the limestone and volcanic tuff that the Mayans used for sculptures, they found that stone tools were practically worthless. The stone choppers they experimented with deteriorated rapidly from the continuous pounding.

Tools of bronze and iron from Chinese foundries were being used in Southeast Asia by this point in time, and we can assume that similar tools would have been available to an Asian colony doing business on the Guatemalan coast. However, there have been no archaeological reports of iron tools found in pre-Columbian sites. This apparent lack of "hard" evidence is not surprising. Considering the rapid rate at which iron deteriorates in tropical climates, it is highly unlikely that iron tools will ever be found regardless of how prevalent they may have been in the past. Exactly when metal crafts reached the New World has been a subject of extensive debate. Copper has been found inside a large ceramic pot dating from the Miraflores archaeological phase in Guatemala (ca. 500 B.C.).[18] As the earliest evidence of metal in Meso-America, it corresponds closely to the time and location suggested for Nu Sun's colony. Gold casting was perfected in the Andes between 1000 and 500 B.C.--possibly predating Nu Sun's arrival and suggesting the influence of other Old-World visitors.[19] By the time of Columbus, gold-working technology was well-established in several areas including Central Mexico, Costa Rica, and the Andes.[20] Copper ornaments, bells, and a few utensils were produced throughout the region,[21] and early Spanish reports indicate that the natives were already mining tin for use in the manufacture of bronze.[22] Surface metal deposits were generally scarce in the region--a factor that must have repressed development of metal smelting and casting technology. Nevertheless, if we are to infer the presence of metal tools from the highly intricate stone carvings of the Mayan Indians, there must have been an ample supply of iron derived from Asian commerce.

Other aspects of Mayan culture provide better clues to the extensive trans-Pacific trade between 500 B.C. and A.D. 200. For example, Mayan ceramics are surprisingly similar to Asian pottery of the same time period (Figures 90 and 91). Not only are the shapes similar, but the motifs used in their decoration also reflect a direct transference of culture from Asia to Mexico.[23] The traditional Asian thunder pattern appears during the Miraflores Phase in Guatemala, and it is accompanied by the "stepped-fret" motif in Monte Alban.[24]

SERPENT RAINBOW
This bas-relief carving from Kaminaljuyu, Guatemala (ca. 400 B.C.), shows the Cosmic Power Sign used as a belt insignia of a sky god. Magic scrolls are also used to represent rain and wind. The *yin/yang* symbol is employed as a serpent knot and as power signs on the Deity's wrists. Two-headed serpent rainbows were also used as a motif in Han China.

The Colonial Period witnessed many changes in the composition of Mayan society. Improved methods of food production and social organization enabled the diverse tribes to establish a more centralized and sedentary existence. Increasing trade and social organization led to greater stability of the villages, while the population increased from several hundred thousand to nearly a million inhabitants.[25] Along with growing prosperity came the establishment of a theocracy, and construction of stone temple mounds by approximately 100 B.C. (Figure 92).

New burial practices seem to have originated during this time period, and it is hardly surprising that the artifacts uncovered by archaeologists are markedly similar to those of the Chinese. Important individuals were interred within stepped chambers using wooden planks in a manner that is characteristic of Chinese burial vaults.[26] Cinnabar and jade were included as primary burial offerings--reflecting a tradition that had been common in China for two thousand years. The appearance of these cultural traits among native Indian tribes soon after Nu Sun's voyage leads to the foregone conclusion that they were adopted directly from Asian colonists.

Also during the Colonial Period, the Confederacy established a new lunar calendar. As a starting date, the priest-astronomers chose a year corresponding to approximately 3000 B.C.[27] The selection of this date for the sequential numbering of years, or the "Long Count," has been one of the enduring mysteries of Mayan civilization. This date actually precedes the beginning of Mayan political organization by more than *two thousand* years.[28] It is hardly coincidental that the ancient Chinese lunar calendar also has an approximate starting date of 3000 B.C. According to Chinese tradition, the lunar calendar commemorates the reign of the legendary Huang-ti, who was the mythical founder of Taoism. Since Nu Sun's Taoist followers probably regarded this date as the legitimate beginning of recorded time, and since they undoubtedly pushed their own traditions upon the Mayan Confederacy, we finally have a logical rationale for why the Mayans chose this unlikely date for the start of their Long Count system.[29]

If we examine the calendars of other societies, we realize that some important date in their history is always used for the beginning. The fact that the Mayan Confederacy adopted the traditional Chinese starting date is yet another example of how closely intertwined the two cultures had become in 500 B.C.

Other traditions adopted from the Chinese included the naming of children after the calendar date of birth and use of the calendar as a divining table for predicting the future.[30] The specific names of the days and the specific fortunes assigned to them were determined by local tradition, and adjustments were made to the cycles of the month and year in accordance with local astronomical observations.

As time went on, the two systems evolved in accordance with the local political and religious history, so that their outward forms gradually diverged. Nevertheless, many historians have remarked about the basic similarities of the Chinese and Mayan calendrical systems, while expressing amazement at the fact that the Mayans seemed to have emerged suddenly from the Stone Age with an advanced sidereal calendar system already so accurate that it must have required thousands of years of observations to produce.[31] Such a feat seems unlikely from the Paleolithic hunting cultures of the Meso-American jungle.

The enigma is finally resolved by our knowledge of Nu Sun's voyage. The Mayan calendar was based on thousands of years of observations, but they were all done in a distant land across the sea--long before the Mayan tribes became the "chosen people" of Meso-America.

A textbook focusing on the subject of Asian influences on the development of Mayan civilization would extend for thousands of pages. Such a volume would be necessary to trace the nuances of how Old-World cultural items were adopted wholesale or modified to meet the demands of the native people. But a book on trans-Pacific exploration such as we have in hand has its limits. The reader who is interested in a more in depth examination will wisely peruse some of the fine references listed in the Bibliography.

For the time being, we shall examine only one of the most common motifs associated with the Omnibus Power Sign tradition. The motif has a three-pronged shape that has been referred to as a "trefoil," or a "celestial symbol."[32] This symbol is one of the most common power signs of the Mayan civilization, and it was derived from Asia, ca. 500 B.C., as a consequence of Nu Sun's voyage. We will refer to it as the Cosmic Power Sign (Figure 93).

Several examples of the Cosmic Power Sign in the context of early Colonial rock carvings are presented in Figures 94, 95, and 96. The symbol typically appears as a band around the neck, or waist, of a religious personage such as a priest, deity, or immortal. It was used as a crown emblem and was occasionally attached to an apron, or phallus. Eventually, the motif became identified with the cosmological concepts of time and celestial energy as manifested in the sun. Consequently, it was used to represent the sun in Mayan murals, and it was used to form the emblem (or cartouche) enclosing the glyphs for each of the twenty day names in the Mayan calendar.

The Cosmic Power Sign has absolutely no antecedents in Olmec symbolism. Consequently, there is no evidence to suggest that it might have been independently developed in the New World. Furthermore, the dramatic influx of Asian religious and cultural traits during this time period, including the Omnibus Power Sign complex, categorically identify an external source (i.e., China) as the origin for this unique motif.

The meaning behind the Cosmic Power Sign betrays an Old-World source, because the symbol presents a highly uncharacteristic philosophical perspective for Paleolithic cultures. Stone-Age societies, like those of the Olmec and the earliest Mayan tribes, have a religious orientation that is typically based upon shamanistic concepts stressing nature worship and a multiplicity of gods. In Colonial Mayan society, however, we see two coexisting systems--one shamanistic, and the other cosmic--just as there was in China during the sixth century B.C. However, during the time period from 1000 to 400 B.C., there were no advanced cultural centers in ancient Meso-America that were even remotely similar to the metropolis of An-Yang. And it was precisely this kind of urban environment that was essential for the rapid development of civilization. The most reasonable explanation for the sudden leap in cultural development in Meso-America is contact with a more advanced civilization, such as those of the Old World.

As we shall see, contact between Asia and Meso-America was both extensive and enduring, and it provided the cultural shock necessary to propel New World societies into a dynamic thrust towards civilization.

ASIA   MESO-AMERICA

A

M

COMMERCIAL PERIOD HIEROGLYPHS

Following the Colonial Period (ca. 200 A.D.), the writing systems of China and Meso-America show few common features due to major revisions and standardizations in both areas. Nevertheless, several notable features are present, including a few similar characters as indicated by the columns at left. The symbols include the *Yin/Yang*, a representation of the Cosmic tree, thunder clouds, the longevity symbol, and the symbol for human being. One feature of classical Mayan hieroglyphs (right) is the use of hands to denote action--a trait that was common in the archaic writing of China (above center).

97

METAL TOOLS

Chisel-like tools that may have been used for stone carving occur in the *codices* (1-3). Other copper tools occur in pre-Columbian burials from Mexico (4 and 5).

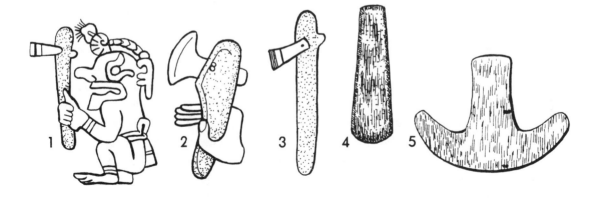

The Long Alliance

Mayan culture exhibits a combination of indigenous and foreign attributes which blend together in ways that tend to disguise Old-World sources. Many travelers to the Orient have been astonished by the striking similarities of style and composition apparent in Asian and Meso-American religious art. Yet they have been unable to make a strong case for direct contact, because native American artifacts and architectural styles are sufficiently divergent from Asian traditions to make independent invention seem a plausible explanation. Certainly, a preponderance of Mayan cultural growth during the Commercial period can be attributed to the genius of Mayan leaders. Nevertheless, it is possible to discern patterns of influence from abroad--however subtle these may be.

Although Chinese contributions dominated the Colonial Period, a variety of Asian contacts seem to have taken place during the Commercial Period. It is evident from the characteristics of artifacts found in Meso-America that Chinese cultural influence declined rapidly following the Han dynasty (202 B.C. to A.D. 220).[1] Meanwhile, commercial ventures expanded from bases around the Gulf of Siam--an area that now includes Indonesia, Thailand, Malaysia, Vietnam, and Cambodia.[2] By the first century A.D., strong religious and cultural forces from India were sweeping into the East Indies. They were followed by an exceedingly rapid rise in population, social development, and commerce. At the same time, Mayan city-states were flourishing in Meso-America.

Hindu colonists spread into Borneo, Malaya, Indo-China and Java, where they established trading centers amid the tropical jungle. By the first century, A.D., the Kingdom of Funan came into being when a powerful monarch united Cambodian city-states; by the seventh century, the Kingdom of Champa controlled the coasts of Vietnam.[3] Other maritime empires and pirate colonies prospered throughout Indonesia as part of a thriving commercial network involving the transportation of gold, grain, slaves, silk, spices, iron, passengers, and religion. Surprisingly, much

EAST ASIA
HINDU-BUDDHIST MONUMENTS

Sculptures of religious figures or nobles were carved into solid rock using metal tools. This Buddhist deity (1) is from Java and dates to about the 9th century A.D. On the front apron is the *yin/yang* knot which was a common symbol throughout the region. The sun pillar (2), from 10th-century India, was also referred to as the "Wheel of Law."

MAYAN MONUMENTS

Mayan sculptures have close parallels to those of Asia. The Cosmic Disk (1) is from the 10th-century Teotihuacan area. In the center of the flaming disk is the unmistakable *yin/yang* motif depicting two encircled dragons with eyes. Other *yin/yang* symbols literally cover the stela of a Mayan noble (2) from Copan, Honduras. The 8th-century stela features two elephants above the noble, and they are surmounted by turbaned *mahouts*, or elephant drivers. Similar themes are common in the HIndu-Buddhist sculptures of Southeast Asia.

STEPPED PYRAMIDS
The 19th-century stone pyramid of Angkor, Cambodia, typifies the architecture of Asian cultures which were in close trade contact with Meso-America. Facades of stone temples from this area feature enormous sculptures of the scroll-headed, mask deity, while the moon served as inspiration behind the symbol of the Great Monad.

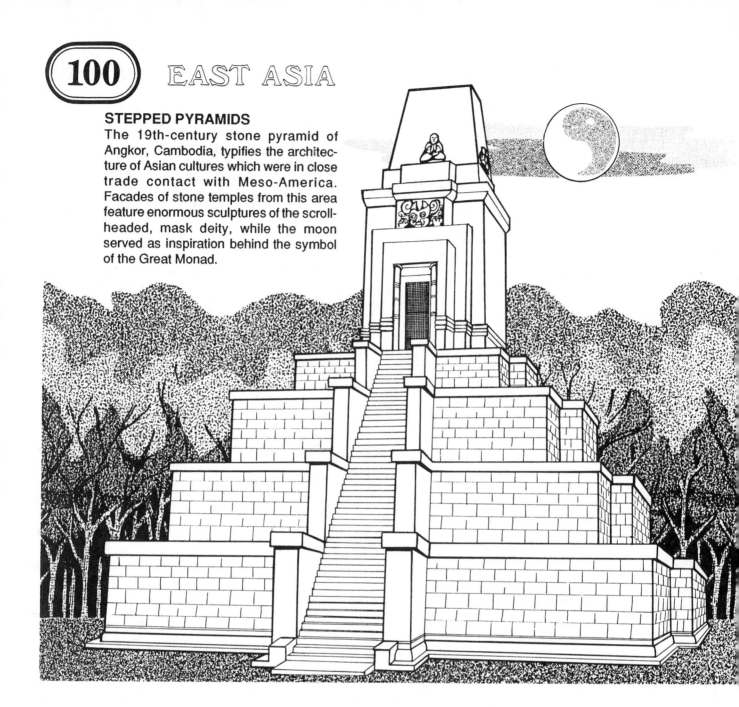

of the cultural, political, and religious growth during this era happened peacefully--as a consequence of the deliberate Indian policy of non-violent commercial expansion.[4]

During this time, two and three-masted ships as large as one hundred and sixty feet from bow to stern sailed the oceans using the seasonal monsoon winds to speed their travel from Indo-China to the outlying islands of the Orient. And wherever the merchants brought the benefits of civilization, jealous rulers sought to compete with the wealth and prestige of the Hindu kings. This obsession with princely grandeur led to the construction of enormous stone palaces with ornate carvings and sculpture. Such a vast growth of imperial buildings and religious shrines required men who were trained in the ancient Hindu craft traditions.

Their buildings and sculptures were largely a reflection of the parent traditions

TEMPLE PYRAMIDS
Hundreds of stone pyramids were con-structed throughout Meso-America. Some have close parallels to temple pyramids of East Asia. Many feature the scroll-headed, mask deity. This one is from Tikal, Guatemala, and dates to the 8th century.

of India, combined with Helenistic influences dating to the third century B.C. invasion by the Greek conqueror, Alexander of Macedonia. Consequently, the presence of distinctive art styles and motifs makes it possible to trace the spread of Hindu stone carving traditions from India to Malaysia, to Indonesia, and from there to the New World. Apparently, Mayan nobles were just as eager to raise colossal stone monuments to the glory of their civilization as were their counterparts in Angkor, Borobudur, and the Indus Valley.[5]

If stone carving and masonry were simple crafts, then it would be reasonable to attribute the simultaneous occurrence of intricate stone sculpture, pyramids, and temples in Southeast Asia and Meso-America to the effects of independent inven-tion. The fact that construction methods and art styles are quite similar could be regarded as the consequence of the tropical environments found in both areas. However, the level of sophistication achieved by both Hindu and Mayan artisans

STONE ARCHITECTURE

Stone building technology spread from India into much of Southeast Asia following the 1st century A.D., reaching its zenith of development between the 12th-15th centuries. Atlantean figures (1) were a common decorative feature. These two are from Sanchi, India, dating to the 1st century A.D. The framed colonnettes (2) are typical of Cambodian buildings, as are corbeled vaults (3) which were popular throughout the region.

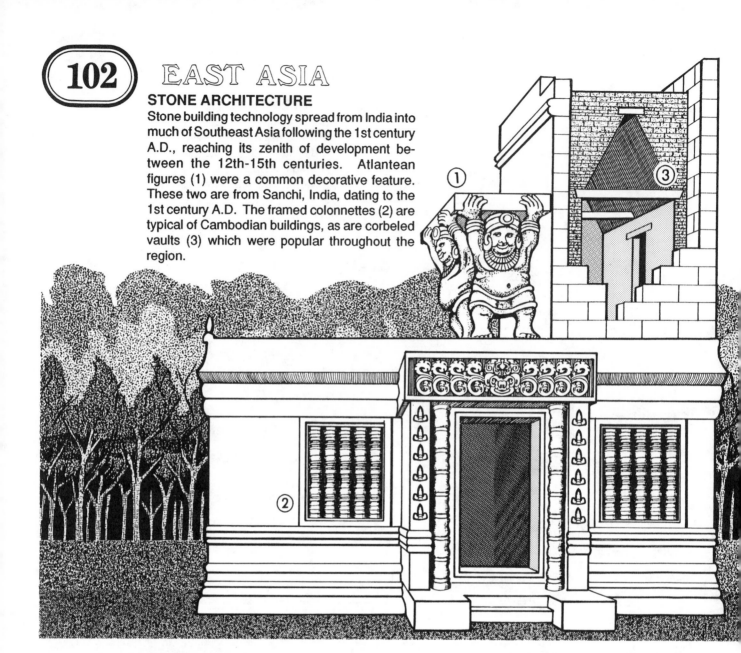

requires a high degree of technological development, rigorous training, and the presence of metal tools.

In the Old World, there is an implicit relationship between the sophistication of stone sculpture and the quality of metal tools. Since tools were the property of tradesmen, rather than nobles, it is not surprising that they are rarely encountered in the archaeological record. They certainly were not the kinds of items to be left in the crypt of a Mayan ruler. Nevertheless, a few authors have identified copper and bronze tools in pre-Columbian archaeological contexts in Mexico,[6] and a few metal tools are portrayed in the thirteenth-century *codices* (Figure 97).

Although the Mayans developed a fairly distinctive art style by the time of the Golden Age of the Confederacy, ca. A.D. 800 to 900, evidence of continued Asian contact is present in the archaeological record. This should not come as a surprise if we consider that Mayan artisans needed to obtain iron tools for use in the manufacture of sophisticated, three-dimensional sculptures. Two examples of artifacts from Asia and Meso-America are presented in Figures 98 and 99. These

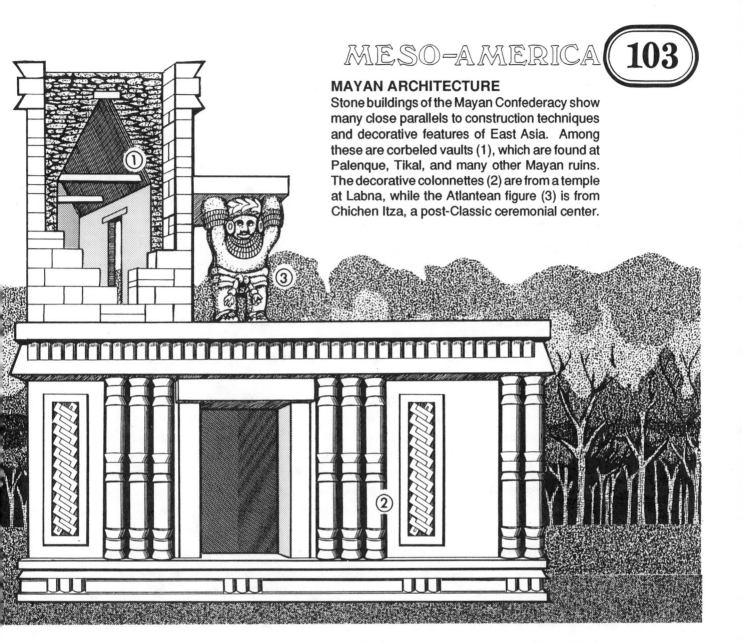

MAYAN ARCHITECTURE
Stone buildings of the Mayan Confederacy show many close parallels to construction techniques and decorative features of East Asia. Among these are corbeled vaults (1), which are found at Palenque, Tikal, and many other Mayan ruins. The decorative colonnettes (2) are from a temple at Labna, while the Atlantean figure (3) is from Chichen Itza, a post-Classic ceremonial center.

Javanese and Mayan sculptures, called "stelae," portray human figures or divinities who were regarded as immortals. They are generally larger than life size and are located in temple courtyards or in front of pyramids as objects of veneration. They frequently incorporate scroll forms, circle shapes (which represented jade or water in both areas), dual-headed serpent bars, dwarf-like figures, elephants, and *yin/yang* motifs. Stela B from Copan, Honduras, is of particular interest due to the presence of two elephants at the top of the sculpture. The sculpture is sometimes referred to as the "Elephant Stela," and some scholars regard it as conclusive evidence of Asian contact, since elephants were not indigenous to ancient Meso-America.[7] Furthermore, the figures mounted on the elephants have turban-like headdresses which are virtually identical to the headgear of Hindu elephant riders, or *mahouts*, of the same time period. However, skeptics contend that the animals on Stela B are actually tropical birds with enlarged beaks.[8]

Such an interpretation might be conceivable, were it not for the presence of numerous other motifs of Asian derivation that reveal the true artistic heritage of

Mayan sculpture. The most significant is the *yin/yang* symbol which occurs on Stela B no less than twelve times. Although the motifs are difficult to see on the actual statue, which has been severely battered in recent years, they are easily identified on castings preserved in the British Museum in London.

The ballcourt marker that accompanies the stela is remarkably similar to stone disks from India which represent the wheel of cosmic law. Indeed, the *yin/yang* symbol is used interchangeably with the cosmic wheel in Asia, while it appears as the central feature of this marker from Teotihuacan.

Architectural designs in Meso-America also reveal Asian influence, although there is a great deal of variation and semi-independent development apparent throughout the Commercial Period. Similarities include aspects of social organization, as well as construction. In both places, the ceremonial centers served as focal points for commerce and religion. Most inhabitants lived in wood and mud structures located at some distance from priestly enclaves which were clustered around towering pyramids. Typically, the temples and pyramids were situated on a north-south axis in accordance with astronomical and astrological guidelines.

Figures 100 and 101 show two pyramids which have been cited frequently as an indication of Southeast Asian cultural influence. They do appear to have similar design features, involving three platform levels and the use of secondary, bastion-like structures, which are built out from the middle of each level. These extensions apparently served the structural purpose of providing reinforcement to the sloping sides of the pyramid. It is a design feature that could have resulted just as easily from independent invention as from transoceanic contact.

However, the presence of scroll-headed deity figures along the facades of temples in both areas cannot be explained so easily. Unlike the bastions which could have been devised as a consequence of similar experiences with building materials, the use of scroll-headed deities has no relationship to structural features. It is a purely symbolic expression, and as such, can be explained only by the religious context from which the symbols were derived. Therefore, the simultaneous presence of these similar motifs constitutes a strong case for trans-Pacific contact and the spread of Asian culture to America.

Other architectural features suggest common origins, although independent invention or derivation from another Old-World source cannot be ruled out as a possible cause. These include the presence of corbeled arches, Atlantean figures,

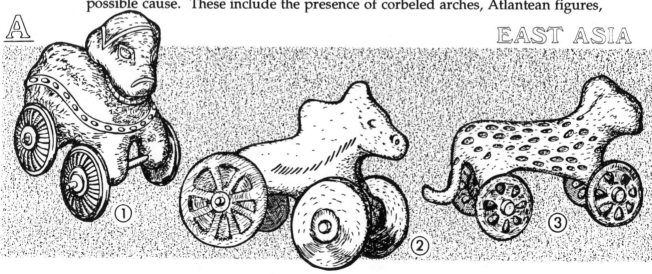

A

EAST ASIA

① ② ③

 EAST ASIA    MESO-AMERICA

104 TOY HOUSES

Clay houses are found in both China and Meso-America, often with little clay figurines inside. Examples from China are prevalent from the 2nd century B.C. through the 6th century A.D. Those from Mayarit, Mexico, date to the 1st and 2nd centuries A.D.

105 WHEELED TOYS

Animals on wheels are present in the archaeological record of India and China (A1 to 3). They also occur in the Late Classic archaeological phase, or Commercial Period, at Mexican sites (M1 to 3). Existence of wheeled toys presents a paradox to those who believed that the wheel was unknown in the New World. The apparent absence of wheeled vehicles is generally attributed to the lack of suitable draft animals.

MESO-AMERICA   M

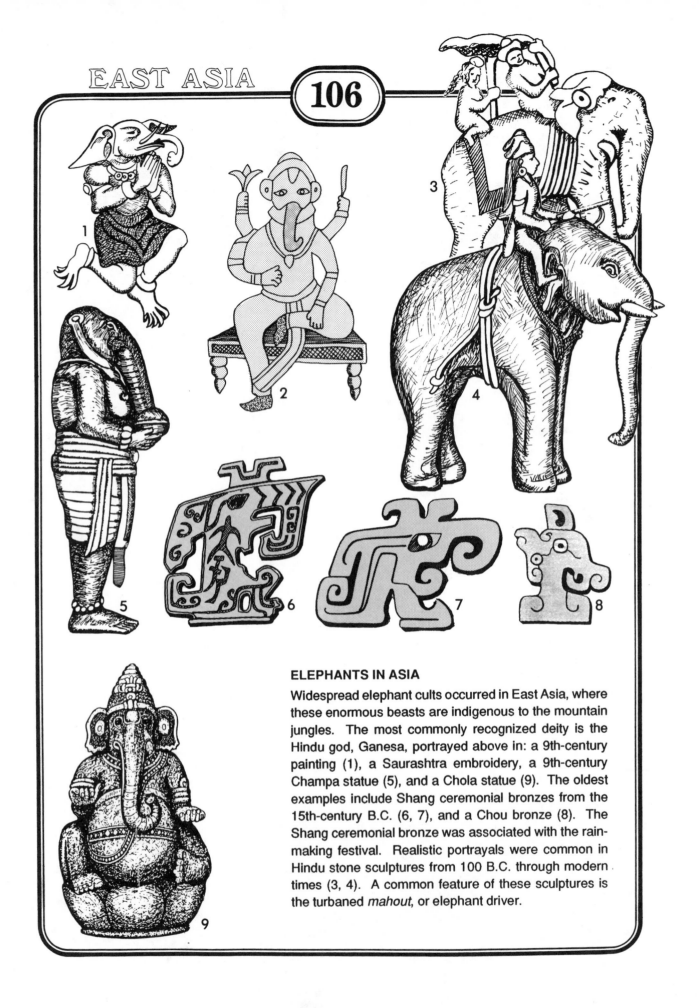

ELEPHANTS IN ASIA

Widespread elephant cults occurred in East Asia, where these enormous beasts are indigenous to the mountain jungles. The most commonly recognized deity is the Hindu god, Ganesa, portrayed above in: a 9th-century painting (1), a Saurashtra embroidery, a 9th-century Champa statue (5), and a Chola statue (9). The oldest examples include Shang ceremonial bronzes from the 15th-century B.C. (6, 7), and a Chou bronze (8). The Shang ceremonial bronze was associated with the rain-making festival. Realistic portrayals were common in Hindu stone sculptures from 100 B.C. through modern times (3, 4). A common feature of these sculptures is the turbaned *mahout*, or elephant driver.

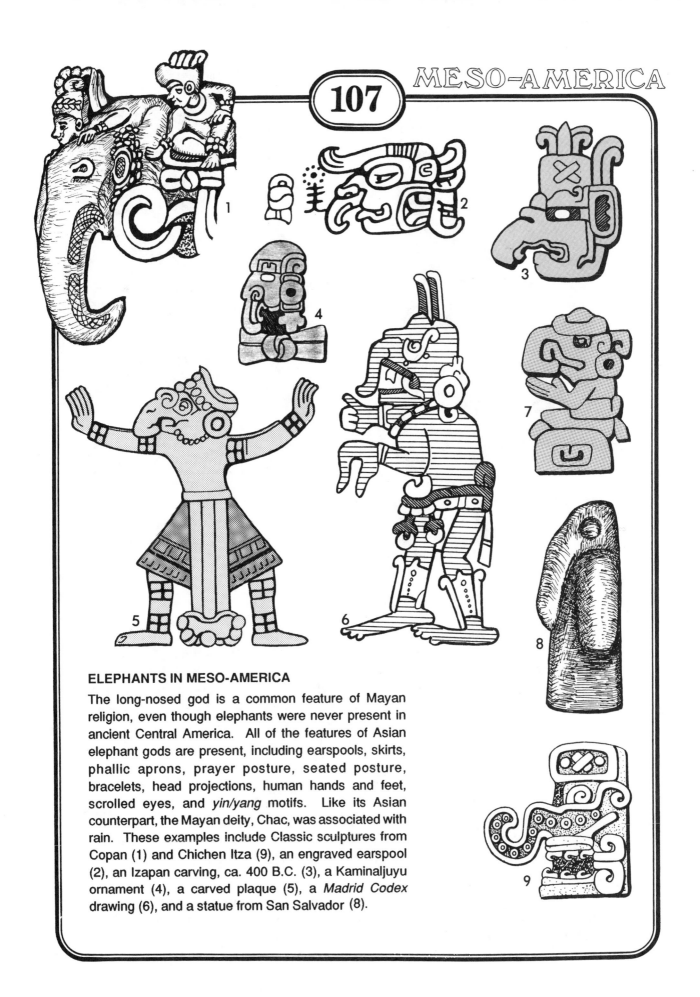

ELEPHANTS IN MESO-AMERICA

The long-nosed god is a common feature of Mayan religion, even though elephants were never present in ancient Central America. All of the features of Asian elephant gods are present, including earspools, skirts, phallic aprons, prayer posture, seated posture, bracelets, head projections, human hands and feet, scrolled eyes, and *yin/yang* motifs. Like its Asian counterpart, the Mayan deity, Chac, was associated with rain. These examples include Classic sculptures from Copan (1) and Chichen Itza (9), an engraved earspool (2), an Izapan carving, ca. 400 B.C. (3), a Kaminaljuyu ornament (4), a carved plaque (5), a *Madrid Codex* drawing (6), and a statue from San Salvador (8).

LOTUS SCEPTER

108 A highly unusual religious motif, the lotus scepter, is shown in the hand of a priest from 10th-century Java (A). A similar theme is apparent at Palenque (M), where a Mayan ruler holds aloft an awkward symbol of his enlightenment.

and colonnettes (Figures 102 and 103). Atlantean figures were present at La Venta, suggesting their introduction prior to 500 B.C. Whether the stone midgets of the Maya were derived from Olmec sources or from later Hindu-Buddhist contacts remains obscure. Nevertheless, the close stylistic similarities apparent in some of the artifacts can only encourage speculation that they resulted from trans-Pacific contact.

There are a wide variety of corbeled arches in both areas, although some are virtually identical. Corbeled arches are easy to construct as they do not require the careful fitting of curved stones and mortar characteristic of the curved, or Roman, arch. They also have the advantage of being able to support a tremendous amount of weight. That was a valuable asset in both Asia and Meso-America, because the arches were placed beneath towering structures of solid stone which reached above the trees like church steeples. The structures served a dual role as beacons for the faithful and as platforms for astronomical observations.

Some scholars regard the presence of colonnettes as being proof of Asian contact, since they serve a purely decorative function in both areas. The validity of this interpretation is diminished, however, when one takes into account that simple decorations invariably occur spontaneously in similar artistic contexts. The presence of columnar supports, rectangular buildings, and pyramids are more easily attributed to the common characteristics of materials available in the natural environment than they are to a singular invention that spread via cultural diffusion.

The same could be said for the presence of similar pottery houses found in Asia and Meso-America (Figures 104) and the wheeled toys from India, China, and Mexico (Figure 105). It is reasonable to expect people in similar climates to develop similar dwellings, just as it is reasonable to expect potters to experiment with the manufacture of clay toys. The principle of the wheel is not far removed from using rolling logs to transport stone building blocks, while the lack of the wagon wheel in Meso-America can be attributed to the absence of suitable draft animals for pulling carts and the scarcity of metal tools for working wood. Both were required in Asia for the development of wheeled vehicles. We should not overlook the fact that the manufacturing of wheels requires a great amount of skill and the support of advanced, metal-casting technology. Ancient America had neither a smelting industry, nor guilds of wheelwrights to produce wheels, while an ample supply of forced human labor reduced the need for wheeled transport.

Contact between Asia and Meso-America is more clearly indicated by the presence of motifs representing the long-nosed Hindu deity, Ganesa--the elephant god. Numerous representatives of the long-nosed god are present in the archaeological record of Asia from 1500 B.C. to the present (Figure 106). In Meso-America, the tradition began in the Colonial Period along the Pacific coast, and it continued throughout the Confederacy (Figure 107). There is no logical explanation for the existence of this peculiar figure in the New World, because there is no local animal with the corresponding strength and massiveness of an elephant to inspire

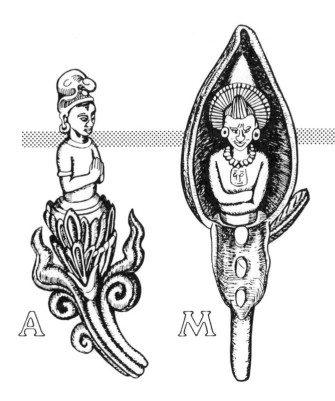

SPIRITUAL ELVES
Miniature divinities are portrayed emerging from lotus blossoms in these examples from Tibet (A) and Jaina (M), a Late Classic Mayan city.

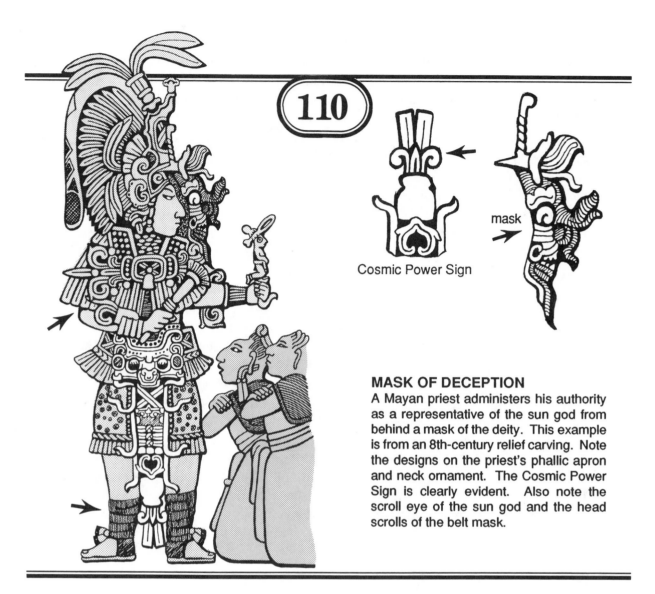

Cosmic Power Sign

mask

MASK OF DECEPTION
A Mayan priest administers his authority
as a representative of the sun god from
behind a mask of the deity. This example
is from an 8th-century relief carving. Note
the designs on the priest's phallic apron
and neck ornament. The Cosmic Power
Sign is clearly evident. Also note the
scroll eye of the sun god and the head
scrolls of the belt mask.

the image of a long-nosed, anthropomorphic god. Nevertheless, the long-nosed god
was so popular among the Mayan tribes that it served as a common decorative
feature of temple facades in the Yucatan peninsula. Furthermore, the Mayans
associated the deity with rain--as did the Shang Chinese.

Asian contact is further indicated by a unique usage of the lotus motif which
Hindus and Buddhists regarded as the point of emergence for cosmic power to enter
the physical world. It was used as a symbol of religious power in both areas, where
it takes the form of the Lotus Scepter (Figure 108). Frequently, the lotus also served
as the point of emergence of Bodhisattvas, or Buddha spirits, and Mayan elves
(Figure 109).

There are other intriguing cultural similarities between Indo-China and Meso-
America that are difficult to explain without accepting direct contact as a causal
factor.[9] These include the presence of a game called *Patolli* which the Mayans
played using a cross-shaped board, markers, and dice. It is similar to the East-Asian
game of *Pachisi*, which also used a cross-shaped playing board, markers, and dice.[10]
Other similarities could be as much the result of independent invention as evidence

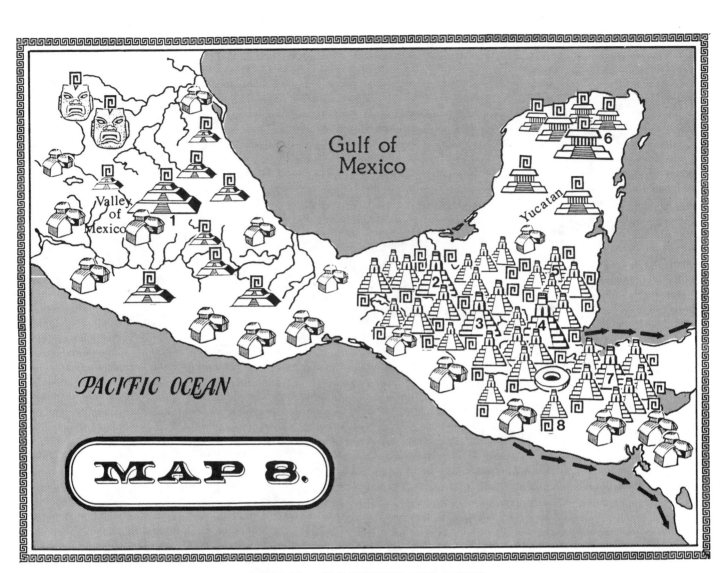

MAYA CONFEDERACY

COMMERCIAL MAYANS

At the height of their development, the Mayans commanded a vast trade network that extended several thousand miles from Teotihuacan in the Valley of Mexico to Venezuela in South America. As many as 15 million people inhabited the Confederacy, which was composed of co-equal city-states. The Omnibus Power Sign spread wherever the Mayans traveled and it was incorporated into most of the indigenous cultures, and it spread along with Mayan conquest and commercial activity.

MAJOR CITIES

1. Teotihuacan
2. Palenque
3. Bonampak
4. Tikal
5. Uaxactun
6. Chichen Itza
7. Copan
8. Tazumal

KEY (8)

 -Mayan temple centers
50-100,000 inhabitants

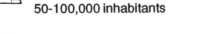 -Mexican ceremonial centers
50-100,000 inhabitants

 -Yucatan temple centers

 -Archaic Olmec tribes

MAYAN TEMPLE OF SCROLLS
This Mayan temple at Hochob, Yucatan, is virtually covered with magic scroll motifs depicting spiritual power. The primary feature is the mask god whose gaping mouth surrounds the doorway. Its eyes are made of scrolls, and two serpents emerge from either side of the head. It is flanked by two scroll-headed guardians.

of Asian contact. These include the use of the royal litter (a hand carried throne), the fan as an emblem of nobility, and the practice of cranial deformation.

Regardless of the degree of contact, the Mayans developed an extremely effective method of inter-city communication, as well as the world's most advanced astronomical profession. Mayan astronomers were able to calculate the time of the solar year with an accuracy exceeding that of European measurements, while they maintained tables for the prediction of lunar eclipses.[11] In A.D. 765, astronomers from throughout the Confederacy met at Palenque to adjust their solar calendars. They knew that the movements of the stars were predictable and methodical. Nevertheless, these learned men also were responsible for perpetuating extensive rituals and "cosmic" ball games which the superstitious commoners believed to be vital to the preservation of the world. Consequently, they were willing to sacrifice their lives, if necessary, to placate the demands of the gods.

What the rituals were really vital for was the preservation of the Mayan state.

Just as Confucius instructed his followers to faithfully observe ritual as a way of maintaining social order, Mayan leaders also used ritual practices and costumes to control their subjects. Numerous Mayan artifacts depict a ruler-priest wearing the mask of a god (Figure 110).

Among the Maya, it was regarded as an honor to die in the service of the state, or in pursuit of religious ecstasy. And priests were expected to engage in self-flagellation as an expression of their devotion to the Mayan religion. The ultimate test of faith came at the end of the ritual ball game. Presumably, the winner of the game, i.e., the one who tossed a rubber ball through a stone hoop, or goal, had the honor of being executed for his victory. To die in such a moment of glory was regarded as a ticket to the highest heaven. Likewise, upon the death of a king or noble, several individuals had the privilege of being sacrificed in order to accompany the revered leader to the afterlife. Those who committed suicide were believed to proceed directly to heaven in recognition of their remarkable act of self-sacrifice, while prisoners of war and criminals could be summarily executed as a way of fostering spiritual purity. In spite of this preoccupation with death as a sacred experience, there is no evidence that the Mayan Confederacy engaged in wholesale human sacrifice. In that respect, they had progressed far beyond their pagan roots.

They had also progressed in many other ways. Commercial activity was extensive, and it reached far beyond the borders of the Confederacy--to Jamaica and Venezuela. Mayan merchants traveled to these distant lands in giant canoes using

DOOR CHARMS
Monumental stone buildings in Southeast Asia and Meso-America feature similar mask gods above the doorways. Serpents, or sea monsters, with scrolls descend on either side. These examples are from a Javanese temple (A), dating from the 8th-14th centuries, and from the Mayan temple at Hochob (B). A similar pattern of usage is prevalent among the Northwest Coast American Indians.

EAST ASIA   MESO-AMERICA

113

NATURE PANEL
A 19th-century Javanese wood carving depicts flowers and trees emerging from a background of magic scrolls. The scroll forms represent the abundant life forces of nature.

slave power and wind. Indeed, the Spanish noticed lateen sails made of cotton on native canoes during the early days of the conquest.[12] Were these the product of independent invention--or the heritage of recent Asian immigrants? The answer is unknown.

Trade between city-states was conducted in accordance with treaties that guaranteed the safety of merchants while providing free nourishment and lodging. Throughout the Confederacy, a system of roadways and way stations provided ready access to all of the major markets and commercial centers. Furthermore, public warehouses sheltered privately-owned supplies of raw materials and manufactured goods. Local villagers maintained the way stations and warehouses in accordance with the mandate of the Confederacy's rulers. Merchants were granted special religious privileges, they had their own patron deity (known as "Ek Chuuak"), they had their own special code of ethics, and they paid no taxes.[13]

During the Commercial Period, the Mayan Confederacy grew from a collection of loosely-knit tribal villages to a union of city-states with as many as fifteen million inhabitants.[14] Their approximate distribution is indicated by Map 8. Agriculture prospered amid a complex irrigation system, while the arts and sciences flourished. And throughout the Confederacy, the Omnibus Power Sign remained the most important motif of Mayan religion. Indeed, its forms and functions continued to increase as magic scrolls evolved beyond the Asian traditions which had typified their earlier development.

Figure 111 shows the scroll-shaped power sign used to cover the facade of a temple at Hochob, Yucatan. This usage suggests themes of fertility and life force. The central deity head (or mask god), served as a door charm. Asian facades show similar designs arranged around temple doorways (Figure 112). Scroll symbols also represented the life force of plants in Asia (Figure 113). Figure 114 shows the scrolls as they appear in a temple mural from Teotihuacan, where they clearly depict the creative life forces of the earth which transform seeds into the vines of growing plants. In this case, scroll motifs indicate the presence of an unseen creative power--the power of life itself emerging from the celestial realm to animate plants and animals.

Most of the motifs introduced by Asian traders during the Colonial Period continued to be used throughout the Commercial Period. Some of them were even adopted by the later Aztec empire--establishing both the importance of the symbols and the fact that they constitute a tradition of usage. It is important to realize that magic scrolls were not a haphazard assortment of motifs used merely for decorative purposes. Nor were they simply the result of some coincidental inspiration from the Cosmic Unconscious--which is a Jungian concept of a psychic linkage among the world's people. It is sometimes used to "explain" the presence of similar myths, beliefs, and symbolism in distant areas of the globe. Although some myths can be attributed legitimately to common psychic phenomena, religious symbols occur in unique historical contexts which invariably brand them with unique features.

Let there be no mistake: the Omnibus Power Sign is a unified complex of motifs representing cosmic and natural forces, and it was consistently used from one generation to the next. It is this reliable pattern of usage that makes it possible for us to trace the development of the symbol complex as new motifs were added. It also enables us to understand the intended meaning of the motifs, because we can examine their patterns of usage throughout the Mayan Confederacy.

FERTILITY SCROLLS

This section from a mural in the Temple of Agriculture at Teotihuacan, Mexico (ca. A.D. 300), uses magic scrolls as symbols of fertility. The scrolls emerge from a cache of seeds, shells, and gourds placed in the ground, and from the scrolls emerge lotus vines and flowers. The mural provides a religious explanation for how living things are able to spring forth from the earth.

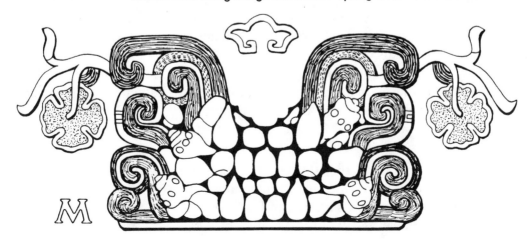

115

PARASOL - SYMBOL OF AUTHORITY

A Mayan ruler (right) holds a miniature umbrella which served as a symbol of authority. This symbolic umbrella had no utilitarian value as a sun shade or protection from rain. The same concept was present in the orient where a *bodhisattva*, or Buddhist angel (above) carried a parasol as a symbol of the presence of Buddha. Note the *yin/yang* symbols on the Mayan parasol and belt insignia (enlarged).

Some examples of the continued usage of the Omnibus Power Sign and other Asian motifs appear in Figures 115 and 116. The Cosmic Duality motif, or *yin/yang* symbol, was used as an emblem on the noble's front apron and on the parasol. The parasol was a traditional Buddhist emblem of authority, while the endless knot was a symbol for longevity. The conch was known as the "voice of Buddha." Bats and the serpent/turtle motifs were prevalent in China from the Chou dynasty onward. The *yin/yang* symbol is sometimes referred to as the "knot" motif, because it often occurs with a piece of rope or fabric representing a joining together of two opposites. It was a common motif in China by the fourth century A.D. Occasionally, the Meso-American knot motif is associated with personal sacrifice in the form of blood letting which took place during flagellation rituals.

The significance of this association becomes clear when we realize the need for personal sacrifice to maintain the union of Mayan tribes. After all, the Confederacy was held together by personal sacrifice, and judging from the many stone carvings portraying the nobility in acts of self-flagellation, the greatest sacrifice was expected from Mayan leaders. The prevalence of this motif throughout the Confederacy is a strong indication that it is indeed one of the most important Mayan symbols. For example, it was used in the hieroglyphic writing at Palenque (Figure 117). The Chinese also used the *yin/yang* in hieroglyphic writing as late as the Ming dynasty, while the swastika sometimes occurs in the form of a double *yin/yang* on Buddhist Tanka paintings.

The incense pipe or smoking tube (Figure 118) was present in China as early as the Shang dynasty where it is seen in the form of carved jade ornaments. Actual tubes which were covered with magic scroll shapes have been recovered from Chou burials and smoking pipes similar to those used for opium or tobacco can be seen on Han dynasty mortuary banners. The religious importance of smoke, besides any intoxicating effects it may have produced, is that mystics believed they could see dragons or spirits in the smoke patterns. This same concept is evident in the way the Mayan priests used smoking tubes.

One of the more popular motifs of India and the West Indies is the *makara*--or long-nosed sea monster. Frequently, it is portrayed with a warrior emerging from

A EAST ASIA

M MESO-AMERICA

116

RELIGIOUS SYMBOLS

Similar religious symbols and concepts abound in Meso-America and the Orient. These include: (1) the endless knot; (2) the conch with scrolls; (3) C-horns placed above the eyes; (4) an angle, or ray, motif representing the sun; (5) the sacred bat; and (6) the serpent/turtle. Asian symbols are from a 19th-century Tibetan conch, or shell horn (A1 and 2), a 17th-century Ch'ing vase (A3), a Shang bronze (A4), a Ch'ien Lung vase (A5), and a Han mirror (A6). Meso-American examples are from a fresco at Santa Rita (M1), a Classic ceramic vase (M2), a relief mural from Tulum (M3), a Mayan bas-relief (M4), a temple facade (M5), and *Codex Laud* (M6). Because religious symbols are highly specific and frequently endure for centuries in the midst of conservative religious traditions, the presence of so many similar symbols between Asia and Meso-America is suggestive of strong cultural connections.

its mouth (Figure 119). Similar motifs in Meso-America depicted men emerging from the mouth of the plumed serpent--which also has an extended proboscis.

In Meso-America the swastika (Figure 120) is a rare symbol that may have originated from Hindu-Buddhist sources. It is unknown in archaeological contexts prior to the Commercial Period when it became a prominent feature of Mayan religious expression. The motif is a major element of Buddhist iconography, and it is probably in this context that the motif spread to the Mayan Confederacy. Nevertheless, there may have been other vectors taken by this motif in its migration from the Old World.

Although the tendency is to look for examples of art motifs which have spread from the Old World to the Americas, it should not come as a surprise that several distinctively American motifs appear to have taken the return trip aboard the ships of Southeast Asian merchants.[15] One monument to the sailing ships of this period could be a stone carving which Thor Heyerdahl uncovered on Easter Island (Figure 121). The time of its origin may fall within the Mayan Commercial Period, however, like most rock carvings, precise dating is virtually impossible.

It was during this active period of trans-Pacific commerce that Asian yams[16] and chicken[17] were apparently brought to the Americas, while the sweet potato, and possibly maize[18] or tobacco were brought back to Asia. The sweet potato, which is a New- World domesticate, was already established as a food crop in Melanesia and Polynesia prior to the time of European colonization in the seventeenth century.[19]

The Asian concept of reincarnation appears to have strongly influenced Mayan art. For example, numerous relief sculptures and painted vases (Figure 122) portray people or deities emerging from scrolled conch shells. Other representations found in Asia and Meso-America depict people emerging from frogs, birds, crabs, serpents, and turtles.

At least three types of motifs have been identified which appear out of context in Southeast Asia--due to the lack of antecedent forms. These include the use of scrolls to represent music (Figure 123), speech scrolls (Figure 124), and phallic aprons (Figure 125). All of these have antecedent forms and well established traditions in Meso-America. Therefore, it seems reasonable to suspect that they

YIN/YANG HEROGLYPHS

Hieroglyphs in the Temple of The Foliated Cross at Palenque (ca. A.D. 645) include numerous *yin/yang* symbols in association with swastikas. Of particular importance is the presence of dragon's eyes which clearly identify an Asian origin for this Mayan motif. The Asian symbol (left) is included for comparison.

118

SMOKING TUBES
Both the Chinese and the Mayans believed that incense smoke could reveal the shapes of spiritual beings. A smoking tube of the Han dynasty (above) portrays dragon clouds, while a Mayan priest holds a smoking tube that reveals the celestial serpent.

were brought back to Asia perhaps in the form of ideas in the minds of priests or artisans. These unique motifs, however, left only a passing impression on Hindu-Buddhist art. It seems that prior Asian traditions were so thoroughly established that these new motifs were never able to gain a strong foothold. They are primarily found in stone carvings on relatively recent temples of Java where they were used for a short period of time between A.D. 900 and 1100. Thereafter, they were apparently ignored by resident craftsmen who relied upon more conventional motifs for their artistic expressions.

Considering the fact that the Mayan civilization achieved a level of near parity with Asian social and architectural development by A.D. 700, it is difficult to ascertain how much of that progress was due to the spread of culture from Asia and how much of it was a consequence of independent achievement on the part of the Confederacy. Certainly, the Maya benefited from Hindu architectural technology which had its roots in both the Indus Valley and Greek traditions dating back to 1000 B.C., or earlier. It is apparent that the Mayans derived some benefit from Asian stone-carving traditions, as was the case with the Elephant Stela and other ornate sculptures throughout the Confederacy. Either Asian stone carvers were imported to work and train local artists, or native Americans were sent to India for training and then brought back by ship to serve their Mayan lords.

The extent to which Mayan culture was influenced by Old-World contacts has yet to be determined. The presence of statues depicting bearded figures, symbols for ships in the *codices*, legends regarding visiting holy men, and the broad ethnic diversity mentioned by the early Spanish chronicles suggest that the Mayan culture absorbed many ideas from abroad. Nevertheless, the basic foundation of Mayan culture was well established during the Colonial Period from a mixture of Olmec, proto-Mayan, and Asian roots.

The preponderance of Mayan culture during the Commercial Period probably represents a growth and elaboration of what had previously existed. For example, it seems possible that the vast network of irrigation trenches and roads of the Commercial Period were independently conceived and brought into being as a

119

CELESTIAL SERPENTS

Serpent motifs from East Asia and Meso-America portray similar themes, including the presence of long, trunk-like noses, beards, scroll eyes, forelegs, warriors emerging from the mouth, and plant forms in the head ornamentation. Scroll forms are abundant in examples from both areas. Those from Asia include a Ch'ing jade carving (A1), a Chou jade (A2), and a 9th-century Cambodian sculpture (A3). Scrolls in these artifacts represent transformational cosmic energy, while examples from Meso-America portray other attributes, such as wind, rain, and sky fire. Examples include a Classic Mayan relief from Yaxchilan (M1) and a portion of the Aztec Monument of The Ages (M2), which is also called The Calendar Stone. The earliest New World occurrence of scrolled serpents can be traced to the Pacific Coast of Guatemala, ca. 500 B.C.

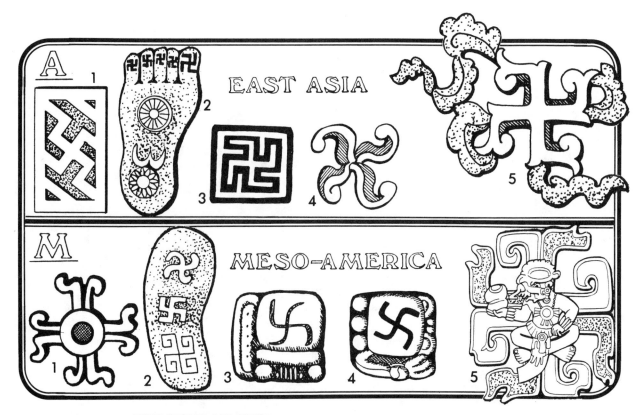

SWASTIKA MOTIFS

120

The swastika is a common Old-World magic symbol attributed to Mesopotamian origins. It was present in the Yangshao culture of Neolithic China, ca. 3000 B.C. The motif represents good fortune, long life, eternity, and cosmic power. Buddhist Tanka paintings of the 20th century portray the swastika as a combination of two *yin/yang* motifs. It was common in the New World only among the Mayans and North American Indians. Asian examples include: 1) a Borobudur stone relief, 2) the footprint of Buddha, 3) a Harappan seal, 4) an Indonesian wood carving, and 5) a Ming embroidery. Mayan examples include: 1) an astrology symbol from a ceramic statue, 2) a stone slab at Mayapan, 3) a hieroglyph from Palenque, 4) a glyph with a *yin/yang* knot, and 5) a stone altar at Copan, Honduras.

natural consequence of a population that exploded from a few hundred thousand to several million. Like most societies, once the essential identity of the Mayans had been established, cultural evolution was primarily of a gradual and superficial nature. Rapid change would have required momentous political events, introduction of significant technological advancements, or drastic disruptions in the environment. Unfortunately for the Mayans, the circumstances of their environment did become drastic toward the end of the eighth century A.D.

The nature of the catastrophe that shattered the New World's greatest civilization has been the subject of debate and controversy--a controversy compounded by a failure on the part of many scholars to consider external influences. In their limited perspective, North and South America were supposed to be pristine continents that were immune from the diseases ravaged the Old World. But the Americas were not immune--neither before, nor after the arrival of the Spanish Conquest in 1519.

GREAT BOATS OF THE PACIFIC

During the 19th century, Easter Island natives wore talismans like the one above, which they referred to as the *Reimiru*, or Great Boat. According to legend, this vessel brought their ancestors to the remote Pacific Island. Other evidence of ancient sailing ships on Easter Island includes a colossal stone carving (right) excavated by Thor Heyerdahl. The statue dates to a period between A.D. 400 and 800, although the age of the petroglyph inscribed on its chest is uncertain. It depicts a three-masted vessel with multiple sails.

REINCARNATION MOTIFS

Numerous artifacts from the Orient and Meso-America depict people emerging from plants and animals. These themes reflect beliefs in reincarnation. Shown here are an illustration from a 19th-century Chinese religious book (A) and a Mayan relief sculpture (M).

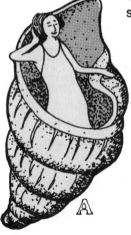

MUSIC SCROLLS

Feline trumpeters occur in the arts of East Asia and Meso-America. A relief carving from 6th-century Thailand (A) incorporates plant forms into music scrolls, indicating transformational capabilities of magic scrolls. A mural from 3rd-century Teotihuacan (M) represents music, or wind.

SPEECH SCROLLS

Stone relief carvings depicting speech, or conversation, have been identified at Tjandi Djago, Java (A). The scroll-shaped symbol is referred to as a *Ju-i*, which represents discussion between Javanese royalty. These symbols, which date to the 10th-15th centuries, are the only known scroll-shaped speech symbols in the Orient. By contrast, speech symbols are very common in Meso-America. The Mayan example is from Cerro de Las Mesas.

125 **PHALLIC APRONS**
Scrolls indicating sexual potency are frequently found in artifacts of the Mayan Confederacy from 500 B.C. to A.D. 900. In Asia, the usage was most common in Cambodia, Vietnam, and Indonesia, ca. A.D. 800 to 1500. Frequently, scroll forms emerge from the front apron. These examples are from a 19th century Chinese painting (A) and a Classic Mayan vase (M).

The collapse of the Mayan Confederacy wasn't due to crop failure--not with the world's most fertile soil and a record of reliable rainfall throughout most of the area.[20] It wasn't the result of an earthquake or a volcano, either. None of the ruins show any sign of a catastrophic event, nor do they show any indication of warfare among the hundreds of city-states.[21] The evidence suggests that the most likely cause for abandonment of the ritual and trade centers was the occurrence of a major epidemic. However, the occurrence of an epidemic is difficult to explain without also accepting the likelihood of foreign contact, because the most conceivable diseases, yellow fever and malaria, have been traditionally regarded as exclusively Old-World maladies. These diseases were presumably absent until the arrival of the Spanish almost six centuries later.[22] Nevertheless, the fall of the Mayan Confederacy was probably due to epidemics of yellow fever, malaria, or other diseases.

Spanish chronicles written during the early 1500's indicate that malaria was already so rampant that the disease must have preceded the arrival of Spanish troops. And a Mayan codex written prior to the Spanish arrival clearly describes the symptoms of yellow fever, indicating that the natives had experienced epidemics.[23] The 1928 epidemic of yellow fever in Rio de Janeiro caused a mortality rate of fifty-nine percent.[24] Since the virus can survive for long periods in mosquito eggs, even when these are left in dried-out water containers, it is possible that the disease was brought inadvertently from Africa or Asia by voyagers who preceded Columbus.

An epidemic of malaria could have had equally severe consequences as yellow fever, although Peruvian native herbalists apparently knew of a cure by 1630. That was the year they introduced Europeans to the Cinchona tree, which is a natural source of quinine.[25] It seems incredible that American Indians were the first to find an antidote for a disease they had presumably known about for less than a century, when that same disease had been reported in Greece during the fifth century B.C. The possibility should not be overlooked that the natives were familiar with the healing powers of the Cinchona, simply because they had already discovered its usefulness during more ancient epidemics.

As many as ten-to-fifteen million natives may have died in Meso-America from epidemics that were as catastrophic as the plagues that struck Europe during the Dark Ages. Commercial activities ceased, writing and calendrical observations were impossible, and there was no common defense against foreign invasion or the beasts of the jungle.

As part of their flagellation rituals, the Mayans used stingray spines and barbed cords which they passed through their tongues or genitals. Whenever epidemics occurred, the rituals would have been more frequent--a religious answer to the unexplained deaths. However, by their own rituals--by sharing spines and barbed cords--they unwittingly spread the virus much more completely than if mosquitoes had been the only vector of infection. There would have been few people strong enough to bury the dead, and quite possibly there were none with the will nor the authority to conduct funerals. Ceremonial centers were abandoned with corpses littering the ground. Many generations passed without priests or ancestors to explain the ancient religion to the young, while glistening pyramids became mysterious monuments to a forgotten past--the symbolic graveyards of a once proud race. Such a catastrophe would have entirely discredited the Mayan religion, as well as the entire cultural and governmental structure associated with it. Consequently, there was no longer the means nor the loyalty required for preserving the Confederacy.[26]

Remnants of the Maya survived in small tribes, and a few managed to build a later civilization at Mayapan and Chichen Itza as allies of the Toltec. But it wasn't the same Mayan spirit that once nourished the Confederacy. Human sacrifice and warfare dominated the new culture.[27] And after the arrival of the Spanish, smallpox epidemics decimated the population once more. By 1525, when Cortez had finished his conquest of Mexico, only a handful of people remained alive in the once densely-populated region around Copan.[28]

Spanish priests paid the survivors one final indignity: cultural exorcism. Led by Bishop Diego De Landa, who was the presiding Judge of The Inquisition, they set fire to all the Mayan libraries, thereby erasing any evidence that may have existed for centuries of Asian trade with the Confederacy. De Landa characterized the burnings as an act of "purification" to rid the Yucatan peninsula of books which he denounced as "works of the Devil." Nevertheless, his contemporaries acknowledged that many of the *codices* were known to be purely historical.[29] The bishop was aided in this atrocity by the zeal of two compatriots, Toral and Zumarraga, who systematically went through the provinces requiring the natives to surrender their written documents or face torture and death. Many natives relinquished their books, only to face torture and death in spite of their obedience.

So it was that Spanish flames consumed the last written testimonials of the Mayan Confederacy--an alliance that had endured for fifteen centuries. Had it not been for the greatest hidden foe of humanity--disease--the course of the Spanish Conquest and all of world history would have turned out differently. But that is a subject for writers of fiction to pursue, while our concern is to reveal the secrets of the past. And one of the most astonishing secrets is the nature of the Omnibus Power Sign. Upon this most unique of world symbol traditions we now focus the exacting eye of science.

The Omnibus Power Sign

We have reached the apex of our investigation. All of the historical interpretations and inferences we have made depend upon the validity of the Omnibus Power Sign as a diagnostic art tradition. We have established that the Shang and Chou mystics of China relied extensively upon magic scrolls to represent their religious beliefs. Furthermore, there is a fairly clear developmental path in Asia leading back to Neolithic power signs and the magic horns of shamans. There is no developmental record in Meso-America, where magic scrolls occur precipitously in the archaeological record between 500 and 100 B.C.

As we have seen in previous chapters, many New-World scroll motifs look similar to contemporary Asian power signs. However, the presence of similar motifs in Asia and Meso-America does not prove that New-World scrolls were derived from Asia, nor does the fact that Asians had sailing vessels which were capable of transoceanic travel actually prove that such voyages occurred.

Speculation regarding possible Chinese voyages to ancient America is not a recent phenomenon. As early as the late 1800's, Ernest Fenlosa noted that the art styles of ancient Mexico and China had distinctive similarities that were indicative of close cultural contacts.[1] More recently, Robert Heine-Geldern and Gordon Ekholm have speculated about two major periods of Asian contact: first from China, and later from Hindu-Buddhist civilizations in the area of the South China Sea. Many other scholars have added their own comparisons of similar motifs between the two ancient cultures leading to a growing archive of intriguing manuscripts. None of these manuscripts, however, get beyond the point of comparing superficial similarities. This is due to an underlying assumption that similarities in form, or style, are sufficient evidence to prove that contact between two areas has occurred. Heine Geldern's comparative study was particularly thorough--but it only scratched the surface of the evidence.

Actual trade goods from the Old World have been found in America, but the discoveries have always lacked adequate verification. For example, Nigel Davies reported that a Chinese soapstone lamp was found in a Mayan mound, but it was close to the surface--leading him to suggest that it may have been buried after the Spanish began shipping goods from the Orient via Mexico.[2] David Kelly reported the discovery, *in situ*, of a Roman figurine at the Mexican archaeological site at Calixtlahuaca (ca. A.D. 200), but he attributed little importance to its presence because there was no way of determining how it got to Mexico in the first place.[3] Jesse Jennings has prepared a fairly thorough chronology of possible Old-World artifacts, although he reports that none were excavated under rigid scientific procedures.[4] Robert Marx has recovered two Grecian amphorae from the bottom of a river near Rio De Janeiro, Brazil, along with thousands of fragments dating to the second century B.C.[5] These artifacts give the impression of being the cargo of an Old-World vessel, however dubious scholars stress there is no proof that any sailors reached shore alive.

Betty Meggers has compared similar pottery fragments from Ecuador and Japan. Called Valdivia ware, the ceramics appear to have similar markings to pottery from the Middle Jomon period of Japan, ca. 300 B.C. However, MacNeish, Nelken, and Davies have questioned the possibility that Asian fishermen could have introduced ceramics to Meso-American aboriginals. Indeed, they cite older ceramic traditions in Colombia, while the radio-carbon dating of Valdivia ware is questionable.[6] Anchor stones found off the southern California coast led to a recent burst of publicity, because they were similar to anchor stones used in Asia. However, subsequent analysis indicated they were left by local fishermen during the nineteenth century.[7] Barry Fell (*Bronze Age America*), William McGlone and Phillip Leonard (*Ancient Celtic America*), and others have accumulated numerous examples of rock inscriptions which appear similar to Old-World writing. Called "Ogam Consaine," the writing has the appearance of scratch marks on either side of a line. Whether or not these constitute evidence of ancient Celtic habitation in the Americas has been a controversial issue--due to the difficulty of dating and interpretation inherent in ancient writing.

Other archaeologists have reported finding numerous Old-World coins, runic inscriptions, metal objects, ceramics, and Mediterranean amber, yet an ardent cadre of skeptics remains unconvinced of their authenticity.[8] The resounding conviction of doubting scholars is that any pre-Columbian voyagers who reached the New World came accidentally in vessels that had been blown off course. That is, there were no deliberate trips to the Americas. Furthermore, the assumption is made that such ancient mariners had no impact on the development of New-World civilization.

In order to answer the valid concerns of the skeptics, we will have to go beyond mere comparisons of similar motifs--that much has been done by many previous authors who sought to establish a link between Asia and the New World. The need for a greater depth of analysis should be self-evident, due to the fact that the mere presence of simple cultural similarities is not proof of a common origin. Whenever two different cultures are examined, there will always be a few incidental motifs that happen to look alike.

OMNIBUS POWER SIGN--
TEOTIHUACAN VARIANT

The transformational quality and multi-dimensionality of the Omnibus Power Sign are clearly evident from mural paintings at the early Mexican civilization of Teotihuacan, ca. A.D. 300. The same bifurcated scroll motif was used to represent wind coming from the mouth of the sky god (1), music from a flute (2), a magic platform (3), bird song (4), life force emerging from a human heart (5), speech or singing (6), creative force coming from the hand of a rain deity (7), and the transferral of life force from a human heart to the mouth of a cosmic coyote (8). The coyote served as a messenger of the gods.

A valid scientific analysis requires exacting standards. We have to look beyond occasional similarities and incidental specimens; we have to examine functional relationships; we have to establish traditional patterns of usage; and we have to identify symbols whose usage is so inextricably linked with religious expression that coincidence, or chance alone, cannot explain their existence. Until we have accomplished these tasks, skeptics will continue to challenge theories of Old-World voyages to the ancient Americas.

Motif Complex and Core Elements

Although the symbols that make up the Omnibus Power Sign complex may be thousands of years old, we are not merely guessing as to their intended meanings. Considerable research has been done in Asia regarding the use of magic scrolls among living artists who inherited the designs from their ancestors. In many cases, such as the use of scrolls to represent cosmic energy in Buddhist art, the traditions have changed little over the last two millennia, and there are written sources available to assist our interpretations.[9] The overwhelming conclusion from scholars familiar with Oriental art is that the scroll motifs represent the many divergent forms of cosmic energy.

Determining the meaning of New-World scrolls is not as easy. The difficulty is due to the fact that few of the artists have survived to tell their story. During the Spanish Conquest of Mexico, priests made notations in the Aztec codices regarding the interpretations given to them by the natives, but the aim of the priests was to stamp out the native religion--not to preserve it for future generations. Their conclusion was that scrolls were used to represent speech, smoke, water, and steam. However, even a cursory examination of the codices is sufficient to verify that there are numerous scroll motifs that do not fit this simplistic interpretation. Indeed, the Mayans and Aztecs also used scrolls to represent falling stars, fertility, life-force, vision, cosmic energy and a multitude of other aspects of existence. Some of these diverse symbolic functions are indicated by Figure 126.

It is apparent that native artisans used scroll motifs to represent anything that they attributed to the supernatural world. That is, they represent spiritual essence.

Thirteen different motifs, or core elements, are present in the Omnibus Power Sign complex as it was used during the time of Nu Sun's voyage. These include Cosmic Duality, Cosmic Power, Cosmic Matrix, Flight, Breath/Soul, Celestial Serpent, Thunderhead, Cosmic Eye, Supreme Being, Cosmic Disk, Cosmic Mouth, Immortality, and Life Force. The standard aspects of these symbols are portrayed in Table 1, which also shows the various types of scroll shapes used in the ancient tradition. The duration of this complex in Asia corresponds to the mid-Chou and early Han dynasties (ca. 700 to 100 B.C.). In Meso-America, the time of origin corresponds to the Middle and Late Proto-Classic archaeological phases in Mexico, Guatemala, Honduras, El Salvador, and Nicaragua (ca. 500 to 100 B.C.).

The following comparative chronologies indicate the presence of specific motif traditions in both areas lasting for more than a thousand years.

TABLE 1.

OMNIBUS POWER SIGN
PRIMARY ELEMENTS ca. 500 B.C.

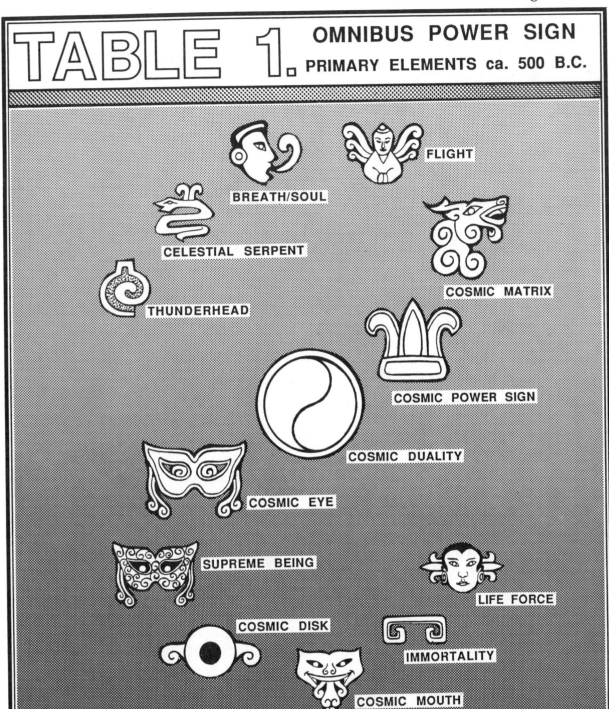

BREATH/SOUL

FLIGHT

CELESTIAL SERPENT

COSMIC MATRIX

THUNDERHEAD

COSMIC POWER SIGN

COSMIC DUALITY

COSMIC EYE

SUPREME BEING

LIFE FORCE

COSMIC DISK

IMMORTALITY

COSMIC MOUTH

The Omnibus Power Sign is a complex of related religious symbols which are all derived from basic scroll shapes. These were used to represent spiritual, cosmic, or magical power. The concept of using a single type of motif to represent every facet of supernatural phenomena apparently originated with Taoist mystics in China, ca. 1000 B.C. Under the auspices of the Chou dynasty, the Omnibus Power Sign complex became the predominant form of religious symbolism throughout the empire and in much of Southeast Asia.

COSMIC DUALITY

The concept of Cosmic Duality was common in most of the ancient world. In the Middle East, the most frequent symbol used to portray this concept was the *caduceus* —two opposed serpents intertwined on a staff. The staff represented the unifying power of natural law.

The Taoist Chinese concept of duality seems to have emerged from early astronomical observations which revealed that all celestial phenomena conformed to invisible cosmic laws. Shang portrayals of cosmic forces (examples A1-3) did not stress duality, while those of the Chou reflected duality as early as 1000 B.C. Example A4 shows the *yin/yang* concept as two scroll-shaped dragons with eyes. Many variations occurred throughout the Orient, where duality is portrayed as circled scrolls, or spirals, using different colors (A7, A10, and A12). Use of stylized dragon eyes with the *yin/yang* symbol became frequent during the Ming dynasty. This usage occurred among the Mayans at Palenque (M9), and at Teotihuacan.

Another variation of the Cosmic Duality motif includes the knot symbol (A9), which represents the joining together of two opposite forces in nature. This motif was present in China by the 4th century A.D., while numerous artifacts indicate that this style persisted through the Ming dynasty. It also occurs frequently in Meso-America, as early as the Formative archaeological phase. It was an enduring tradition that was adopted by the Aztecs.

A third variety of duality symbolism includes the Cosmic Disk motif with two ribbons passing through a central hole (A8). Often, the Cosmic Disk was portrayed in Han mortuary art along with two dragons representing *yin* and *yang*. Consequently, dragons and ribbons were used interchangeably to show a linking of cosmic forces.

In Meso-America, the earliest examples of this motif occur ca. 500 B.C. in artifacts found along the Pacific Coast of Guatemala, at Kaminaljuyu (M2 and 4), at Santa Lucia Cotzumahualpa (M3), and at Izapa, Mexico (M1). There are no motifs remotely similar to the Cosmic Duality symbol in Olmec art, prior to 500 B.C., indicating that it did not emerge from an Olmec cultural base.

Although the knot symbol is by far the most prevalent variety in Meso-America, other kinds are found in great abundance. Hundreds, if not thousands, of examples of this motif are present throughout the region--an indication of the central role it played in Mayan and Aztec religion. Example M10 is from the shield of Quetzalcoatl--representing the spring winds and rain. A similar relationship of symbol and meaning existed in ancient China, where the scroll represented the life-giving qualities of spring rains.

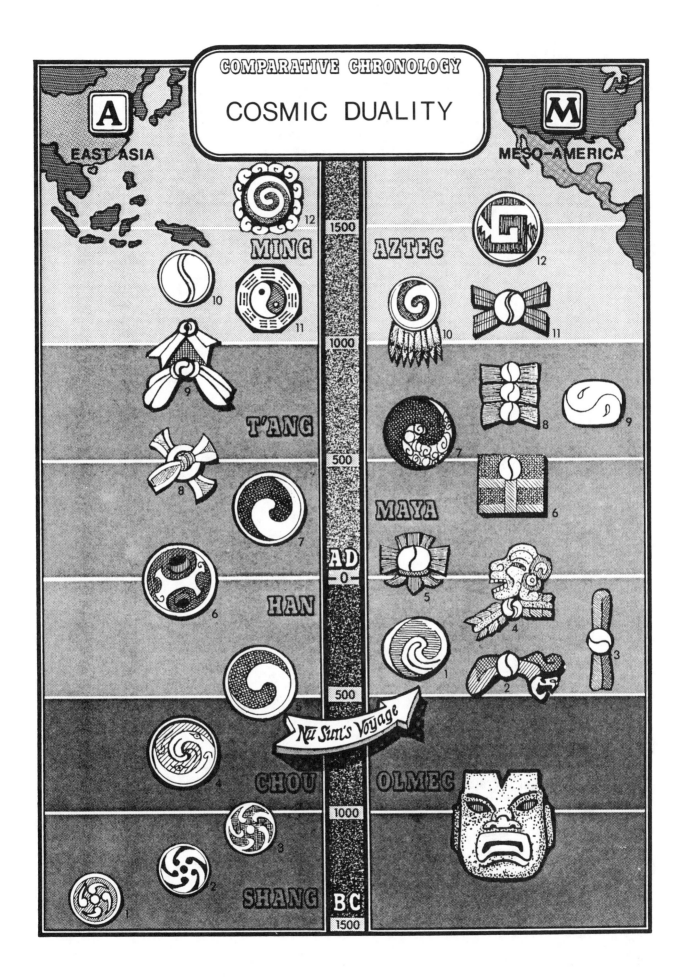

COMPARATIVE CHRONOLOGY

COSMIC DUALITY

A — EAST ASIA

M — MESO-AMERICA

MING

T'ANG

HAN

CHOU

SHANG

AZTEC

MAYA

OLMEC

Nü Sun's Voyage

1500
1000
500
AD
0
500
1000
1500
BC

COSMIC DUALITY IN ASIA

The *yin/yang* symbol was originally used to represent the union of complementary forces. A common form was the *yin/yang* knot, which Buddhists wore as a symbol for enlightenment (1, 9). The smaller circles within the circled scrolls (2-5) represent the eyes of dragons. The motif was used as an emblem on Chinese religious scepters (2), crowns (6), and Buddhist objects associated with the Cosmic Power Sign (8, 9). The motif represents serpent power on the earspools of a Hindu king (7), while flaming motifs represent cosmic power, creation, or enlightenment.

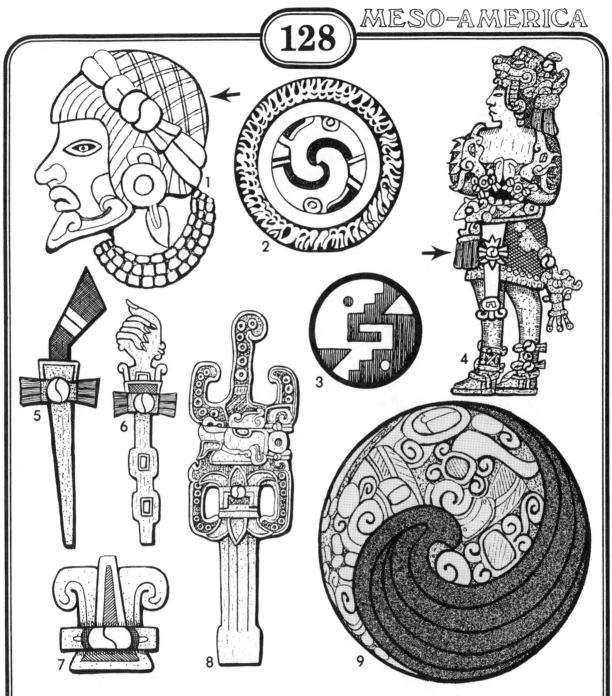

MESO-AMERICAN DUALITY MOTIFS

Ancient motifs have many similar functions to the *yin/yang* motifs of East Asia. The *yin/yang* knot adorns headdresses (1), phallic aprons (4), and religious scepters of the Mayans (8), and the Aztecs (5, 6). A stone sculpture from Teotihuacan (2) depicts the *yin/yang* at the center of a cosmic wheel of fire--a usage that is similar to Asian motifs in Figure 127 (3, 6). The wheel of fire and an Aztec war shield (3) include dragon eyes. A Mexican carving (7) and a Mayan engraving (4) show the motif in association with the Cosmic Power Sign. A Mayan ceramic bowl (9) portrays half of the surface as a void (*yin*), while the other half overflows with power signs (*yang*).

COMPARATIVE
CHRONOLOGY

COSMIC POWER

The Cosmic Power Sign represents the emergence of invisible forces into the physical world. The earliest Chinese artifacts to exhibit this motif occur during the Shang dynasty, ca. 1500 B.C. (A1). The symbol is not commonly seen in China following the Han dynasty, asreligious reformers adopted Buddhist symbolism. The Hindu culture of India retained the motif, however, leading to frequent usage in Southeast Asia between 100 B.C. and the present. It is commonly used as a base for the cosmic tree, from which the sun emerges (A6 and 13). Consequently, the triangular motif in the center is regarded as a representation of fire, or the sun. Examples A5 to 9 and 11 to 14 are from India, while A10 is from Vietnam. The scrolls flanking the central flame element represent either lotus blossoms or celestial serpents. These motifs are often used interchangeably in Asian art.

The earliest examples from Meso-America occur in archaeological sites along the Pacific Coast of southern Mexico, and Guatemala: Monte Alban (M1); Cerro de Las Mesas (M2); Kaminaljuyu (M3); Chiapas de Corzo (M4); and Izapa (M7). All of these have been attributed to the Pre-Classic archaeological phase between 500 and 100 B.C. The motif was extremely popular in the region, where hundreds of examples have been reported in Mayan and Aztec ruins. The symbol's association with the sun is evident from M18 which is a conspicuous feature of the Aztec Sun Disk.

COSMIC POWER SIGNS
An emblem from a 10th-century Chinese crown (1) depicts a the birth of creation as a cosmic fireball emerging from the mythical Mount Meru. The motif is also associated with the Cosmic Disk, which is portrayed in a Han jade (2) and in a mural from Teotihuacan (3). The mural makes use of the disk, Cosmic Power Sign, and thunder bird to explain how rain comes from the sky.

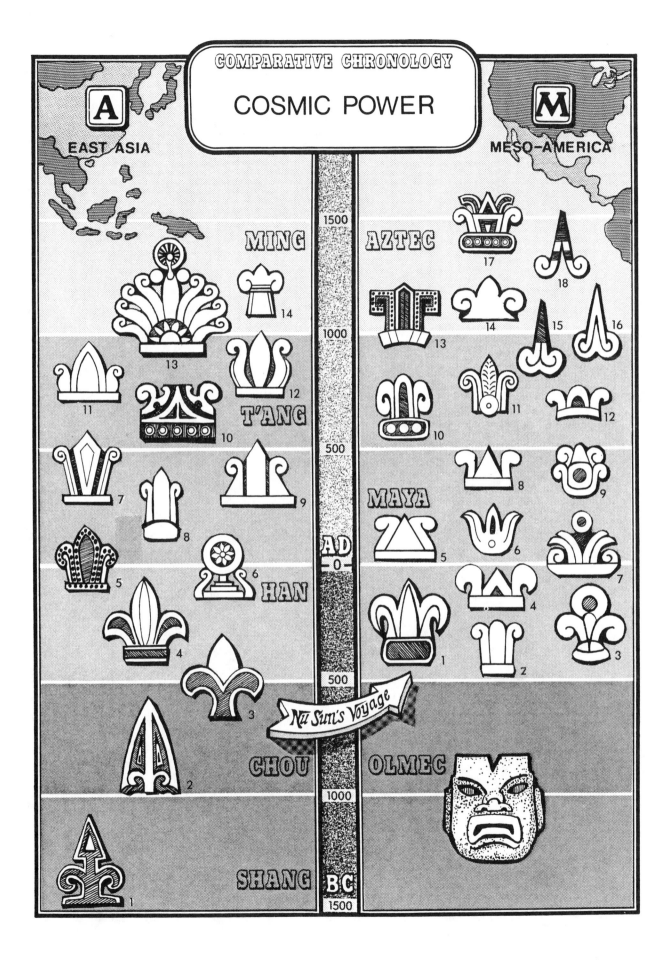

COMPARATIVE
CHRONOLOGY

COSMIC MATRIX

The Cosmic Matrix is identified as a background of scrolls from which a human being, deity, sacred animal, or plant seems to emerge. The Chinese tradition of this motif matrix can be traced back to Neolithic *pi* disks (A1), which were covered with scrolls. Later bronze artifacts of the Shang and Chou dynasties were also covered with scrolls, but they have dragons portrayed in high relief against the scroll background (A2 and 4). Sometimes, a three-dimensional dragon arises from the scroll matrix as though it were emerging from clouds. Indeed, these scrolls are often identified as "clouds," but their actual symbolic function is to explain the emergence of spiritual beings into the physical world.

Human figures are frequently associated with scroll backgrounds in Han mortuary art (A5). This usage is reflected in the earliest Meso-American artifacts depicting humans, immortals, or deities surrounded by clouds (M1-3). These are from the archaeological sites of Izapa and El Baul near the Pacific Coast. Their time of occurrence ranges from ca. 500 B.C. to A.D. 100. Use of this motif to show emergence of spiritual beings was widespread throughout the region. Numerous artifacts, such as a ceramic vessel from Teotihuacan (M4) and a marble vase from Ulua, Honduras (M6), are completely covered with scrolls except where small human figures are present. The tradition persisted through the Aztec empire in Mexico, and it is still present in Oriental art.

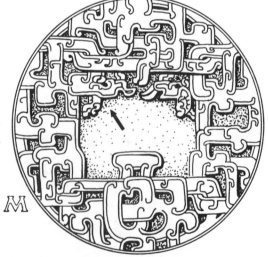

COSMIC MATRIX
Dragon heads emerge from a matrix of scrolls in a 19th-century Vietnamese woodcarving (A) and in a relief carving from Early Classic Kaminaljuyu, Guatemala (M).

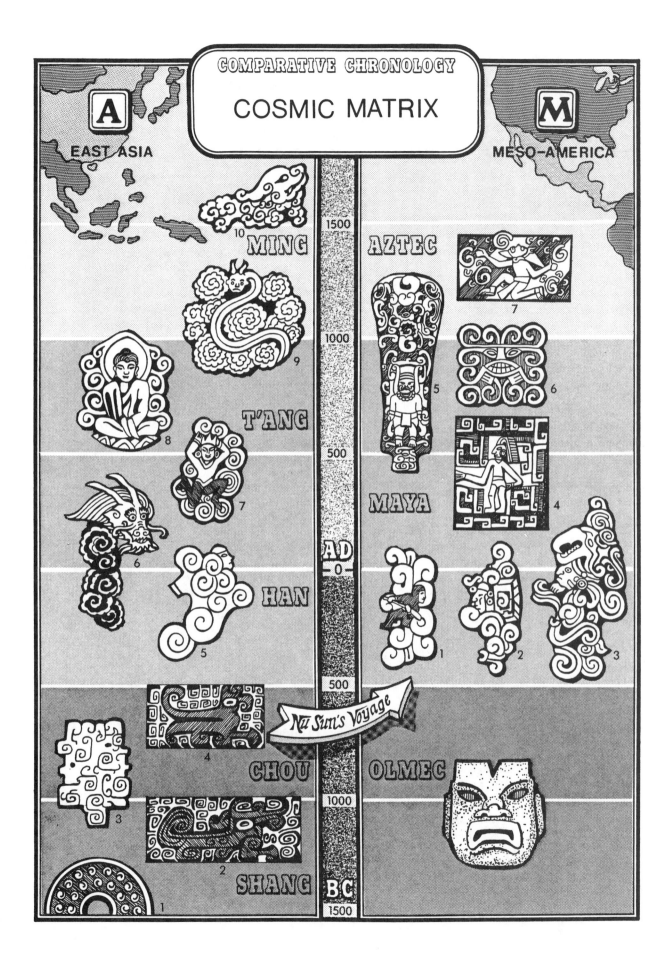

COMPARATIVE CHRONOLOGY

COSMIC MATRIX

A EAST ASIA

M MESO-AMERICA

MING

T'ANG

HAN

CHOU

SHANG

AZTEC

MAYA

OLMEC

Nu Sun's Voyage

1500
1000
500
AD
0
500
1000
1500
BC

FLIGHT

Examples of scrolls representing flight occur by the Shang dynasty in China, where they represented bird wings (A1 and 2). Often, serpents were combined with feathers to represent flight as a power of the Celestial Serpent. This tradition lasted into the Chou period (A3), before stylized scrolls became the primary symbol for flight. During the Han dynasty, scrolls in the shape of "flying scarves," or ribbons, represented the heavenly flight of angels, immortals, dragons, sacred horses, and unicorns (A6-8). Scrolls were sometimes used to represent the wings of sacred lions (A8) or they were used in conjunction with miniature winglets of huge lion statues (A9).

The earliest Meso-American flight scrolls (M1 and 2) occurred at Izapa, on the southwestern coast of Mexico, ca. 500-100 B.C. After the Colonial Period, flight scrolls rarely appear in the archaeological record in association with human beings. A stone statue from Teotihuacan (M4) has back scrolls that are similar to Asian lion scrolls (A9), while scroll wings are commonly found on birds and bats.

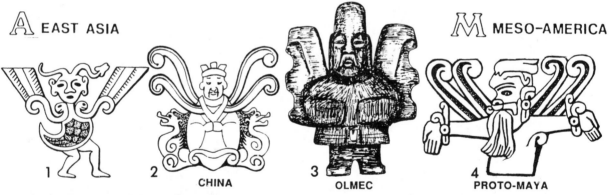

𝔸 EAST ASIA

1

2
CHINA

3
OLMEC

𝕄 MESO-AMERICA

4
PROTO-MAYA

131

HUMAN FLIGHT

Scrolls attached to the shoulders of humans generally represent a spiritual quality that makes possible heavenly flight, or transcendence. These examples include a Chou bronze (1), a Han mirror (2), an Olmec statuette (3), and an Izapan carving (4). Although three examples of winged Olmec men have been found, none have scrolls--suggesting that the Mayan scrolled-wing tradition was an Asian import.

COMPARATIVE CHRONOLOGY

FLIGHT

A — EAST ASIA

M — MESO-AMERICA

MING

T'ANG

HAN

CHOU

SHANG

AZTEC

MAYA

OLMEC

Nu Sun's Voyage

1500

1000

500

AD
0

500

1000

BC

1500

COMPARATIVE CHRONOLOGY

BREATH/SOUL

Ancient Asian symbols representing the soul, or the breath of the soul, can be identified from their similarity to motifs used in historic times. Scrolls projecting in front of the mouth have been identified in the context of esoteric Buddhist art as depicting breath, or the soul (A14 and 15). Two forms of this motif are common: one projecting in front of the mouth, and the other curving up behind the mouth. The latter form is typically employed where the nature of the art medium prevents extending the scrolls in front of the mouth. This is primarily true of three-dimensional stone sculptures.

The earliest Asian example is from Shang China (A1). It was near the beginning of a tradition that can still be seen in Chinese dragon masks that have scroll motifs curving from behind the mouth. Following the Han dynasty adoption of the Buddhist ribbon, some auspicious beasts have a ribbon in their mouths to represent the heavenly soul.

There are no examples of this symbol in Olmec art. The earliest Meso-American artifacts with Breath /Soul motifs occur at Kaminaljuyu, Guatemala, near the Pacific Coast (M1 and 2), ca. 500-100 B.C. The tradition of usage continued through the Aztec empire up to the present, and examples of the motif can be seen in the folk arts of the region. The backward curving mouth scroll is frequently used with serpents (M10) and is not to be confused with the serpent-tongue which is typically portrayed in addition to the Breath/Soul motif.

132

SUN BIRDS
Bird and sun combinations are common to East Asia and Meso-America. Hindu scroll motifs represent the fiery breath of the sun. Examples include a Han tapestry (1), a 17th-century Hindu carving (2), a Teotihuacan mural (3), and a drawing from the *Nuttal Codex* (4).

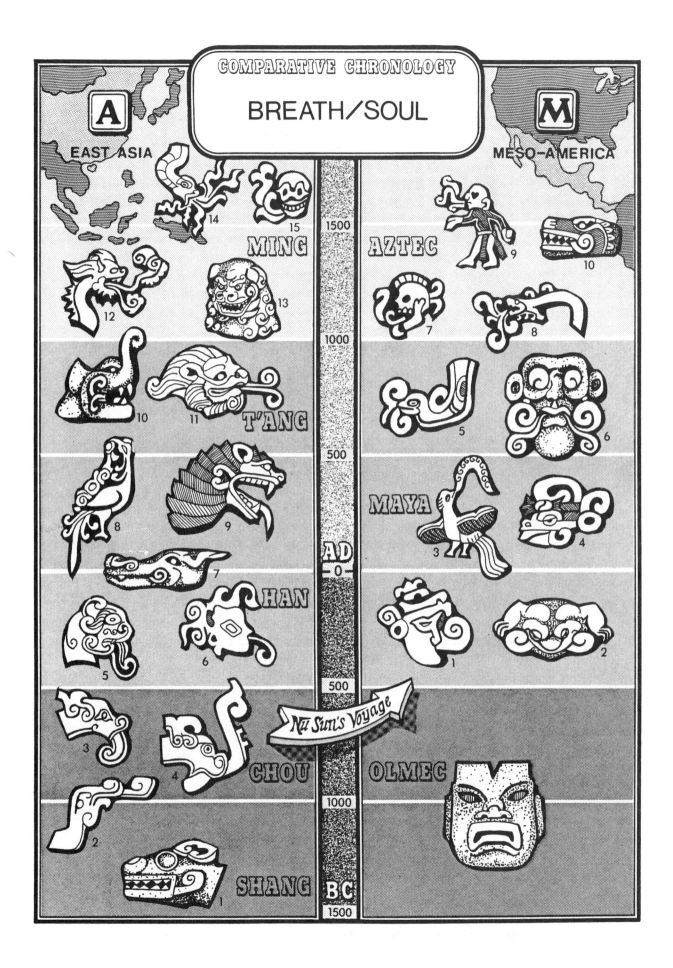

CELESTIAL SERPENT

Many ancient societies have a superstition that attributes lightning to a supernatural sky serpent. Other spectacular meteorological phenomena, such as cyclones and rainbows, are commonly attributed to this mythical creature. It is also not unusual for this beast to be represented with two heads at opposite ends of its body. What differentiates the Asian Celestial Serpent is the presence of scrolls which typically emerge from behind the head, or neck. Occasionally, they occur elsewhere along the body. These scrolls represent the power of magical flight, or transformation--as the serpent may take on the form of cloud scrolls or plants.

The earliest Asian artifacts featuring the Celestial Serpent occur in The Shang period (A1). Example A4 has been identified as a representation for a rainbow, while the Serpent Bar motif (A6-8) is a common motif associated with royalty. Following the Han dynasty, serpents and dragons were typically embellished with cloud scrolls to represent their power of flight and magical transformation.

In Meso-America, one of the earliest forms of this motif occurs near the Pacific Coast at Kaminaljuyu, Guatemala (M2). It has a curved shape and with rain clouds at both ends indicating that it was used to represent a rainbow. The time period of this relief carving is ca. 500-300 B.C. The double-headed serpent bar also became popular in Meso-America as a symbol of royal and religious power after A.D. 500. Mayans used the scroll-embellished serpent to represent their mythological hero Kulkulkan, while the Teotihuacanos used a feathered serpent (M4) to represent a similar spiritual being called Quetzalcoatl. This tradition was common throughout the region until the end of the Aztec empire and is still popular in contemporary folk art.

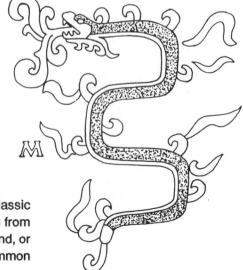

CELESTIAL SERPENTS
These serpent motifs from 9th-century Tibet (A) and Post-Classic Chichen Itza (M) show a similar usage of scrolls emerging from the body to depict flight, or spiritual power. Fiery breath, wind, or lightning is indicated by mouth scrolls. These are common themes in both Asia and Meso-America.

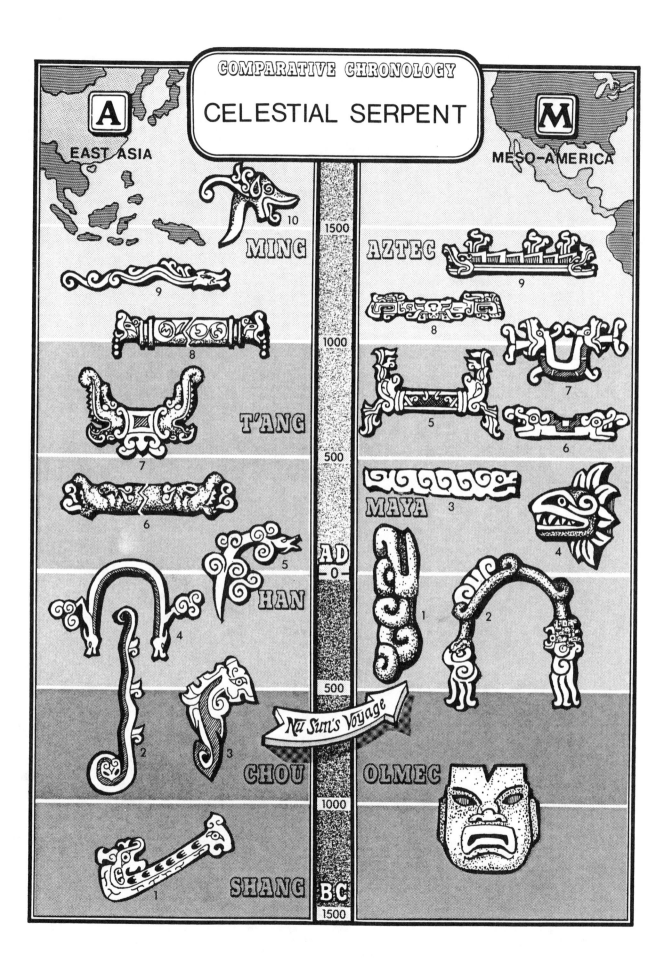

COMPARATIVE CHRONOLOGY
CELESTIAL SERPENT

A EAST ASIA

M MESO-AMERICA

1500

MING

AZTEC

1000

T'ANG

MAYA

500

HAN

AD
0

Nu Sun's Voyage

500

CHOU

OLMEC

1000

SHANG

BC

1500

THUNDERHEAD

The Thunderhead motif is one of the most common features of Oriental art. The motif's ancestry can be traced back to the Shang dynasty, ca. 1500 B.C., where it was portrayed emerging from a dragon's mouth (A1). This unusual motif, which has the form of a peaked scroll, represents the creative potential of spring rains--an interpretation that is clearly supported by the context of its usage. The peak may represent sky fire, or lightning. The tradition was well established in Chou bronze castings, although its greatest popularity seems to have occurred during the Ming dynasty. Even today, it is a common motif in Chinese rugs, tapestries, ceramics, and jade (A11). Throughout the remainder of the Orient, it is a relatively rare motif.

The earliest artifacts from Meso-America which bear this motif occur at Izapa, Mexico (M1 and 2), and Kaminaljuyu, Guatemala (M3), ca. 500-100 B.C. The association of the peaked scroll and rain water is clearly indicated by a mural at Teotihuacan (M6). This association included the Celestial Serpent at Xochicalco, Mexico, where the scrolls comprise the serpents body (M11).

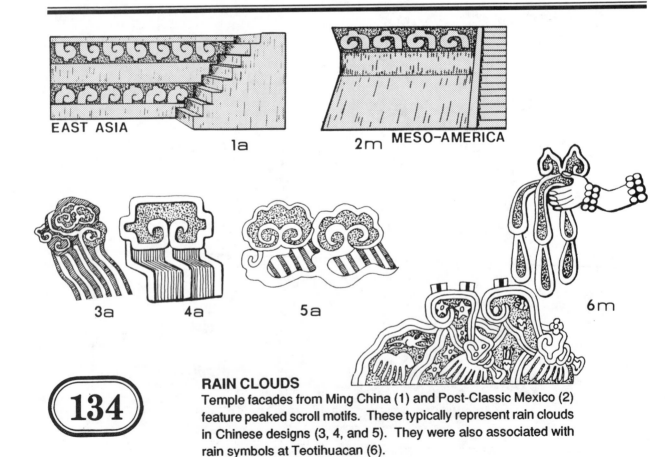

EAST ASIA

1a

2m MESO-AMERICA

3a 4a 5a 6m

134

RAIN CLOUDS
Temple facades from Ming China (1) and Post-Classic Mexico (2) feature peaked scroll motifs. These typically represent rain clouds in Chinese designs (3, 4, and 5). They were also associated with rain symbols at Teotihuacan (6).

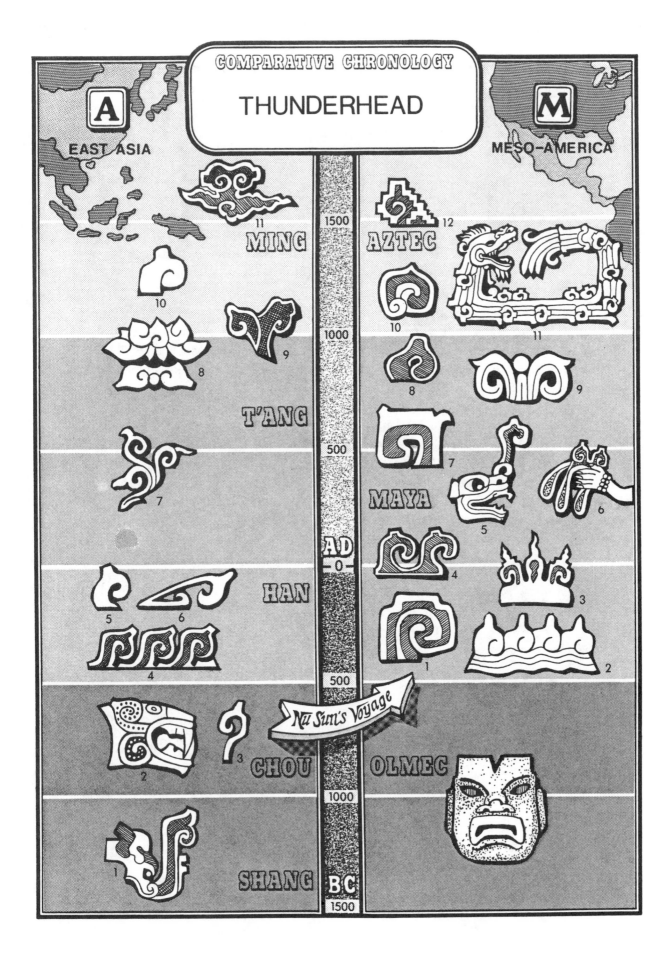

COMPARATIVE CHRONOLOGY

THUNDERHEAD

A

EAST ASIA

M

MESO-AMERICA

1500

MING

AZTEC

1000

T'ANG

500

MAYA

AD
0

HAN

500

Nü Sun's Voyage

CHOU OLMEC

1000

SHANG BC

1500

COMPARATIVE CHRONOLOGY

VIII

COSMIC EYE

The Cosmic Eye motif is one of the world's most unusual symbols. It takes the shape of a scroll, which does not look like an eye at all. Indeed, most artists choose the more common form consisting of concentric circles--as these more realistically portray an iris and pupil. Use of a scroll to represent the eye makes no sense outside of the context of an Omnibus Power Sign tradition. Within the context of such a tradition, the scroll can be regarded as a representation of cosmic vision.

The earliest known examples are from the Shang dynasty (A1 and 2). Like other scroll motifs, this one lost favor during the Han cultural revolution. After the 2nd century A.D., it was rarely seen in China, although it gained popularity in Malasia (A9-12). It was frequently used to portray the eyes of deities, immortals, and *makaras* — which were long-nosed sea creatures (A11).

The Cosmic Eye motif was not used in Olmec art, leading to the conclusion that it was not an indigenous development. Between 500 and 100 B.C., the tradition spread to Meso-America. Early examples have been discovered at Izapa, Mexico (M1 and 3), and at Kaminaljuyu, Guatemala (M2 and 4). Both places are situated along the Pacific Coast. The most extensive usage of this motif occurred during the height of the Mayan Confederacy, between A.D. 4-900. As was the case in Asia, the motif was used solely to represent the eyes of immortals, deities, and auspicious beasts. It was not used to represent the sight of mortals.

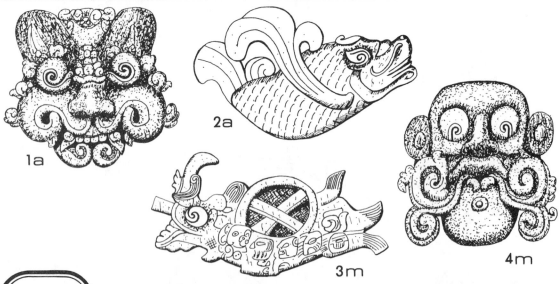

135

SCROLL EYES
Scroll-shaped eyes are common in Southeast Asia and in the Mayan Confederacy. Examples are from: Indonesia, ca. A.D. 1300 (1); China, ca. A.D. 1800 (2); Jaina Island (3); and Copan, 782 A.D. (4).

COMPARATIVE CHRONOLOGY
COSMIC EYE

A — EAST ASIA

M — MESO-AMERICA

MING

T'ANG

HAN

CHOU

SHANG

AZTEC

MAYA

OLMEC

Nu Sun's Voyage

1500
1000
500
AD
0
500
1000
1500
BC

SUPREME BEING (MASK GOD)

The Supreme Being motif, or god-head mask, is common in ancient Asia and Meso-America. What differentiates the Asian Supreme Being from mask gods found elsewhere in the world are the abundant scrolls that comprise the mask. Eyes, ears, horns, mouth, and teeth may consist of scroll patterns. Sometimes, these have the connotation of clouds, spring rain, or creative forces. Both Asian and Meso-American motifs lack a lower jaw, while others portray two serpents emerging from the sides of the mouth.

The earliest known Chinese forms occurred in the Shang dynasty (A1 and 2). It was an extremely frequent motif in Chinese bronze castings up to 200 B.C. (A3 to 6). Thereafter, it continued as a common motif on jade carvings and ceramic vessels (A7, 9, and 12). It was also a common theme in Mortuary art (A8), and it gained widespread usage as an architectural ornament in Indonesia between A.D. 8-1500.

Olmec cultures featured a mask god, however, it was embellished with bracket motifs--not scrolls. The earliest known examples of the scroll-headed masked god in Meso-America occurred near the Pacific Coast between at Monte Alban (M1), ca. 500 to 100 B.C. The motif gained widespread usage, particularly during the Commercial Period of the Confederacy. It was during this time that the symbol was used as the central architectural facade of Mayan temples (M4, 6, and 7).

MASK GODS
The presence of a divinity represented by a mask is indicated by repetitions of the same head pattern. Scrolls play a central role in these designs on a Shang ceremonial bone (A) and on a Mayan temple facade (M). The facade features Chac--the rain god of the Yucatan.

A   M

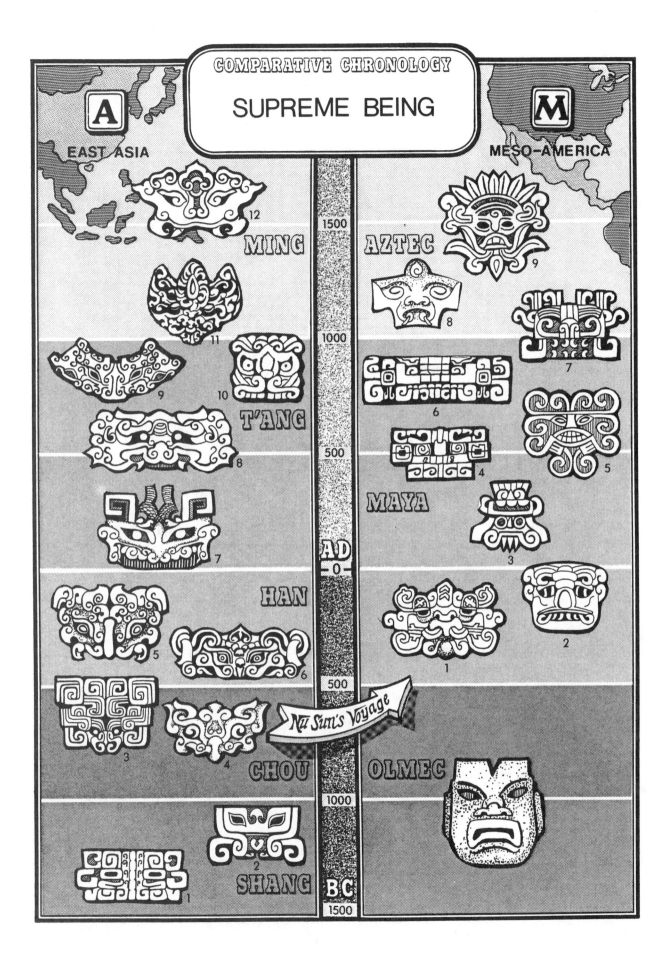

COSMIC DISK

The Cosmic Disk is a common motif in the archaeological records of both the Orient and Meso-America. It is characterized by a central hole and scrollwork that either embellishes the surface or emanates from the center of the disk. Sometimes, dragons or serpents embellish the surface of the disk, while on occasion, they may rise up from the surface or plunge through the hole. The hole represents a cosmic passageway used by spiritual beings to move between the spirit world and the realm of mortals. It also represents the heavenly source of water and thunderstorms. The motif was commonly employed in both Asia and Meso-America as a religious object that was held in the hands, as mirrors, as earspools, or as a celestial object representing a source of water, light, or cosmic energy.

The origin of the disk symbol can be traced back to the Neolithic Age in China, ca. 3000 B.C., at which time *pi* disks (A1) were used in ceremonies pertaining to astronomy and mysticism. These disks are often covered with a scroll matrix representing cosmic energy (A1 and 5). Chou artisans introduced the usage of scrolls emerging from the central hole, and it was this form that spread to Meso-America.

Disks are common throughout the world, and they occur in Olmec ruins. However, Olmec disks do not have the scroll forms that are characteristic of Asian motifs. The earliest Meso-American artifacts with Cosmic Disks are from Kaminaljuyu, Guatemala (M1), and Izapa, Mexico (M2). These are Formative-phase archaeological sites located near the Pacific Coast. The time period is between 500 and 100 B.C. Many of the variations that occurred in the following centuries show striking similarities to those of Asia, such as A6 and M6, A4 and M8, and A15 and M12.

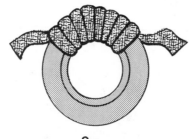

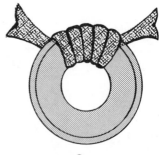

1a   2m   3m

DISKS AND RIBBONS
A Han dynasty *pi* disk (1) and Cosmic Disks from Aztec Mexico (2 and 3) are tied at the top with ribbons. This was a Buddhist tradition to symbolize holiness. Similar disks were attached by ribbons to the clothing of priests in both areas.

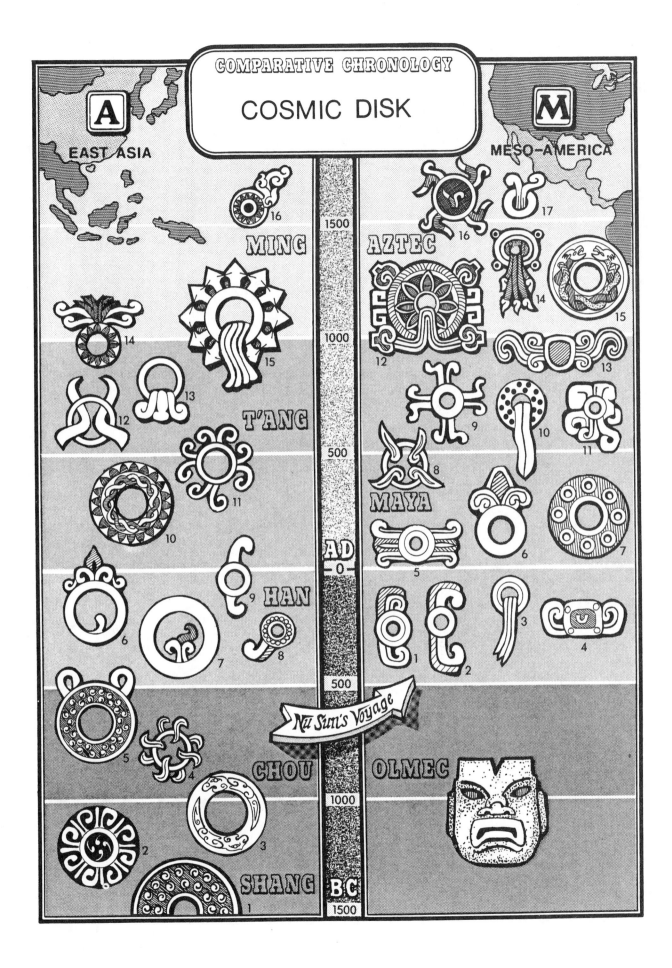

ASIAN DISKS

Cosmic Disks portray the means by which invisible forces enter the physical world. The hand-held disk serves as the source for heavenly water, or the spring rains, while serpents and dragons embellish the surface of disks, or pass through the central hole. Examples include a Javanese sculpture (1), a Chou jade (2), a 5th-century B.C. *pi* disk (3), a Han mortuary carving (4), a 6th-century Chinese sculpture (5), a Nepalese bronze (6), and a Sung porcelain (7).

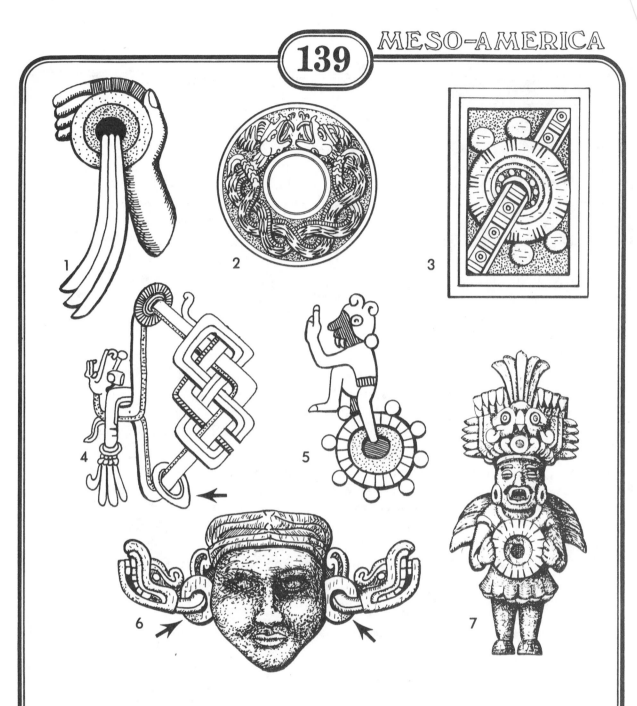

MESO-AMERICAN DISKS

Disks are used to portray the emergence of deities, rain water, and celestial serpents into the physical world. Their forms reflect those of Asia, although serpents generally replace dragons in similar compositions. Examples include a carving from Cerro de Las Mesas (1), a ballcourt goal from Chichen Itza (2), a Mixtec relief carving (3), a Mayan mural (4), an Aztec illustration (5), a Mayan sculpture (6), and a ceramic statuette from Monte Alban (7). Hand-held disks are common in the Mayan region, as are serpents emerging from earspools.

COSMIC MOUTH

The Cosmic Mouth has three basic forms. The most common variety portrays a stream of scrolls emerging from the mouth of the Supreme Being, or sky god, to represent water or creative forces. A second variety pictures the deity's mouth with an emerging Cosmic Disk, while the third variety features a human being, serpents, or plant forms emerging from the opening. Consequently, the mouth is used to depict the means by which cosmic forces emerge from the invisible, spiritual realm. These traditional patterns occur in both Asia and Meso-America.

The earliest Asian artifacts showing the Supreme Being with a mouth full of scrolls occur in the Chou period (A2). Nevertheless, the concept may derive from Shang dragon motifs (A1). The tradition continued to spread throughout Southeast Asia where the scrolls were often portrayed as plant forms (A9), celestial serpents (A5), or as gushing fountains of water (A7). Another peculiar use of the Cosmic Mouth portrayed the emergence of the Cosmic Disk (A4, 8, and 10). This usage is also reflected in Meso-America (M4 and 6).

Olmec cultures had a very common expression regarding the mouth of their supreme being, however, they used bracket motifs to represent creative forces--not scrolls. The mouth/disk combination is also absent from Olmec religious art. The earliest Meso-American forms of the Cosmic Mouth of scrolls occurred during the Formative archaeological phase (between 500 and 100 B.C.). Example M1 is from a tripod ceramic vessel found in Guatemala, while M2 and 3 are from Guatemalan stone carvings excavated from the Pacific coastal region. The range of forms that emerge from this tradition are strikingly similar to Asian motifs.

COSMIC MOUTH
A Tibetan banner (A) from the early 20th century, and a Teotihuacan mural (M), ca. A.D. 300, show bifurcated scrolls emerging from the mouths of sky deities. These extended scrolls often have a transformational quality which involves serpents or plants.

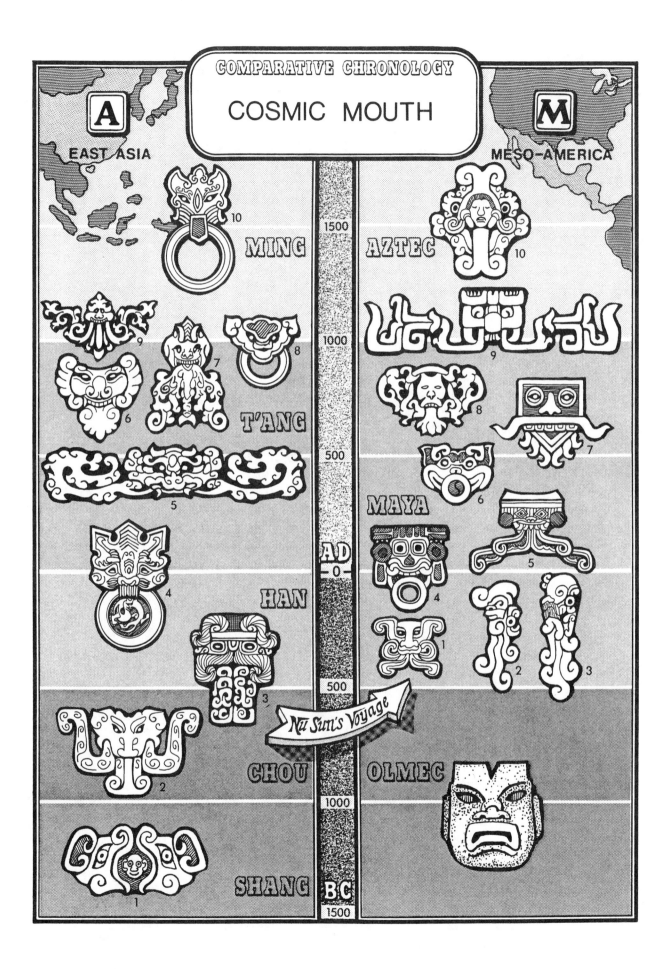

COMPARATIVE CHRONOLOGY

COSMIC MOUTH

A EAST ASIA

M MESO-AMERICA

MING

T'ANG

HAN

CHOU

SHANG

AZTEC

MAYA

OLMEC

Nu Sun's Voyage

1500

1000

500

AD
0

500

1000

BC

1500

IMMORTALITY

The Immortality motif has a long history in China dating to the Shang dynasty (1500 B.C.), or earlier. Its meaning is well-established as a consequence of its uniform usage over time and the interpretive reliability of the context in which it has been used. Many living Chinese can identify the bar with curled ends as a symbol for "long life," while ancient inscriptions (A1) confirm the representation of "longevity." The symbol is frequently associated with tombs (A5) and with depictions of Taoist Immortals, such as the Queen of the West (A7). In this instance, the symbol is used as a throne and its function is to represent immortality. The same usage was also common in Meso-America. For example, the motif was used to represent the throne of the Aztec Queen of Heaven (M11) and the throne of the Water Goddess (M14).

The meaning ascribed to this symbol is confirmed by other Asian and Meso-American examples. For instance, it appears on the temple platform of Confucius and the halo of Buddha (A10). A Classic Mayan ceramic vessel of the Colonial Period used the symbol to indicate footprints on the Road of Death—presumably to indicate the path of immortality. It was commonly used in Asia to embellish thrones and platforms for ruler-priests, indicating their heavenly status of immortality.

The earliest known examples of this motif in Meso-America are from archaeological sites near the Pacific Coast, ca. 500-300 B.C. Example M1 is from a stone relief carving found at Kaminaljuyu, Guatemala, while M2 and 3 are from Izapa, Mexico. The tradition spread throughout the region during the Commercial Period (A.D. 200-900) and persisted through the Aztec empire where numerous examples appeared on stone carvings (M9), and in the codices (M11, 12, and 14).

It remains one of the most common symbols of the Orient, where it is used extensively in wood carvings. Few examples of this ancient craft have survived, although a wooden bell stand (A5), dating to the 5th century B.C., is evidence of a tradition that has endured for over two thousand years. The only reason why we are able to compare this tradition to that of the early Mayans is that they had enough concern for the future to carve some of their designs in stone.

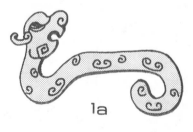

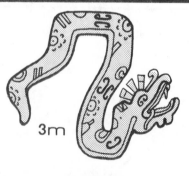

1a 2a 3m

SERPENTS OF IMMORTALITY
The Immortality motif is used in conjunction with the Cosmic Serpent on Chinese vases (1 and 2), ca. the 17th century, and in the Mayan *Madrid Codex* (3), ca. A.D. 1100.

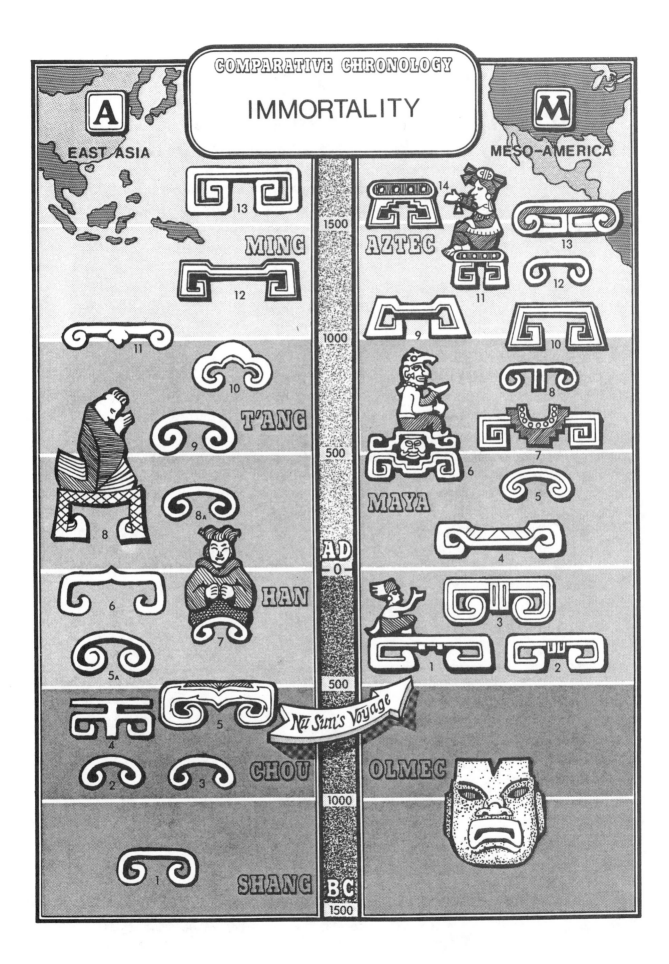

COMPARATIVE CHRONOLOGY

LIFE FORCE

Life Force scrolls have a variety of forms, although there are several characteristic types. These include the portrayal of Cosmic Power Signs emanating from the top, back, or temple region of the head (A2), the use of scrolls with skulls (A14), and the placement of scrolls coming from other areas of humans and animals (A5).

The motif first appeared in Chinese art during the Shang dynasty, ca. 1500 B.C., where it is used in conjunction with the elephant god (A1). Often, the crown scroll was used interchangeably with miniature dragons (A7), or cosmic serpents. This leads to the inference that these motifs are early manifestations of the Oriental concept of *Kundalini*, or "serpent power," which is regarded as the source of conscious and life force among contemporary Buddhists. Following the Han dynasty, the symbol was rarely used in China, although it achieved widespread usage in Malasia. Later Buddhist traditions converted the scrolls into ribbons that projected from the sides of the head (A15 and 16).

Life-Force scrolls are unknown among Olmec cultures. The earliest Meso-American examples of this motif occur at archaeological sites near the Pacific Coast, ca. 500-300 B.C. Example M1 is from Kaminaljuyu, Guatemala, while M2, 3, 4, and 6 are from Izapa, Mexico. Example M6 is from Monte Alban. Note that M1, 3, and 5 all have variations of the Cosmic Power Sign, as do several Asian examples (A2, 6, and 10). Examples M7 through 10 are from Classic Mayan archaeological sites, while M13 is from the *Nuttal Codex*. Variations of these symbols are still present in Meso-American folk art and in the esoteric Buddhist arts of Tibet and Nepal. It is in this refuge located far from the tyranny of Chinese rulers that many of the ancient practices and religious symbols survived long after cultural reformers banished them from the empire.

A

M

LIFE FORCE SKULLS
A Tibetan silk embroidery of the 19th century (A) is remarkably similar to a Classical Mayan vase painting (M) depicting scrolls emerging from a human skull. These scrolls represent life force.

EAST ASIA

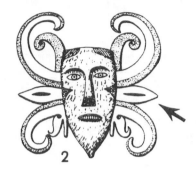

ASIAN LIFE-FORCE SYMBOLS
Spiritual power, holiness, and life force represented by this collection of Asian artifacts.
Cosmic Power Signs are featured with several specimens, including Chou bronzes (1
and 4), a Timor mask (2), a 4th-century B.C. Chinese painting (7), and the Bali supreme
being (10). Dragon scrolls are featured on a Han jade (3), while flame scrolls erupt from
a Chou jade (5) and a Javanese skull (6). *Kundalini* serpents and ribbons are reflected
in the body scrolls of a Shang jade statuette (8), and a Chou figurine (9).

MAYAN LIFE-FORCE SYMBOLS
Asian traditions are reflected in many Mayan and Toltec artifacts. The Cosmic Power
Sign is featured in temple facades at Hochob (1) and Casa de Los Monjas (2). It also
appears with the Celestial Serpent (3). Similar head scrolls occur with skull motifs from
Chichen Itza (4) and Copan (5). Flame scrolls emerge from figures at Tikal (6) and
Copan (7), while body scrolls are found on a Toltec vase (8) and objects from Chichen
Itza (9 and 10). These body scrolls often have attributes of serpents--much like their
Asian counterparts.

TABLE 2. OMNIBUS POWER SIGN

COSMIC DUALITY	COSMIC POWER	COSMIC MATRIX	FLIGHT
I.	II.	III.	IV.
asia			
meso-america			

SUPREME BEING	COSMIC DISK	COSMIC MOUTH	IMMORTALITY
IX.	X.	XI.	XII.
asia			
meso-america			

ASIAN AND MESO-AMERICAN COMPONENTS

ca. 500 B.C.

BREATH/SOUL	CELEST SERPENT	THUNDERHEAD	COSMIC EYE
V.	VI.	VII.	VIII.

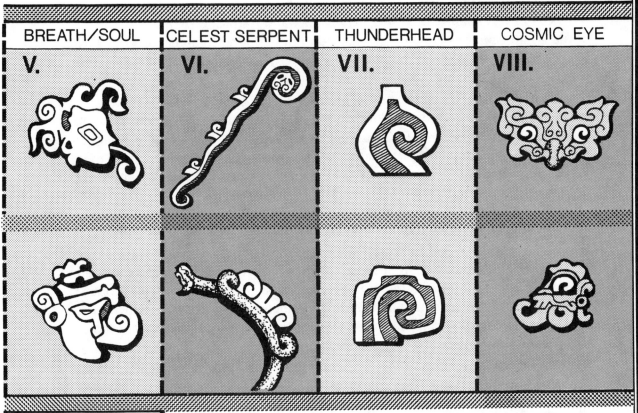

LIFE FORCE
XIII.

This table compares motifs from Asia (ca. 900 B.C. to A.D. 200) and Meso-America (ca. 500 B.C. to A.D. 200). Most of the examples occur between 700 and 400 B.C.

These examples represent specific motif traditions in both areas. The close similarity of each tradition is suggestive of a possible cultural contact between Asia and Meso-America. The close similarity of all 13 components of the Asian Omnibus Power Sign to those of Meso-America is conclusive evidence of fundamental cultural contact.

An Asian source would not be indicated if archaeological data revealed a developmental history for these motifs in the New World. However, this is not the case. All 13 traditions trace their New-World origins to the Pacific Coast of southern Mexico and Guatemala at the same approximate time period, ca. 500 to 100 B.C. The developmental path of the corresponding Asian motifs extends for two thousand years, suggesting that the sudden appearance of all 13 traditions in Meso-America is not attributable to independent invention. The location of their origin indicates that they were not a product of the Olmec culture--whose primary religious centers were situated along the Gulf of Mexico.

Summary of the Chronologies

The same pattern is apparent in all of the chronologies. There is a developmental sequence in Asia extending back in time to 1000 B.C., or earlier. In Meso-America, however, the archaeological record is virtually barren of magic scrolls until about 500 B.C. In a very short span of time, between 500 and 100 B.C., all of the components of the Asian Omnibus Power Sign tradition can be found in archaeological sites along the Pacific Coast of southern Mexico and Guatemala, with the heaviest concentrations occurring at Izapa and Kaminaljuyu.

The pattern of occurrence of these motifs is highly indicative of the manner in which magic scrolls gained popularity as the preeminent Mayan religious symbol. They formed the very core of Mayan religious expression. Furthermore, many of the motifs were adopted by the later Aztec rulers--who also added their own variations. The result is that New-World symbols exhibit increasing complexity until the early sixteenth century.

The situation in Asia was quite different. Chinese reformers of the Han dynasty gradually eliminated most of the archaic motifs and replaced them with more acceptable symbols of Buddhist derivation. The most popular replacement was the heavenly ribbon, which had its origin among the Ionian Greeks who had followed Alexander into northwestern India.[10] Some artisans tried to strike a compromise between the old scroll style and the Buddhist symbols, by using ribbons which were convoluted into scroll shapes. In the long run, ribbons won out as the motif of choice to represent heavenly power in East Asia.

As religious symbolism in Meso-America grew more varied, the symbolism of China became more refined and conservative. The result of these cultural changes is that comparisons between the scroll motifs of Asia and Meso-America are bound to show vastly differing components--except for one specific span of time: 500 to 200 B.C. That is one reason why the existence of the Asian Omnibus Power Sign in America has gone undetected for so long.

A summary of the corresponding motifs of the Omnibus Power Sign as it appeared in East Asia and Meso-America during the Colonial Period is presented in Table II. The results of this comparison are nothing less than astonishing. All thirteen motifs are virtually identical. The statistical probability of any single type of motif occurring in both areas is roughly fifty percent--assuming there had been no contact. Two motifs might have a probability of occurring together twenty-five percent of the time due to chance alone. However, for all thirteen motif traditions to be present in both areas at the same time has the unlikely probability of only one in ten thousand.

But art is never the consequence of simple random selections of motifs. Art is more like a river whose characteristics derive from a confluence of many streams and brooks forming an enduring pattern of styles and cultural conventions. That is not to say that styles and conventions do not change. However, among the ancients, certain religious traditions lasted for a considerable length of time. If they changed at all, it was often due to some major, identifiable event in the socio-cultural environment, such as the advent of Buddhism in China.

The association between the Omnibus Power Sign in Asia and Meso-America is supported by more than just the similarity of their forms and the patterns of their occurrence. It is supported by a congruence of symbolic function. That is, in both areas, similar motifs are used in a similar manner to represent virtually identical religious beliefs. This aspect of their relationship is indicated by Figures 127 through 144. These illustrations show a high degree of similar usage. For example, similar Thunderhead motifs are used to decorate the sides of pyramids, *yin/yang* motifs occur on scepters and phallic aprons, hands hold the Cosmic Disk that spews forth water, or the disks are wrapped in Buddhist-style ribbons, and Cosmic Power Signs erupt from the heads of human figures, skulls, and deities.

For Neolithic Mayan tribes to develop a complex tradition that was virtually identical to the Asian Omnibus Power Sign without close contact would have been virtually impossible. Likewise, for the Omnibus Power Sign to have acquired the importance that it did, to the extent that all thirteen motifs became the primary religious symbols of the Mayan Confederacy, would have required very close contact with Asian artists for a substantial period of time. On these two conclusions, i.e., the degree of complexity and the degree of similarity, rest the validity of Nu Sun's voyage and the theories concerning subsequent periods of colonial and commercial contact. The reader can judge whether or not the conclusions are reasonable.

Regardless of the fact that China seems to be the apparent source of the Omnibus Power Sign in Meso-America, true science demands that we consider every alternative explanation, regardless of how unlikely it may seem. Therefore, we must evaluate alternative hypotheses that might explain the sudden appearance of the tradition in ancient Mayan territory. Presently, there are two possibilities that are worthy of our attention. The first one suggests that the omnibus tradition is not unique at all, in which case we would expect to find magic scrolls used as omnibus power signs throughout the world. The second hypothesis is that some other culture besides East Asians may have brought the tradition to Meso-America. These two alternatives are the subject of our final chapter.

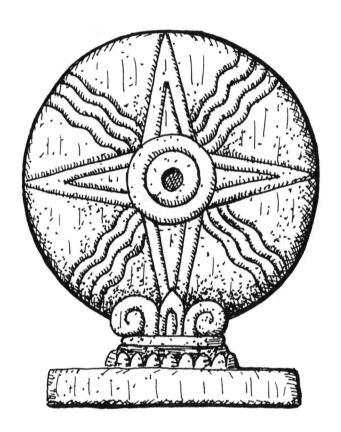

The Case for World Scrolls

It is time to focus our attention on the world as we seek alternative sources for the Omnibus Power Sign in Meso-America. Since our major concern is to determine who else besides the East Asians may have brought the Omnibus Power Sign to Meso-America, it is reasonable to focus our attention on those cultures that were far enough advanced to mount seagoing expeditions between 500 and 100 B.C. Those are the inclusive dates given by anthropologists for the production of Izapan carvings which form the preponderance of our evidence for the beginning of the Omnibus Power Sign in Meso-America. In this regard, the Egyptians, Greeks, Phoenicians, Carthaginians, Celts, Persians, and Hindus are the primary candidates.

It should come as no surprise that scroll motifs are abundant among these cultures during the sixth through the second centuries B.C. Nevertheless, it is possible to categorize scrolls into basic types of motifs--just as has been done with the Omnibus Power Sign in Asia. The use of categories is a common scientific procedure, which enables us to undertake a sensible examination of the evidence.

The most prevalent type of Old-World scroll is very similar to the Cosmic Power Sign. It is commonly known as the Sacred Tree motif (Figure 145). This motif consists of a pair of outward curving scrolls with a palmette leaf in the center. It occurs with great abundance in the arts of Phoenicia, Rome, Greece, Mesopotamia, Persia, and India. Some forms of this motif have a triangular element between the scrolls, with the consequence that it appears identical to the Asian Cosmic Power Sign. At other times, a series of scroll forms arise from the base motif to form a tree, and this is often surmounted by a symbol for the sun. The origin of the motif is generally attributed to Mesopotamia ca. 3000 B.C.[1]

Like its Far-Eastern counterpart, the Sacred Tree motif sometimes culminates in the emergence of the sun between the two scrolls (Figure 146), indicating that the motif serves the function of explaining the emergence of cosmic forces into the

OLD WORLD SACRED TREES

The sacred tree motif of ancient Mesopotamia and the Mediterranean is similar to the East-Asian Cosmic Power Sign in its basic form which includes an angular flame element between two scrolls. The flame element is associated with the sun, and with concepts of emerging cosmic energy, while the scrolls are associated with a very ancient concept of cosmic duality. This concept of duality was sometimes portrayed in the form of two serpents intertwined about a staff, which represented natural law. Its most commonly recognized form is the Greek *caduceus*, which was the scepter carried by the god Mercury. These examples are from: Rhodes--5th century B.C. (1); Cyprus--8th century B.C. (2); Romania--4000 B.C. (3); Nimrud (4, 5); Iran--500 B.C. (6); Italy--700 B.C. (7); Greece (8); and Phoenicia (9, 10).

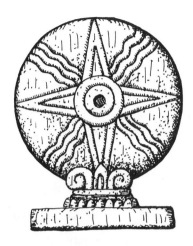

ASSYRIAN SUN DISK

Old-World symbolism typically associated the sacred tree with the sun disk. Presumably, the tree represented an invisible pillar of cosmic law that held the sun aloft in the sky. In this bas-relief from Nabupaliddina, ca. 900 B.C., the sun is portrayed resting upon or emerging from the sacred tree motif.

physical realm. However, similar motifs found on Romanian ceramics (ca. 4000 B.C.) lack this association with the sun and probably represent a somewhat different concept.

Presumably, if the Romans or Phoenicians were responsible for bringing magic scrolls to the New World, the classic Mediterranean style of Sacred Tree would have been adopted by the Mayans, instead of the Oriental *cieba*. The same situation holds true for other scroll motifs found in Mediterranean art. For example, scrolls were occasionally incorporated into the wings of birds and sphinxes (Figure 147). However, the feathers do not have the shape of stylized scrolls that are characteristic of East Asia. Greek artists were quite realistic in their portrayals of flying horses and dragons, giving them huge wings modeled after those of a colossal eagle. The Chinese aeronautical artists, however, would have used a few scrolls or cloud forms to convey the message of the cosmic power of flight--and this is the style that we find in the early days of the Mayan Confederacy.

Mediterranean and Mesopotamian cultures also used scrolls to represent the concept of life force. Some of these are similar to Asian Life-Force motifs, while others look like the body scrolls of Meso-American artifacts (Figures 148, 149, and 150). Nevertheless, most examples from civilizations outside of East Asia appear

MYCENAEAN SPHINX

This 14th-century B.C. ivory carving portrays a winged lion deity with a wing scroll. This usage reflects a tradition common among Mediterranean cultures: scroll motifs are used to embellish realistic wings, rather than being used independently to represent flight--as occurred in 10th-century China.

OLD-WORLD HEAD SCROLLS

Scrolls associated with life force, cosmic power, and the sun were present in numerous Mediterranean and Mesopotamian locations, including: the Minoan culture (1), ca. 1500 B.C.; Assyria (2); Egypt (3), ca. 1000 B.C.; Greece (4, 5); and Iran (6), ca. 500 B.C. Egyptian designs typically employed realistic serpents and sun symbols.

SCYTHIAN MAGIC SCROLLS
Nomadic tribes using horses for transportation spanned the distance between Asia and eastern Europe, carrying cultural influences and trade goods in both directions. These artifacts from eastern Europe of the 6th century B.C. show eye scrolls and mouth scrolls typical of Chinese artifacts of the same time period.

to be unique items. That is, they do not seem to comprise major artistic traditions--with the singular exception of the Sacred Tree, or Cosmic Power Sign. The situation is quite different from what we encountered in the art of China and Meso-America. In both areas, all thirteen elements of the Omnibus Power Sign constitute prolific art traditions.

As time went on, some of the Chinese scroll styles spread to India, although India had a well-established cultural identity that resisted most Chinese influences. Likewise, a few Chinese motifs were eventually incorporated into Persian art as a consequence of trade along the Silk Road through Central Asia. Scythians also brought East-Asian motifs into Europe as they migrated westward from Asia. Some of these motifs were later incorporated into Danish and Celtic art styles.[2]

In more recent times, elements of the Omnibus Power Sign and Mesopotamian symbols have spread throughout the world, as architects and artists have expanded the vistas of their own creative pursuits. This borrowing of motif traditions has given the impression that magic scrolls are indiscriminate symbols which are universally present in nature, or occur in the Jungian cosmic unconscious. This

ETRUSCAN LIFE FORCE SYMBOLS
One of the common themes of magic scrolls in Mediterranean cultures is the representation of life force. The creative forces of nature were indicated by plant form scrolls which emerged from the ground, the sky, or from animals.

TABLE 3.

WORLD SCROLL SURVEY ca. 500 B.C. *

					OPS ELEMENT								
	I.	II.	III.	IV.	V.	VI.	VII.	VIII.	IX.	X.	XI.	XII.	XIII.
MARITIME POWER — EGYPT		⚜											
CELT		⚜						R				🌀	R
ETRUSCAN/ROMAN		⚜		R								🌀	👤
OLD WORLD — PHOENICIA CARTHAGE GREECE		⚜		R								🌀	👹
PERSIA		⚜		R									R
HINDU		⚜											
EAST ASIA/CHINA	☯	⚜	🐉	👼	👂	🐍	🌀	🎭	🦋	◦	👺	🌀	👹
NEW WORLD — PROTO-MAYA	☯	⚜	🐉	👼	👂	🐍	🌀	🎭	🦋	◦	👺	🌀	👹
OLMEC													

Key: ▨ ABSENT   R – RARE   🌀 – ABUNDANT

This Table is a synopsis of major scroll traditions present among maritime nations ca. 500 B.C. Although scroll motifs are plentiful throughout the world, the specific magic scroll elements of the Omnibus Power Sign complex were quite limited in their geographical distribution. The complete absence of these 13 elements in Olmec art prior to 500 B.C. and the sudden appearance of all 13 among the proto-Mayan peoples near the Pacific Coast of Meso-America, ca. 500 B.C., clearly indicate the strong cultural relationship between the Mayans and the Chinese at that critical turning point in New-World cultural development.

*Table Three summarizes a review of over one million artifacts.

perception, however, is totally inaccurate, as we can see by examining the patterns of artifacts and motifs present ca. 500 B.C.

A summary of data collected during the author's world scroll survey is presented in Table 3. More than a million artifacts were examined in the course of a thorough review of documents and collections available in several museums and libraries mentioned in the credits. The lack of association between Meso-American and Mediterranean cultures is strikingly apparent. On the other hand, the close association with East Asia is conclusive. This is not to say that other Old-World cultures did not make significant contributions to New-World civilization. The available evidence suggests that numerous contacts took place, although their level of influence has not yet been determined.

What this diagram clearly indicates is that the contact between East Asia and the Mayan tribes of Guatemala was very intimate. It had to be in order to result in such a close pattern of similarity in the usage of the Omnibus Power Sign components. And, it was precisely this kind of intimate contact that served as the germination of Mayan civilization.

吉星

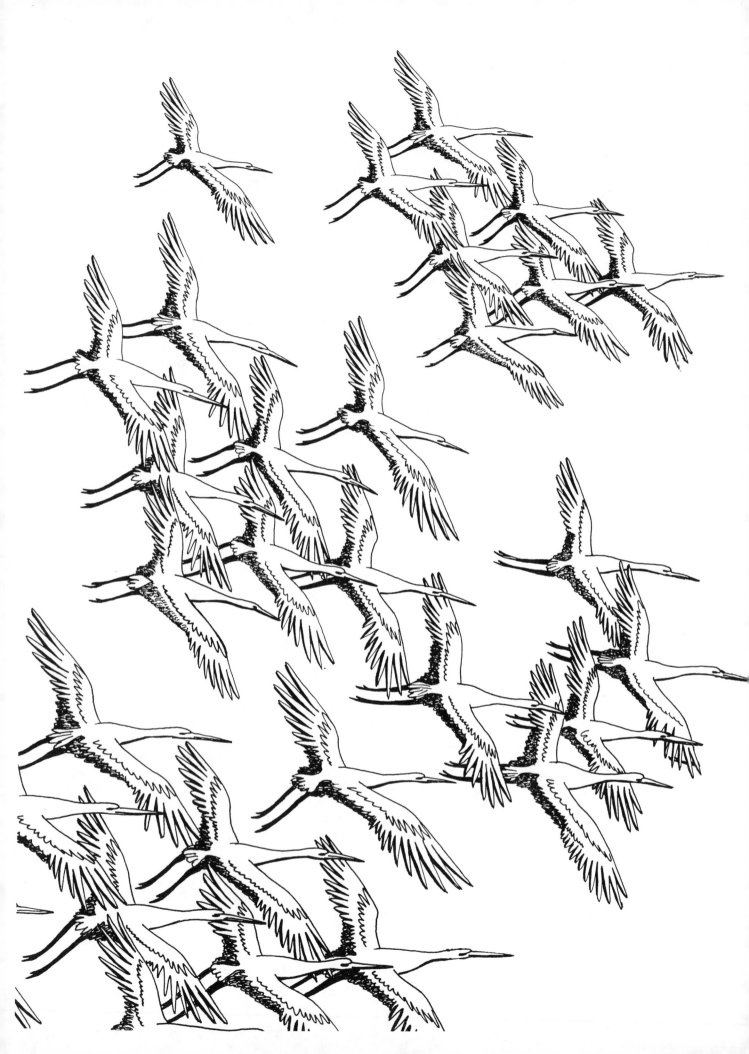

Epilogue

The story of America's past is not yet complete. Although we have added many of the missing pieces as a consequence of our examination of the Omnibus Power Sign, many pieces remain to be found in the infinite puzzle of antiquity. We have reviewed ample evidence of Asian involvement at the inception of Mayan civilization, although the precise roles played by indigenous tribes and Asian merchants remain subjects for further investigation. Consequently, the most significant finding of our study is that the appearance of civilization in the Western Hemisphere can no longer be regarded as an indigenous phenomenon. That is not to say that such an evolutionary process was impossible--only that it did not happen the way many scholars once believed.

Other voyagers traveled to the Americas in the centuries before Columbus, although the evidence of their expeditions is often scarce or cloaked in fable. Be that as it may, we should not ignore their contributions to the development of New-World cultures. If we are to take a rational, scientific approach to the examination of the evidence for such voyages, there is no place for ridiculing those who propose diffusionist theories of cultural development. In the past, they have often been referred to as "deluded amateurs" and "romantics," although the test of time has proven them to be more accurate than their critics could have ever imagined.[1] Much work lies ahead in our efforts to reconstruct an accurate picture of ancient American culture before the last remaining artifacts are lost to decay. It will require tolerance of divergent theorists and a cooperative effort, if we are to salvage what we can of the secrets of our ancestors.

Meanwhile, the simplistic belief that America was a "virgin land" at the time of the Spanish Conquest must be abandoned. It seems apparent that the importance of the Columbus voyages has been grossly exaggerated out of a misconception that the viceroy was the first significant explorer to cross the Atlantic, that he was God-ordained to discover the New World, and that he had no prior knowledge of what he would encounter across the ocean. That is, it is assumed that he crossed the Atlantic simply out of faith, believing that God would steer him in the right direction.[2] All of these beliefs are wrong.

In the past, these false beliefs have prevented an accurate appraisal of evidence regarding other voyagers to the ancient Americas. Indeed, even the practice of science has suffered from a tyranny of dogmatic narcissism conditioned by an ethnocentric perspective of the world. This unscientific mind-set has preconditioned many historians, educators, and politicians into a pattern of thinking that invariably ignores the truth, while distorting reality into a more palatable fantasy. Consequently, the homeless suffer in the streets--while politicians and bankers build vacant office buildings; zealots urge expanding the arsenals--while avenues for peace go unexplored; and citizens cry out for more prisons--while the unemployed and the destitute are forced into lives of crime.

In light of the conclusive evidence that Old-World voyages to the Americas were not an unusual occurrence, we must question the motives of those who have tried to portray Columbus as a saint.[3] Indeed, some authors have characterized his expeditions as romantic, God-inspired acts of salvation for the benefit of native peoples, when in fact, they were brutal acts of aggression perpetrated by men obsessed with a lust for gold.[4] The mis-

211

conception that Columbus was the "discoverer" of America is grounded in ignorance and sustained by avoidance of the truth. Consequently, what many believe to be the history of America is seriously flawed and must be reevaluated if we are to clearly understand both our past and our destiny.

This reevaluation may well change how we regard ourselves as a nation of people led by divinely-inspired will.[5] Such a belief has no basis in reality. Furthermore, it is hazardous to our social well-being, because it attributes the actions of our leaders to supernatural power. We are not alone in this dilemma: it is a common problem faced by many of the world's nations. The consequence of such beliefs is that we excuse ourselves, and our leaders, from a responsible assessment of our social behavior. Indeed, by basing our assessments of the world around us upon false assumptions, we often chain ourselves into repeating past mistakes. Meanwhile, we ignore steps that must be undertaken to adequately prepare for the future.

The world is changing, and we must change along with it in ways that encourage economic freedom for the disadvantaged in our own country and economic independence for all the world's people. Civilization is at the threshold of a new horizon of growth--and for that, we need a new vision of the future. Perhaps that vision can emerge from a clearer vision of the past.

Chapter Notes

Chapter 1

1. Worcester (1971) indicates that Chinese ship dimensions were often modified in order to circumvent tax codes. 2. According to Sullivan (1984, 54), King Cheng ordered the execution of Chou scholars in order to eradicate the memory of his predecessors.

Chapter 2

1. Thompson (1979, Historical Table) indicates the presence of Buddhist motifs in China ca. 200 B.C., while Soothill (1929, 93) cites the formal introduction of Buddhism in A.D. 58. He also suggests that there may have been an exchange of philosophy between Indian Buddhists and Chinese Taoists during the 6th century B.C., as a result of trade contacts (1929, 82). 2. The Author identified the Meso-American Omnibus Power Sign in his Master's Thesis at the University of Wisconsin--Madison, in 1969. He noted that the native Americans used scroll forms to represent speech, as well as other aspects of magic and spiritual forces. The nature of the symbol as a comprehensive motif representing spiritual power in Meso-America was disclosed in The Spirit Sign, published in 1974. This interpretation was independently confirmed by Norman (1976, 69) and Freidel (1985, 5-30; also in Schele: 1986, fn-50). The presence of an Omnibus Power Sign in Asia was unknown in modern times until the Author's discovery at the University of Hawaii, in 1987. 3. Casal, et al., (1980) indicate the similarity of curvilinear scroll patterns on the surface of Thai and Chinese ceramics of the late Neolithic to the early Bronze Age in China. 4. Barrow (1984) has interpreted the Koru to represent magic and life force. The Koru is a scroll-shaped motif found abundantly in Polynesia. 5. Bamboo records of comets are present in China by the 2nd century B.C. (Wood: 1985). 6. Ch'en (1964, 27) suggests the presence of Taoists in China by the reign of Huang-ti, who was one of the Legendary Emperors between 2-3000 B.C. Soothill (1929, 47) also notes the presence of followers of Tao prior to the 6th century B.C. Tao is translated as the course, or way of nature, as natural law, or as the invisible law (Soothill: 1929, 47; and Thompson: 1979, 6). 7. Keightley (1983, 550) and Watson (1971, 59) indicate that jade was probably imported from Baikalia along the Amur Valley to An-Yang, because there were no known sources in China. 8. Smith (1979) indicates that the old lunar calendar of the Chinese began with Huang-ti, ca. 2698 B.C. Grump: 1962, iii) has suggested an error factor of about 200 years in calculation of Chinese dates, which would set the starting date to about 2900 B.C., or earlier. 9. Ch'en (1964, 27) notes that Huang-ti, the Yellow Emperor, and Lao-Tzu are regarded as the founders of Taoism. 10. Te-K'un (1960, xxi). 11. Grousset (1959, 12). 12. Keightley (1983, 252) cites the Thailand bronze discovery reported by Barnard (1977, 58).

Chapter 3

1. Te-K'un (1960, 1). 2. Knightly (1903, 551). 3. Sullivan (1984, 16) indicates that the chenjen were court diviners and scribes. Although some authors believe that Taoism did not begin until the 6th century B.C., Soothill (1929, 47) indicates that the belief in Tao and many associated practices that later formed the basis of the religion were already in existence by 600 B.C. 4. The Book of Changes is a guide for the interpretation of patterns or numbers that occur from throwing coins, dice, or sticks which are presumed to reflect the balance of forces pertaining to an event or situation. The interpretations are attributed to Fu Hsi, a legendary ruler between 3000-2000 B.C. (Sullivan: 1984, 13). 5. Toynbee (1973, 113). 6. Sullivan (1984, 17) notes human sacrifice on a gigantic scale. One ruler was buried with 100 retainers and an elephant. 7. According to Sullivan (1984, 17), oracle bones show that scholars knew the precise length of the year. 8. Van Heusden (1952, 53).

Chapter 4

1. Te-K'un (1960, xxiv) believes the takeover was not a popular revolt against a tyrant but rather an act of planned conquest later justified by Chou propaganda. 2. Sullivan (1967, 10) and other scholars date the beginning of the Chou dynasty to 1030 B.C., although the official Chinese dating is presently 1111 B.C. 3. Estimating the population of ancient lands is an inexact practice. Cohen (1973, 282) reports a Chinese population of 150 million by the 16th century. The pattern of extensive settlement and large urban centers of more than 100,000 inhabitants during Chou times suggests that a figure of 14 million for the population ca. 500 B.C. is not unreasonable. A census in A.D. 2 counted approximately sixty million Chinese subjects (Toynbee, 1923, 38). 4. Knightly (1983, 81) reports the domestication of soybeans by the Chou dynasty. 5. Knightly (1983, 81) reports the presence of crop rotation by the 5th century B.C. 6. Smith (1979, 33) and Knightly (1983, 247) report casting of iron ca. 700 B.C. 7. Worcester (1971, 20) places the first arrival of foreign

influence by sea at 650 B.C. He notes a mention of "Thina" by Erathostenes in 250 B.C., and says that Alexandrian entertainers went there by sea during the 2nd century B.C. **8.** Some scholars question the existence of Lao-Tzu (Ch'en: 1964, 24), while others indicate that the name may be an alias for a philosopher who did exist at the time. Thompson (1979, 6) calls him an older contemporary of Confucius. **9.** According to Sullivan (1984, 19-26), t'ao-t'ieh (or taotie) masks represented tigers or water buffalo. While some have referred to the motif as a "monster," or a "glutton," he believes they are actually related to Tibetan devils which play the arcane role of protectors of the sacred truth.

Chapter 5

1. Davies (1979, 104-20) indicates that during the 3rd century B.C., sea captains were dispatched to a distant land in search of the plant of longevity. Thompson (1979, Time Chart) indicates that tales about immortals living on offshore islands occurred by 500 B.C. **2.** Worcester (1971, 16), Shao (1976, 11), and Heine-Geldern (1966, 293) report that Emperor Shih Huang of Ch'in ordered Hsu Shih to voyage to the "Isle of the Blest" in 219 B.C. One purpose of this voyage was to establish the source of the legendary ling chih, or magic mushrooms, which were regarded as the herb of immortality. The Koreans also had a legend about magic mushrooms which they called pullocho (Covell: 1981). Based on these legends, Heine-Geldern suggests that the drug trade was an important part of Asian-American commerce. **3.** Doren (1971, 117; citing Needham: 1971, 439) indicates that the pictogram for boat looks similar to the shape of a river junk--which it probably originally represented. Worcester (1971) suggests that the pictogram for "sail" has a modern derivation, while Needham has traced the pictogram to Shang times. Mc Grail (1981, 58) also indicates the pictogram for sail was present in the late 2nd millennium B.C. **4.** Worcester (1971, 11). **5.** Heine-Geldern (in Wauchope: 1966, 292). **6.** Gibson (1948, 17) attributes the evolution toward the plank-built boat to emergence of bronze-age metallurgy and invention of the saw. Weiner (1986, 263) attributes a large part of man's emergence from the Stone Age to the export of Cypriot copper to Egypt. Casson (1971, 30) indicates that nautical developments closely followed the development of metal technology in the Mediterranean. Glob (1967, 157) attributes the vast development of shipping networks in Denmark between 1500-500 B.C. to the presence of bronze. **7.** According to Worcester (1971, 7), the traditions of junkmen indicate that shipbuilding on the Yellow river antedates that of the Yangtze which preceded the building of oceangoing junks. **8.** Solheim (1982, 182) and

Covarrubias (1954, 33) indicate the spread of Dongson culture into Southeast Asia ca. 750 B.C. **9.** Bellwood (1979, 185). **10.** Bodrogi (1972, 19). **11.** Ballinger (1978, 109). **12.** Leung (1979, 103). **13.** Ballinger (1978, 109). **14.** Temple (1986, 187). **15.** Karnow (1962, 31). **16.** Darion (1976, 30). **17.** Ballinger (1978, 109). **18.** Ballinger (1978, 125) and Dieter (1976, 17) note similarities in 2nd-century Indian vessels primarily with ancient Egyptian vessels--indicating that Indian ship designs were probably derived from Egyptian contacts prior to Alexander's arrival in the 4th century B.C. Also, the Indians used caravel planking which was typical of Roman construction. **19.** Cohen (in Toynbee: 1973, 281). **20.** Worcester (1971, 21) indicates the probability of Phoenician voyages to China by 650 B.C., although he sees no evidence of major impact on Chinese ship designs as a result of that contact. **21.** Worcester (1972, 22) indicates that the whitewash used on ships around Chinchew, China, contains wood oil extracted from the poisonous seeds of Dryandra cordifolia which prevents attack by sea worms. Its use is recorded as far back as the 14th century, although who invented the process is unknown. Some form of worm and barnacle preventative must have been in use during ancient times to preserve the hulls of Chinese ships. **22.** Mangrove bark acted as a preservative due to its tannin content. A set of sails would usually be replaced after two years of use because they gradually became worn and brittle (Worcester: 1971, 73).

Chapter 6

1. Sullivan (1984, 28) notes a close similarity of Shang art to the arts of Siberia, Alaska, British Columbia, and early Meso-America. **2.** Nocturnals consist of a sighting tube and a gauge with three spokes for alignment with known constellations. Stone artifacts in the shape of these gauges are present in the archaeological record of China from 2000 B.C. Similar objects are still in use throughout the world--primarily by amateur astronomers and boy scouts. **3.** Ballinger (1978, 73) indicates that the Chinese traded for Siberian mammoth tusks. **4.** Bandi (1969, 76) notes that iron from 3rd century B.C. China may have reached settlements along the Bering Sea by the Okvik phase. Bandi (1969, 76) notes that the discovery of an iron point on an engraving tool at Uelen, on Cape Dezhner in Siberia, indicates the probable accessibility of iron in the Okvik and Old Bering Sea cultures of the Alaskan Eskimo. He indicates a Chinese reference for iron working along the North Pacific by the 3rd century B.C. **5.** Covarrubias (1954, 187-9) and Patterson (1973, 115-7) indicate that the Northwest Coast art style was too well developed by the 19th century to be a recent phenomena--i.e., it was not consequence of

European contact. Patterson suggests that the similarity of ancient stone artifacts to historic wood carvings substantiates a great antiquity for the craft. Recently found wood carvings dating to the 3rd and 4th centuries A.D. from British Columbia and northern Washington State indicate that the basic wood-carving style was already in existence by that time period (Fladmark: 1986, 22-3). The carvings have scrolls and themes typical of ancient China. **6.** Covarrubias (1954, 189) and Paalen (1944) indicate that Captain Cook observed the Northwest Coast natives using non-European iron tools with such dexterity that they must have been in use for a long period of time. **7.** Quimby (1985, 1) mentions several Japanese shipwrecks reaching the North American Coast in historical times, as well as the use of iron by natives prior to contact with Europeans. **8.** Worcester (1971, 100) indicates that the controversy as to whether or not the Chinese invented the mariners compass is unresolved, although he indicates the presence of magnetized devices used by geomancers at a very early date, presumably by 1500 B.C. Ballinger (1978, 74) indicates that the magnetic needle was known in China ca. A.D. 800. Temple (1986, 150) cites evidence that the Chinese were using the magnetic compass for navigation ca. A.D. 850, while the directional properties were known by the Han dynasty. **9.** Toynbee (1973, 134) notes that Chinese star maps were far in advance of anything known in Europe as late as the 10th century A.D., although nautical records are known to have been used by the Greeks in the 6th century B.C. (Ballinger: 1978, 126). There were other navigational aids known to ancient sailors, including stars, the sun's point of rising on the horizon and its angle of movement across the sky, use of "shore-sighting" birds, sounding rods to measure the depth, and a mariner's own knowledge of wave patterns which apparently played a role in the settlement of Polynesia. Also, during certain seasons, mariners could follow the migratory patterns of birds and cloud formations or perceive land hundreds of miles away by the way the sky reflected the earth below (Morrison: 1971, 34-5; and Ballinger: 1978, 127). **10.** Ballinger (1978, 124) notes that water transportation is at least as old as the Mesolithic in Europe--about 5000 B.C., while migration patterns along the islands of Indonesia between 40,000 and 10,000 years ago (Richardson, 1986-14) suggest an earlier use of water-craft in Asia. Presumably, oceangoing rafts were used at an early date, while dugout canoes may be an invention of the Late Neolithic, ca. 3000 B.C. **11.** A Greek temple facade (ca. 500 B.C.) shows a tusked gargon mask having serpents emanating out of both sides (Johnston: 1976, 98). Although the motif is similar to the Asian kalamakara it does not seem to have been used as a door charm--which was a typical usage in Asia and

ancient America. **12.** Campbell (1983, 320), Covarrubias (1954), and others have indicated the similar function and placement of the makara, sisiutl, and Mayan mask god symbols. Stewart (1986, 102) clearly shows the sisiutl around a doorway, while Holt (1967, 1) shows a Javanese makara in a similar fashion. Some Northwest Coast Indian sisiutls also make use of the scroll-eye motif--which is another highly unique Asian trait (Inverarity: 1967, 14).

Chapter 7

1. According to Bernal (1969, 39) and Wicke (1971, 24), Olmec frontier markers extend as far south as El Salvador. **2.** Davies (1979, 123) suggests that any Asian traveler unlucky enough to land in ancient Mexico would have become the main entre at a cannibal's feast. **3.** Coe and Diehl (1980, 392) report cannibalized remains at the Olmec site of San Lorenzo. **4.** Examples of brown-skinned inhabitants of Meso-America are present in the murals of Bonampak and Teotihuacan. Heyerdahl (1952, 287-8) cites several examples of black-skinned warriors and fair-skinned people with beards and yellow hair in Mexico prior to Columbus. See also, Covarrubias (1954, 25). **5.** Gardner (1986) dates the San Lorenzo ceramic phase to 1200-900 B.C. Inverted volutes which occur during this phase constitute the only known use of scrolls prior to Nu Sun's voyage. There is no apparent connection between this rather simplistic scroll usage and the appearance of the 13-motif Omnibus Power Sign ca. 500 B.C. **6.** Flannery (1983, 87) notes that the population of Monte Alban, ca. 500 B.C., is estimated at 3-7,000. Heizer (1960, 219; in Wicke: 1971, 88) estimates the population of the 350 square-mile area around La Venta at 18,000. Coe and Diehl (1980, 388) estimate the population of San Lorenzo phase A at 1000 people based on the pattern of house mounds. **7.** Coe and Diehl (1980, 388) report no evidence of writing at San Lorenzo. Bernal (1969, 114) reports no evidence of calendrical inscriptions, writing, or the Long Count at either La Venta or San Lorenzo, while Moreno (1959, 1031) believes that the Long Count eventually passed from the early Mayans to descendants of the Olmec. **8.** Morrison (1971, 5). **9.** Casson (1971, 105).

Chapter 8

1. Coe and Diehl (1980, 392) indicate that the primary Olmec weapons were probably wooden clubs and fire-hardened spears. Dart points are rare and arrow points of obsidian do not occur in the San Lorenzo chronology until the Villa Alta phase ca. A.D. 900. **2.** The source of most Chinese jade has not been determined, and until spectroscopic analysis rules out an American source for even a few of the thousands of jade artifacts, the possibility exists that Nu Sun may have initiated jade trade with the New World. The Gulf of Fonseca is near Montagua--the primary Guatemalan jade source used by the Maya (Abel: 1981, 173). It is on the main coastal route the Maya used to export jade to Costa Rica. Weaver (1972, 291) suggests that narcotic plants may have been imported from Mexico to China in ancient times. He cites Mountjoy (1969) as expressing a similar view and further suggests that a ready market awaited such imports. Jennings (1978, 641) suggests that Chinese voyages to Mexico, between 500-300 B.C., may have been related to Taoist trade in magic mushrooms or "drugs of longevity." **3.** The time periods indicated by the present investigation compare very closely to those derived independently by Robert Heine-Geldern (in Wauchope: 1966). Heine-Geldern suggested a period of Chinese influence from Late Chou (ca. 500 B.C.) to Late Han (ca. A.D. 220), and a period of Indo-Chinese influence from the 2nd century A.D. to the 10th century. He suggests that the Tajin Scroll Style of Veracruz is a derivative of a Late Chou style ca. 300 B.C. He sees a start of Chinese influence in Meso-America, ca. 700 B.C., by means of a woodcarving tradition. Woodcarving was the primary means by which Chinese art came to influence the art of Borneo and Fiji. **4.** Morley (1946, 17) indicates that Mayan speakers currently number two million persons with twenty-four separate languages and numerous dialects. **5.** Benson (1977, 141) believes that use of the bow and arrow slowly diffused from Asia via Alaska prior to the 13th century A.D. It appears at that time in Mazapan--a Late Classic city of Yucatan, Mexico. Covarrubias (1954, 28) and Baldwin (1947) postulate arrival of the bow and arrow by 300 B.C. from China, while Miles (1963, 36) suggests a date of A.D. 500. Morley (1956, 209) indicates that the bow and arrow were present at Tikal prior to A.D. 800, on the basis of graffiti found in Temple II. **6.** A Han dynasty funeral cloth shows that the Chinese were smoking pipes at least by the 2nd century B.C. (Lowe: 1979, 6). **7.** The legend of Hui Shen's expedition to Fu Sang indicate that the merchants of the distant land paid no tax (Davies: 1979, 104). **8.** Like the Chinese, the Mayans attributed the origin of writing to a mythical cultural hero. The Mayan hero is identified as "Itzamna" (Morley, 1946-195). He is often portrayed with magic scroll power signs around his head. **9.** Cheng Te-K'un (1960, xxviii) indicates that the Chinese used bamboo tablets for writing in the 4th century B.C., and Benson (1977, 12) indicates the use of bark paper as a common trait between Asia and ancient Mexico. Toynbee (1973) indicates the use of wooden strips for writing in A.D. 100. Other materials included silk and cotton cloth which were used as early as 800 B.C.

10. Stuart and Stuart (1977, 26) indicate that Izapan art (ca. 500 B.C.) is the first to include two critical elements of classical Maya--the calendar and hieroglyphic writing. Bernal (1969, 156) indicates the origin of hieroglyphic writing at Monte Alban, Oaxaca, or Kaminaljuyu, Guatemala, suggesting that it predates Olmec hieroglyphs. He calls this area the cradle of writing in Meso-America. **11.** Von Hagen (1960, 29) cites the simultaneous spread of glyph writing, bark paper, the calendar, dated monuments, common trade and a common written language--indicating the presence of a strong political alliance that had no single capital but consisted of many co-equal city-states. **12.** Thompson (1950, 72; in Norman: 1976, 195) identifies the <u>ceiba</u> as the sacred tree of the Mayans as do most others, but Norman indicates the breadnut tree as a possible alternative. **13.** The Olmec used rough metallic surfaces for reflective objects, and they may have known about the magnetic properties of hematite, or loadstone, ca. 1000 B.C. However, these objects were very poor by comparison to the cast bronze mirrors of the Chinese, and their use of loadstones was of trivial importance without the kind of calibrated dials available to Taoist geomancers. Some Chinese mirrors are capable of allowing energy waves to pass through creating the illusion that light has passed through metal (Temple: 1986, 41). These "magic mirrors" were in use by the 5th century A.D. **14.** Willey (1966, 104) indicates that the Olmec capital of La Venta was destroyed and monuments defaced, ca. 400 B.C., during the Middle Pre-Classic archaeological phase. Coe and Diehl (1966) indicate that internal social upheaval occurred ca. 900 B.C., and abandonment of San Lorenzo took place ca. 400 B.C., after the Olmec were overrun by unknown invaders. **15.** Blanton (1980; in Wenke: 1984, 366) calls Monte Alban the capital of a new confederation, ca. 200 B.C., with a population of about 17,000. **16.** Bernal (1969, 113) indicates that Monte Alban, where scroll motifs are found in abundance (ca. 500 B.C.), is primarily "proto-Mayan" and essentially independent of the Olmec capital in Veracruz. Proskouriakoff (1968, 119) and Kidder (1973, 56), however, regard Izapan art as transitional between Olmec and Maya--leading to their assumption that the scroll motifs at Izapa could be an Olmec derivative. Scrolls are also present at the beginning of the Monte Alban subculture, whose origin Coe (1984, 81) places at 500-450 B.C. There is some dispute among archaeologists regarding the beginning of the "Izapan style" which is a term used to refer to the earliest rock carving using scrolls as a major part of the composition. Norman (1976B, 324) indicates that most Izapan rock carvings were done as a unit between 300-200 B.C.

Miles (in Norman: 1976) dates the Izapan style between 100 B.C.-A.D. 100. Gore (1984, 26) and Stone (1972, 122) have suggested that the Chalcatzingo rock carving known as the "King" may have been done prior to the Izapan style due to its Olmecoid features. The composition (Figure 84) features an array of scroll-forms that have been variously described as gas, wind, steam, and blessings. If Gore's dating of 600-400 B.C. were correct, it would constitute the earliest scroll forms in Central Mexico. However, since the King is a petroglyph whose date of origin has been guessed at by comparing its style to that of other artifacts, it cannot be regarded as a reliable indication of when or where scroll forms first appear in the New World. Indeed, the dates that others have attributed to this petroglyph range from 1000 B.C. to A.D. 100. Luckert (1976, 23) and Quirarte (1973; citing Parsons) place the King petroglyph at a period in time substantially later than Izapa--indicating that the Izapan style as the earliest known expression of magic scrolls (i.e., the Omnibus Power Sign motif complex). Indeed, the style of scroll forms used in the Chalcatzingo carving are most similar to those of the Temple of Agriculture at Teotihuacan, with a date of A.D. 200-300. Dates for the so-called "Olmec Paintings" of Oxtotitlan Cave, which include a possible "speech scroll," are suspect since there is no reliable method for dating rock paintings. Gore (1970) called them the "earliest speech scrolls" in Mexico, while admitting a rather shaky dating by means of his own artistic impressions. Covarrubias (in Grove: 1970) indicated a much later date for Oxtotitlan--i.e., post-Olmec. 17. Lewenstein (1987, 61-2) reported that experiments using bi-facial chert choppers as stone tools proved them to be inadequate for carving relatively soft volcanic tuff. She noted a deterioration rate of 30-65% in three hours of use. 18. Smith (1944, 36) reported that field hands found copper in a ceramic pot dated to the Miraflores Phase (ca. 500 B.C.), however, he assumed that the presence of copper at such an early date was impossible. At least he had the wisdom to mention the discovery in his field report. 19. Heyerdahl (1978, 345) reports the presence of Mayan ceramics dated to 2600 B.C., indicating a spurt of cultural development that is possibly related to Ecuadorian sites where Meggers identified the intrusion of Shang-era immigrants with ceramics similar to the Jamon style of Japan. Some critics regard the ceramics as being too simple in their design to be regarded as proof of Japanese voyages. Willey (1966, 23) noted Jamon ware similar to Valdivia ceramics in Ecuador, ca. 3000-2500 B.C., indicating possible introduction from Japan. Meggers (1966, 94) attributed the introduction of ceramic house models, a Buddha-like statue, ceramic headrests, and panpipes at the Ecuadorian site of Bahia to trans-Pacific Asian contact ca. 500 B.C. This dating is based on radio-carbon analysis, and the proximity to the suggested Nu Sun expedition should not be overlooked.

20. According to Willey (1966, 23), metal working technology, including lost-wax casting, welding, and alloying, appears in Peru during the mid-first millennium B.C. He indicates that these complicated methods of working metal "cannot be dismissed lightly," suggesting that they may be an Old-World import. Leonard (1967, 122) indicates the presence of copper smelting in Peru by the 1st century A.D., bronze alloys by the 5th century, and copper smelting in Meso-America by A.D. 900. Benson (1977, 138) indicates gold casting in the Andes as early as 1000 B.C. 21. Benson (1977, 138) and Thompson (1937, 94). 22. Thompson (1937, 95) indicates that both Peruvians and Mexicans knew how to make bronze. He also assumes this to be a fairly recent invention made prior to the Spanish Conquest. Covarrubias (1954, 43) indicates that bronze was used for making ornaments in Argentina prior to the Spanish Conquest, while the Berlin Museum contains numerous artifacts of pre-Columbian bronze, including shields with mask designs. Thompson (1937, 94) identified the presence of several copper implements in native Mexico, including bells, money tokens, and crescent-shaped hoes. Beirne (in Riley, et al.: 1971, 8, 20) identified the Mayan use of a copper-tanged axe from an illustration in one of the codices. 23. Heine-Geldern (in Wauchope: 1966, 282-3) indicates that Chinese ceramics of the Han period and Guatemalan ceramics of the Teotihuacan III style are virtually identical. 24. Muser (1978, 147) indicates that the "stepped fret" first appears in Monte Alban II vessels ca. 350-100 B.C., and thereafter it becomes a popular motif with its greatest use in post-Classic architecture at El Tajin and Tula. It is also frequently used in Mixtec codices. 25. Wenke (1984, 355-62) indicates a population of about 1000 at San Lorenzo, ca. 950 B.C., and a population of about 2,500 around La Venta, ca. 500 B.C. By 200 B.C., Monte Alban had become the capital of a new confederation with a population of about 17,000 people (Blanton, in Wenke: 1984, 367), while Teotihuacan had a probable population of 200,000, ca. A.D. 500. (Blanton, 368). 26. Covarrubias (1954-48) notes the similarity of Guatemalan tombs of the Miraflores archaeological phase with those of Shang tombs in China. 27. Willey (1966, 135) indicates that the starting date for the Mayan Long Count Calendar is about 3113 B.C., according to the Goodman-Martinez-Thompson correlation (which is supported by radio carbon dating from Tikal). However, there is an error factor from several decades to several centuries in the calculations of when the Mayans first began their calendar. Smith (in Knightly: 1983) notes that the Chinese Old Lunar Calendar was based on a starting date of 2698 B.C.,

in celebration of Huang-Ti, while Gump (1962, iii) indicated an error factor of 200 years, or more, in calculating the starting date which could be as early as 2900 B.C. Muser (1978, 91) suggests that the Long Count system originated in the Uaxactun-Tikal area of Guatemala, while Benson (1977, 99) placed the origin at ca. 500 B.C. further east in Oaxaca or Veracruz. Most authors indicate a 5th-to-6th century B.C. time of origin along the west coast of Guatemala. **28.** According to Ferguson (1984, 6) the Long Count calendar was not established until after 300 B.C.-- long after the Mayans supposedly inherited the Olmec calendar which doesn't exist in the archaeological record. Von Hagen (1960, 177) notes that the early starting date of the Mayan Long Count, at 3111 B.C., is unlikely to be the result of native ingenuity, because: "Archaeology reveals that at this time, the Maya as such did not even exist." **29.** Proskouriakoff (1968, 124) notes a 260 year discrepancy between the traditional Mayan calendar of the Peten and that of coastal Indians. By adjusting the start of the Mayan lunar calendar by this amount of time, to 2751 B.C., there is an obvious overlap with the range of starting dates for the Chinese lunar calendar, i.e., 2698 to 2900 B.C. Consequently, it is possible that the starting dates refer to the same event in the mythical past of both cultures.

30. Kirchoff (in Reed: 1966, 42) indicates a close resemblance of Chinese and Mayan calendars, based on the use of animal symbols, use in divination, and the patterns of major time dimensions. Humbolt (in Vining: 1885) also notes the similarity of Asian and New World calendars. **31.** Tompkins (1976, 346) notes that the Mayan calendrical system emerged so sophisticated that it indicates thousands of years of previous careful astronomical observation--a feat unlikely to have been accomplished by the primitive Mayans. Heyerdahl (1952, 645) indicates that the Maya had determined the length of a solar year to be 365.2420 days which is more accurate than the Julian calender of 365.25 days. This was achieved by observing that the sun and moon obtained the same relative celestial position every 6940 days. **32.** Parsons (1965, 1; in Norman: 1976, 117).

Chapter 9

1. Jennings (1978, 641) indicates that Chinese influence was strong at Teotihuacan, but it declined rapidly following the Han dynasty. **2.** Heine-Geldern (1966, 284) suggests that Southeast Asian merchants had contact with Chinese sailors who were engaged in trans-Pacific trade and began taking a similar route to the New World across the North Pacific ca. A.D. 200. He cites the appearance of the Buddhist lotus motif at Amararato in India--a center

for expansion into Indonesia--and the later appearance of the motif among the Maya by A.D. 700. **3.** Karnow (1962, 31). **4.** Karnow (1962, 31) indicates that the Hindus carried on a deliberately peaceful program of expansion with a focus upon establishing mutually beneficial linkages and intermarriage for the purpose of promoting commerce. **5.** Heine-Geldern (1966, 293) sees parallels between the bursts of civilization in the jungles of tropical Asia and Central America--suggesting the influx of considerable numbers of immigrants from Asia. In both places there occurs a sudden rise of advanced civilization in jungle environments. **6.** Thompson (1937, 84-95) indicates that copper axes and hoe blades have been found in Oaxaca where they were reportedly used as currency. He further indicates that the natives mined tin and knew how to make bronze, however, he assumes this to be a fairly recent pre-Columbian enterprise. Beirne (in Riley, et al.: 1971, 8.20) indicates that the Mayans had copper tanged axes. **7.** Extermination of mastodons occurred during the end of the last Ice Age, ca. 9000-5000 B.C., at the hands of big game hunters and the more temperate climate. **8.** Spinden (in Bernal: 1980, 114) regards the animals on Stela B as birds. **9.** Weaver (1972, 293) and Ekholm (1964) note similar lotus motifs, tiger thrones, phallic sculptures and sacred tree motifs in classic Mayan and Hindu-Buddhist civilizations. They also trace fresco techniques and wheeled toys to Han, China. Willey (1966, 21) indicates the presence of similar blowguns, pan-pipes, star-shaped maces, pottery house models, and pottery headrests. **10.** Davis (1979, 114). **11.** Willey (1965, 633) indicates that the Mayans had eclipse tables and could describe the synodical revolution of Venus. **12.** Von Hagen (1960, 29, 78, 90) indicates that the Mayans made trips of 2-3000 miles by slave-powered canoes up to 80 feet long and carrying 40 men. **13.** Von Hagen (1960, 87) indicates that merchants were regarded as a special class with their own rules of conduct, and they paid no tax. **14.** Adams (1986, 435) indicates that the population of the Maya may have reached 16 million in an area of 10,000 square miles. **15.** Heine-Geldern (1966, 292) suggests that merchants from India had vessels up to 160 feet long for use in their trans-Pacific crossings. These ships were three-masted and had more than six times the cargo capacity of the caravels used by Columbus. **16.** Willey (1966, 22) indicates that the Southeast Asian yam, which is found in South America, may or may not be of pre-Columbian origin. **17.** Carter (in Riley, et al.: 1971, 194-97) indicates that linguistic similarities and cultural characteristics indicate the pre-Columbian importation of chicken from Asia to the Americas. **18.** Jeffreys (in Riley, et al.: 1971) notes the pre-Spanish presence of corn in China and indicates that it may have been brought by Arabs. Corn was apparently widespread in Asia by the 14th century, leading other scholars to suggest that it was brought there by Indo-Chinese traders. **19.** Willey (1966, 22) indicates the possibility that the sweet potato was brought from America to Asia in pre-Columbian times. **20.** Reed (1966, 244). **21.** Von Hagen (1960, 206,210) reports no evidence of warfare among Mayan cultural centers abandoned between A.D. 900-1000. **22.** Reed (1966, 245). **23.** Von Hagen (1960, 105) and the Encyclopedia Britannica (1954/23, 883; and /14, 706) indicate that the issue of whether or not malaria was present or absent prior to the Spanish Conquest is unknown. **24.** Encyclopedia Britannica (1954/23, 883). **25.** Encyclopedia Britannica (1954/14, 706). **26.** Anton (1970, 44) cites an official Spanish report indicating that only seven Mayan Indians survived the plague in Copan during the Conquest. **27.** Von Hagen (1960) reports that human sacrifice became a major factor only in the Toltec-Mayan alliance at Mazapan and Chichen Itza from the 10th-15th centuries A.D. **28.** Coe (1984, 55) reports approximately two million living Mayans who speak several mutually unintelligible dialects. **29.** Von Hagen (1960, 201-5) indicates that De Landa's fires consumed many books which were known to contain purely historical records. This occurred in 1562, at the hands of De Landa's cohorts, Toral and Zumarraga (Westheim, et al.: 1972, 380).

Chapter 10

1. Fenollosa, Epochs of Chinese and Japanese Art, 1908. **2.** Davies (1979, 122). **3.** Kelly (in Riley, et al.: 1971, 60) reports the discovery of a Roman figurine head (ca. A.D. 200) in archaeological context at Calixtlahuaca, Mexico. **4.** Jennings (1978, 622) notes the possible presence of Chinese artifacts or inscriptions at Teotihuacan and at other sites. **5.** Gardner (ed.:1986, 17) indicates that Aegean or Roman amphorae were found 15 miles from Rio de Janeiro representing a vessel that may have been blown off course. **6.** Davies (1979, 69-70) indicates that an older Ecuadorian pottery style, San Pedro, has no parallel to Japanese ceramics, and there is an earlier type of ceramics in Colombia. **7.** According to Frost (A:35/1, 1982, 24-9), analysis of the Palos Verdes anchor stones found off the southern California coast indicates that they are of local manufacture from stones characteristic of Monterey Shale, which is common in the area. **8.** See for example, Hawley (1949), Snodgrass (1985) and Medley (1964). **9.** Norman (1976, Part II) and Freidel (1985, 5-30; also in Schele: 1986, 60) both indicate the use of the scroll motif to represent multiple concepts relating to spiritual forces. These follow the Author's 1974 publication of The Spirit Sign, which indicated that

spiritual essence was the common theme of Meso-American scroll motifs. The spiritual meaning behind Asian scroll motifs has been suggested by numerous authors. For example, Govinda (1974, 62) discusses how energy scrolls arise from the lotus blossom and produce the varja, or cosmic thunderbolt of Buddhist symbolism, which forms around the invisible, mythical Mount Meru at the center of the universe. Hempel (1983) indicates that flames arising from Buddhist symbols represent a sacred quality. Hung (1987, 276) identifies the scrolls arising from seated figures on a Han mirror as "wings," while Tubner (1973, 89) calls them "flying scarves." Snodgrass (1985, 301) indicates that the projecting mouth scrolls of a gander represent the fiery breath of the sun--regarding 19th-century sculptures from India. Pope (1971) gives a similar interpretation for the scrolls emanating from a gander's mouth on a Persian plate from the 19th century. **10.** According to Ch'en (1964, 15) hellenistic motifs were brought to Buddhism by way of Ionian Greeks living in northwestern India.

Chapter 11

1. Goldsmith (1929, 22) suggests that the stylized sacred tree motif was derived from Assyria. **2.** According to Ch'en (1964, 15), Scythians spread Chinese symbols towards Europe and India between 600 and 100 B.C.

Epilogue

1. Rowe (in Davies: 1979, 1) characterizes the theory of cultural diffusion as a "wave of the past," and he views its adherents as being "deluded." Morley (in Robicsek: 1972, 71) referred to a scholar who identified Oriental motifs on the Elephant Stela as a "scientific discard." Such personal attacks have no place in the realm of scientific investigation. **2.** Marble (1980, 23) and Fell (1983). According to Marble, Columbus is said to have been aware of African, French, Portuguese, and German voyages between Guinea and Venezuela prior to his own expedition. O'Gorman (1961, 40) regards the acceptance of Columbus as the discoverer of America as a false belief encouraged by historians. According to Deacon (1966, 2), Didorus Siculus in 100 B.C. reported that the Phoenicians had discovered a "Large, sweet, fertile land opposite to Africa... about 10,000 furlongs from the African Coast." Tell (1976, 214) indicates that a Roman Navy faced larger Celtic ships in 55 B.C. and that these vessels substantiated claims of Celtic settlements in New England during the 1st millennium B.C. According to a popular legend of the Middle Ages, Saint Brendan discovered lands across the Atlantic in the 6th century A.D. These were often indicated as Saint Brendan's Island on charts during the years preceding Spanish voyages to the New World (Morrison: 1942, 26). There were also legends about Portuguese voyages in the 8th century (Morrison, 1942, 80), and in 1535, there was an account of a Portuguese pilot who supposedly informed Columbus about virgin lands rich with gold across the Atlantic. Irving (in O'-Gorman: 1961, 28) attributed the "discovery" of America to Columbus because he was the first European of consequence to make the trip and because European migrations followed. He notes the prior voyages of the Norwegians, but claims they were of little importance because they "abandoned" the settlements. Humbolt (in O'Gorman: 1961) likewise regards the Norse voyages as accidental, or of little consequence. However, Chapman (1981, 69-85) has made a strong case for a continuous Norse presence in the New England area and further south. European maps of the early 16th century refer to "Norse Villa" and "Vinland"--indicating that Europeans were aware of Norse settlements in the New World. Deacon (1966, 80) reported Hernando Desoto's discovery of abandoned forts attributed to "fair-skinned" people living with the Indians, while Fingerhut (1984, 87) indicates that Columbus heard reports of black-skinned natives living on the islands, and a spear point sent back to Spain had the same proportion of gold, silver and copper as alloys produced in West Africa. Balboa also encountered black people near the Isthmus of Panama. Lundstrom (1966, 105) notes that the King of Portugal maintained that the lands across the Atlantic belonged to him--based on a claim of prior discovery. However, the Spanish monarchs prevailed upon the Spanish Pope Alexander VI to acknowledge their sovereignty based on the documentation of the voyage of Columbus. When Alexander VI issued the new Bull, Portugal threatened to go to war. A compromise agreement, the Treaty of Tordesillas, gave Portugal access to Brazil and acknowledged the Portuguese claim of prior discovery. 3. Duff (1936, 248) calls Columbus an "Immortal," suggesting that his tremendous achievement rendered the atrocities he committed to a level of unimportance.

4. Zinn (1980, 7) indicates that a history of Columbus by S.E. Morrison (1975) is a romantic story about a man Morrison admits committed genocide. Morrison (1942, 308) paints a glorious portrait of Columbus as the first voyager to the New World. Columbus believed he had discovered the Garden of Eden--due to the innocence of the natives (Wasserman: 1930, 166). Nevertheless, upon his own order, the Indians who revolted on Hispaniola had their noses and ears cut off and were pressed into slavery to mine gold (Wasserman: 1930, 181). According to Wasserman (1930, 148), Columbus imported blood hounds to hunt down reluctant Indian slaves. Zinn (1980, 1-11) indicates that Columbus was primarily interested in seeking gold in the New World. He had the hands cut off Indians who failed to produce their required quota so that many bled to death. De Las Casas (in Duff: 1957, 244) reports the Indian losses at 12 million on the continent and 3 million on Hispaniola. He further indicates that 30 islands in the neighborhood of Puerto Rico were entirely depopulated. 5. According to Robertson (1980, 25), most Americans believe that their nation is rich and mighty because of its "God-given" inspiration. Such a belief usually ignores the possibility that all nations are divinely inspired and simultaneously led by worldly self-interest.

BIBLIOGRAPHY

Adams, Richard E., ed. *Origins of Maya Civilization.* Albuquerque: University of New Mexico Press, 1977.

Asche, G., et. al. *Quest for America.* New York: Praeger, 1971.

Bernal, Ignacio. *The Olmec World.* Berkeley: University of California Press, 1969.

Casson, Lionel. *Ships and Seamanship in the Ancient World.* Princeton: University Press, 1971.

Casson, L., R. Claiborne, & J. Thorndike. *Mysteries of the Past.* New York: American Heritage, 1971.

Chapman, Paul H. *The Norse Discovery of America.* Atlanta: One Candle Press, 1981.

Covarrubias, Miguel. *The Eagle, The Jaguar, and The Serpent.* New York: Knopf, 1954.

Davies, Nigel. *Voyagers to the New World.* Albuquerque: University of New Mexico Press, 1979.

Fairservis, Walter Jr. *The Roots of Ancient India.* New York: MacMillan, 1971.

Fell, Barry. *Bronze Age America.* Boston: Little, Brown & Company, 1982.

Fingerhut, Eugene. *Who First Discovered America?* Claremont, CA: Regina Books, 1984.

Fong, Wen, Ed. *The Great Bronze Age of China.* New York: Alfred Knopf, 1980.

Govinda, Lama. *Foundations of Tibetan Mysticism.* New York: Samuel Weiser, 1974.

Groslier, Bernard. *Art of Indo-China.* New York: Crown Books, 1962.

Hau, Qian, C. Meyi, and R. Suicher. *Out of China's Earth.* New York: Henry Abrams, 1981.

Heyerdahl, Thor. *American Indians in the Pacific.* London: George Allen, 1952.

Early Men and the Ocean. London: George Allen, 1978.

Huntington, Susan. *The Art of Ancient India.* New York: Weatherhill, 1985.

Irons, Veronica. *Indian Mythology.* New York: Bedrick Books, 1967.

Jennings, Jessse. *Ancient Native Americans.* San Francisco: Freeman, 1978.

JiaJim, Zhu. *Treasures of the Forbidden City.* Hong Kong: Commercial Press, 1986.

Joraleman, Peter D. "Olmec Iconography," in *Studies in Pre- Columbian Art and Archeology, No. 7.* Dumbarton Oaks, Washington D.C., 1971.

Keightley, David, ed. *Origins of Chinese Civilization.* Berkeley: University of California Press, 1983.

Knobl, Kuno. *Tai Ki.* Boston: Little, Brown & Company, 1975.

Landstrom, Bjorn. *The Ship.* New York: Doubleday, 1961.

McGlone, W.R, and P.M. Leonard. *Ancient Celtic America.* Fresno, CA: Panorama West Books, 1986.

McGrail, Sean. *The Ship: Rafts, Boats & Ships.* London: National Maritime Museum, 1981.

Miller, Mary E. *The Art of Meso-America from the Olmec to the Aztec.* London: Thames & Hudson, 1986.

Norman, V. Garth. "Izapa: An Introduction," in *Papers of the New World Archeological Foundation.* Brigham Young University, Provo, Utah, 1982.

O'Gorman, Edmundo. *The Invention of America.* Bloomington: Indiana University Press, 1961.

Pal, Pratapaditya. *The Art of Tibet.* New York: The Asia Society, 1969.

Proskouriakoff, Tatiana. "Olmec and Maya Art: Problems of Their Stylistic Relation," in Benson, Elizabeth, ed., *Conference on the Olmec*. Washington, D.C.: Dumbarton Oaks, 1968.

Quirarte, Jacinto, "Izapan Style Art: A Study of Its Form and Meaning," in *Studies in Pre-Columbian Art and Archeology*. Washington, D.C.: Dumbarton Oaks, 1973.

Rawson, Jessica. *Ancient China*. New York: Harper & Row, 1980.

Reader's Digest. *The World's Last Mysteries*. Pleasantville, NY: 1982.

Riley, C., J. Kelley, C. Penniglan, and R. Rands, eds. *Men Across The Sea*. Austin: University of Texas Press, 1971.

Shao, Paul. *Asiatic Influences in Pre-Columbian Art*. Ames: Iowa State University Press, 1976.

Smith, G. Elliot. *Elephants and Ethnologists*. New York: Dutton, 1924.

Soustelle, Jacques. *The Olmecs*. New York: Doubleday, 1984.

Te-K'un, Cheng. *Archeology in China*. Toronto: University Press, 1963.

Temple, Robert. *The Genius of China*. New York: Simon and Schuster, 1986.

Torr, Cecil. *Ancient Ships*. Chicago: Argonauts Inc., 1964.

Toynbee, Arnold, ed. *Half The World*. New York: Hold, Reinhart, and Winston, 1973.

Von Hagen, Victor. *World of the Maya*. New York: Times Mirror, 1960.

Van Over, Raymond. *Chinese Mystics*. New York: Harper & Row, 1973.

Watson, William. *Early Civilization in China*. London: Thames & Hudson, 1966.

Wicke, Charles R. *The Olmec*. Tucson: Unviersity of Arizona Press, 1971.

Worcester, G. *Junks and Sampans of the Yangtze*. Annapolis: Naval Institute Press, 1971.

Yetts, Percival. *Symbolism in Chinese Art*. New York: The China Society, 1912.

Zimmer, Henrick. *Myths and Symbols in Indian Art and Civilization*. New York: Pantheon Books, 1946.

Zinn, Howard. *A People's History of The United States*. New York: Harper & Row, 1980.

List of Sources

KEY:AA/*Arts of Asia* – AAA/*Archives of Asian Art*
AP/*Asian Perspectives* ARCH/*Archaeology*
AR/*Artibus* – HO/*Horizon*
OA/*Oriental Art*   OCS/*Oriental Collector's*
OR/*Orientations*   NK/*Nederlandishe Kunst*

A: Asian Sources M: Meso-American Sources
P: Plate   NWC: Northwest Coast Indian

CHAPTER ONE
1. Honey (1922, 55) and Vasselot (1922a, 38.2).

CHAPTER TWO
2. Nilsson (1968, 112), Snellgrove (1978, 165), and Paddock (1966, 151). **3.** Takacs (1930, 244) and Burckhardt (1961, 10). **4.** Seler (1908, 69). **5.** A: d'Argenie (1973, 19); Plum Blossoms, Ltd., Hong Kong; Lowry (1973, 42); Newark Museum (1971); Davidson (1950, 19); Price (1983, 5); Hung (1987, 277); and Jickeng (1984, 143). M: Ferguson & Royce (1974, 55-7); Kircheberg (1956); Robicsek (1978, 175); Campbell (1974, 179); Pasztory (1978, 3); Bernal (1969, P-98); Randall (1985, 18); and Seler (1915). **6.** 1--Casal (1980, 18); 2 & 3--Chang (1968, 138); 4--AR (35/1, 1973, 146). **7.** Pevsner (1968, 2.B); Wood (1985, 261); Weng and Boda (1982, 148). **8.** Parrinder (1971, 2); Fairservis (1971, 17); Rawson (1980, 58); Fairservis (1971, 23); Zhongmin and Delahaye (1985, 83). **9.** Gryaznov (1969, 141); AP (7/1, 1963, 3); Siren (1929, P-20). **10.** Zong: Rawson (1980, 23). Pi: Smith (1979, 75). **11.** Grimal (1965).

CHAPTER THREE
12. 1--Te-K'un (1960, 11); 2--Watson (1966, 44) and Te-K'un (1960, 41); 3--Wenuri (1976, 74); 4--Watson (1979, 580); 5--Hansford (1968, 15); 6--Dore (1914, 171). **13.** Te-K'un (1960, 7). **14.** Te-K'un (1960, 35); Cauldron: Hau, et al. (1981, 25). **15.** Top: Barnard (1972, 11). Left: Campbell (1968, 16). Right: Pruden (1958, P-4). Bottom: Niblack (1889, VIII). **16.** Left: Te-K'un (1963, 153); Van Heusden (1952, 21). Right: Te-K'un (1963, 21). **17.** Covarrubias (1954, 15). **18.** De Young Museum (B60-J657). **19.** Te-K'un (1963, 153). **20.** Buerdeley (1966, 115). **21.** Campbell (1983, 324).

CHAPTER FOUR
22. 1--Xuegin (1985, 40); Smith (1979, 243); Watson (1979, 270); 2--Cotterell (1981); 3--Morant (1931, P-3); 4--Kim (1948, P-2); 5--Jenyns (1951, 37); 6--Laufer (1912, 189). **23.** Watson (1979) and Willetts (1965, 92). **24.** Xuegin (1985, 56); Jenyns (1951, 11). **25.** Cotterell (1981). **26.** Te-K'un (1963, 1). **27.** Toynbee (1973). **28.** Visser (1948, 157); Rawson (1980, 101). **29.** Shoten (1969, P-32). **30.** HO (1969, 62); Adolf (1948, 94). **31.** 1--Salmony (1963, 415); 2--Watson (1979, 588); 3--OCS (1976, 47); 4--Weng and Boda (1982, 154); 5--Watson (1951, 36); 6--Kuwayama (1983, 5b); 7--Watson (1979, 587). **32.** Kim (1948, 2); Jinhua (1985, 9). **33.** Visser (1948, 129). **34.** NK (12/6, 1927, P-1). **35.** 1--Watson (1961, 67); 2--ChiLu (1968, 118); 3--Kidder (1964, 3); 4--Randall (1985, 18); 5--Fong (1984, 9); 6--Newark Museum (1971, P-54); 7--Strzygowski (1930, 290).

CHAPTER FIVE
36. 1--Zimmerman (1923, 40); 2--Zimmerman (1923, 24); 3--AA (5/4, 1975, 78); 4--Covell (1981); 5--Carle (1940, 126). **37.** 1 & 2--McGrail (1981, 36-37); Ross (1916, 145); 3, 4, & 5--Worceter (1971, 10-11). **38.** Left: Xuegin (1985, 27); Right: Consten (1952, 6). **39.** Jaspers (1925). **40.** Inset: Cotterell (1975-76); Bodterson (1964); Cotterell (1975, 77). **41.** Solheim (1982, 4). **42.** 1--Dieter (1976, 6); 2--Dieter (1976, P-II); 3--Giteau (1976, 77). **43.** Peralta (1980). **44.** Gibson (1948, P-4); Temple (1986, 187). **45.**

Cohen (1973, 281); Bodterson (1964, 34); Loehr (1980, 82); Lundstrom (1961, 219); Sullivan (1965, 51); Smith (1979); Toynbee (1973, 42); Van Nouhuys (1926, 280). **46.** Author. **47.** Left: Frankfort (1948, 41); Center: Moscati (1965, 19); Right: AA (1951/V, 20). **48.** 2--Hay (1973); 3--Star (1974, 18). **49.** Worcester (1971, 336).

CHAPTER SIX
50. Los Angeles Co. Museum, Annual Report (18/23). **51.** Kempers (1959, 233). **52.** AA (3/28, 1975, 176). **53.** 1--Loewe (1979, 21); 3--Huntington (1985, 5.8); 2 & 4--Bandi (1969, 26). **54.** Left: Siren (1929, P-6); Center and Right: Covarrubias (1954, 47). **55.** Haida Villages: Keithan (1973, 11) and Halpin (1981, 12); Fishing Boats: Waterman and Coffin (1920, I); Swanton (1905, 17); and Keithan (1973, 104). **56.** Swanton (1905, XXI); Keithan (1973, 100); Swanton (1905, XXI); and Keithan (1973, 98). **57.** Pijan (1931, 391). **58.** Asia: 1--Rawson (1980, 95); 2--AR (3/28, 1975, 176); 3--Willetts (1965, 136); 4--With (1920, 26a); 5--Rawson (1980, X, 65). Northwest: 1--Stewart (1986, 91); 2--Campbell (1983, 335); 3--Inverarity (1967, 1c); 4--Stewart (1986, 115); 5--Pijan (1931, 374). **59.** Asia: 1--McBain (1984, 91); 2--OA (2/2, 1949, 63); 3--Rawson (1980, 117); 4--Rawson (1980, 50); 5--Rawson (1980, 80); 6--Covarrubias (1954, 22). Northwest: 1--Garfield and Forest (1948); 2--Keithan (1973, 122); 3--Keithan (1973, 122); 4--Keithan (1973, 122); 5--Stewart (1986, 102); 6--Stewart (1986, 114); 7--Campbell (1983, 331). **60.** McBain, (1984, 91); Keithan (1965, 146). **61.** Pijan (1931, 374); Coe and Diehl (1980, 494, p126, p258). **62.** Top: Covarrubias (1954, 18) and Campbell (1983, 320); Bottom: Inverarity (1967, 14). **63.** Top: Siren (1929, P-6A, B); Bottom: Stewart (1986, 112); NWC Scroll Eye: Inverarity (1967, 78).

CHAPTER SEVEN
64. Colossal head: Bernal (1969, P-10); Stone tools: Peterson (1959, 6); Coe and Diehl (1966, 233, 282); House: Paddock (1966, 39); La Venta site plan: Weaver (1981, 5); Ceramics: Gove (1984, 7-24); Warrior: Grove (1984, 40). **65.** Top: Grove (1984, 9); Center: Grove (1984, 33); Bottom: Grove (1984, 34). **66.** Left: Willey (1965, 7); Top: Lothrop (1961, 4); Center: Bernal (1969, P-68); Right: Willey (1965, 9); Cranial deformation: Coe and Diehl (1980). **67.** Willey (1966, 3.27). **68.** Covarrubias (1957, 29). **69.** Adams (1977, 20). **70.** Bernal (1969, 11) and Willey (1965, 19). **71.** Coe and Diehl (1966, 138-170); Sabloff (1981, 5.8-10); Wauchope (1965, 3); Koru: Barrow (1984, 44). **72.** Bernal (1969, 45, 58); Soustelle (1984). **73.** 1--Burland (1976, 44); 2--Schele (1986, P-32); 3--Soustelle (1984); 4--Coe and Diehl (1980, 494); 5--Westheim, et al. (1972, 17). **74.** Large Head: Bernal (1969, P-68); Top Row: Stewart (1986, 115); Pijan (1931, 374); Bernal (1969, P-68); Burland (1976, 44); Burland; Bottom row: Pasztory (1978, 34c); Soustelle (1984); Willey (1965, 9; Pasztory (1978, 34f); Schele (1986, P-32). **75.** Grove (1984, 8). **76.** Center: Coe and Diehl (1966, 315); Right: Bernal (1969, 139).

CHAPTER EIGHT
77. Bernal (1969, 48). **78.** Chinese: Harvard (1947, P-11); Republic (1969, 48); Parrinder (1971, 3); Laufer (1909, 305); Te-K'un (1960, VI); Dieng (1985, 7); Weyer (1965, 379); Honey (1922, 108). Tuxtla: Wicke (1971, 4). **79.** Wicke (1971, 4); Joraleman (1971, 26); Seler (1902, 454);

Knorozor (1963, 615); Spinden (1957); Norse: Gelling (1969, 26). **80.** Hezerdahl (1952, 295); Westheim, et al. (1970, 37); Seller (1908, 61); Carnegie (1969, 9); Paddock (1966, 188). **81.** Stone (1972, 66). **82.** Coe (1984, 57). **83.** Paddock (1966, 21). **84.** Coe (1984, 17); China: Hackmack (1973, 8). **85.** Bernal (1969, 4). **86.** Lothrup (1964, 16); Highwater (1983, 227); Bes: Gray (1964, 64). **87.** A1--Ridley (1978, 32); A2--OA (10/2, 1964, 110); A3--Zimmerman (1923, 21); A4--Campbell (1974, 76); A5--Laput (1912, 119); A6 & A12--Plum Blossoms, Ltd., Hong Kong; A7--Rawson (1980, 60); A8--Kempers (1959, 233); A9--Toynbee (1973, 193); A10--Vandier and Nicholas (1983, 61) and Karnow (1962, 116); A11--Tay (1983, 12); A12--Plum Blossoms, Ltd.; A13--Newark Museum (1971), or Rawson (1980, 101); A14--Agrawlaq (1965a, 35); M1 to 14--Norman (1976, 165). **88.** Vidder, Jennings, and Shook (1946, 141). **89.** Joraleman (1971, 26); Covarrubias (1964). **90.** China: Covarrubias (1954, 25); Laufer (1909, XI). Meso: Covarrubias (1954, 25); Emmerich (1963, 143). **91.** China: Te-K'un (1963, 34.20). Meso: Covarrubias (1954, 20); Stepped fret: Muser (1978, 147). **92.** Bernal (1969); Wauchope (1965, 2). **93.** Agrawla (1965a, 36); Pal (1972, 3); Dixon (1959, 6); Ferguson and Royce (1977, 12). **94.** Emmerich (1963, 89). **95.** Bernal (1969, 35). **96.** Emmerich (1963, 72).

CHAPTER NINE

97. Knorozov (1963, 534); Beirne (1971, 8.20); Knorozov (1963, 535); Thompson (1937, P-40) (last 2). **98.** Statue: With (1920, 150); Disk: Snodgrass (1985, 7). **99.** Disk: Coe (1984, 45); Statue: Shao (1976, 227); Adams (1971, 48) with reconstruction based on Darvas (Stela A after Maudslay and Catherwood). **100.** Groslier (1962, 105) and Kircheberg (1956, 571). **101.** Morley (1946, 70) and Kircheberg (1956, 570). **102.** Colonettes: Broslier (1962, 167) and Swaom (1966, 59); Corbeled Vault: Broslier (1962, 137); Atlanteans: Pelican History of Art/India (p95/6.5). **103.** Colonettes: Pijan, (1946, 738 & 721); Corbled Vault: Joyce (1920, 74) and Morley (1946, 34); Atlantean: Weaver (1981, 28A). **104.** Munsterberg (1924, 369); Adams (1977, 18). **105.** A1--Ghosh, 1954-27; A2--Knobl, 1975; A3--Ghosh, 1954-4. M1--Davies, 1979-11; M2--Von Winning, 1968-277; M3--Knobl (1975). **106.** 1--National Library, Paris (1973, 372); 2--Shamija (1971); 3--AA (4/2, 1974, 27; 4--Agrawala (1965a, 38); 5--Heine-Geldern (1966, 14); 6--Watson (1962, P-10); 7--Watson (1961, 23); 8--Watson (1962); 9--Balasub (1963, 22). **107.** 1--Stela B at Copan after Maudslay; Wauchope (1965, 2); 2--Coe (1967, 24); 3--Adams (1977, 21); 4--Wauchope (1965, 8); 5--Heine-Geldern (1966, 14); 6--Wauchope (1965, 13); 7--Heine-Geldern (1966, 14); 8--Hein-Geldern (1966, 14); 9--Chichen Itza. **108.** Rawson (1967, 197); Reed (1966, 267). **109.** Rhie (in AA, 15/1, 1985); Robicsek (1981, 50). **110.** Willey (1966, 3.73). **111.** Pijan (1946, 720); Robertson (1963, 73); Weaver (1972, P-30). **112.** A--Holt, (1967): M--Pijan (1946, 720); NW Indians--Stewart (1986, 104). **113.** Albrecht (1925, P-15). **114.** Vaillant (1962, P-62). **115.** A--Vandier-Nicholas (1963, 61); M--Fuente (1970). **116.** A--Lowry (1973, 42); Lowry (1973, 42); Te-K'un (1963, 153); Hartman (1969, P-39); Marchanson, Ltd., London; Campbell (1974, 76). M--Joyce (1920, 79); Robicsek (1978, 175); Fuente (1970); Robicsek (1978, 145); Proskouriakoff (1963, 31); Seler (1923, 699). **117.** Ferguson and Royce (1977, 55-7). **118.** A--Loewe (1979, 7); M--Westheim, et al. (1970, 122). **119.** A--Hartman (1969, 199); NK (12/9, 1928, 287); Parmentier (1927, 65); M--Robicsek (1978, 48); Campbell (1974, 130). **120.** Asia: NK (12/10, 1928, P-1); MacQuitty (1969, 44); Fairservis (1971, 12); Wagner (1959, 63); Ostasiatica Museum, Stockholm. Meso: Dockslader (1964, 82); Goldsmith (1929, 106); Ferguson and Royce (1977, 52-7); Robicsek (1972, 98). **121.** Ellis (1836, 295); Heyerdahl (1958, 169). **122.** Dore (1914, 134); Seler (1908, 2). **123.** AA (14/5, 1984, 52); Miller (1973, 24). **124.** With (1920, 123 & P-119); Willey (1965, 15); Ju-i Symbol: Medley (1964, 49). **125.** Sarraut (nd, 208); Robicsek (1978, 175).

CHAPTER TEN

126. Miller (1973, 270); Toscano (1970, 186, 2 & 3); Nicholson (1967, 24); Covarrubias (1957, P-31); Leonard (1967, 37); Miller (1973, 172); Coe (1962, P-32). **127.** 1--Agarawala (1979, 75); 2--Hobson (1929, 7); 3--Author's collection; 4--Visser (1948, 157); 5--Toynbee (1973); 6--Turner (1974, 355); 7--AA (5/6, 1975, 52); 8--Newark Museum (1971); 9--Froneck (1969, 11). **128.** 1--Nicholson (1967); 2--Coe (1984, 45); 3--Diego Rivera

Mural, Mexico, D.F.; 4--Larousse (1963); 5 & 6--Campbell (1974, 179); 7--Sejourne (1962, 38); 8--Nicholson (1967); 9--Benson (1967, 86). **129.** 1--AA (6/3, 1976, 11); 2--Nai (1983, 30); 3--Westheim, et al. (1972, 370). **130.** Sarraut (nd, 43); Pasztory (1978, 9). **131.** 1--Waterburg (1952, 23); 2--Hung (1987, 277); 3--Benson (1981, 7); 4--Norman (1976, 3.11). **132.** 1--Hay (1973); 2--Snodgrass (1985, 219); 3--Miller (1973, 362); 4--Nuttal (1975, 83). **133.** Raunig (1982, 186); Spinden (1975, 21). **134.** 1--Toynbee (1973, 57); 2--Vaillant (1935, 31) and Joyce (1920, 13); 3--Ishkustro (1956, 18); 4--OR (14/10, 1983); 5--Chinese Literature (4, 1987, i); 6--Lothrop (1964). **135.** 1--AAA (37, 1984, 25); 2--AA (5/4, 1975, 63); (3) Coe (1967, 68); 4--Shao (1976, 215). **136.** A & M--Covarrubias (1954, 12). **137.** Rawson (1980, 175); Seler (1960, 533). **138.** 1--Ions (1967, 51); 2--OCS (1976, 81); 3--OCS (1976, 47); 4--Siren (1929, 99); 5--Willetts (1965, 131); 6--British Museum (1988); 7--Munsterburg (1924, 397). **139.** 1--Bernal (1969, 23); 2--Kricheberg (1956, 344); 3--Seler (1960, 223); 4--Joyce (1920, 79); 5--Nicholson (1954, 11); 6--Seler (1960, 23); 7--Paddock (1966, 151). **140.** A--Pal (1983, 45); M--Miller (1973, 270). **141.** Hartman (1969, P-40); Palace Museum (1977, 7); Stierlin (1981, P-210). **142.** Pal (1969, P-39); Robicsek (1981, 112). **143.** 1--Salmony (in AAA, 1945, 37); 2--Kebudayaan (nd); 3--Shao (1976, 225); 4--Zhongmin and Delahaye (1985, i); 5--Hansford (1968, 8); 6--Kempers (1959, P-232); 7--Salmony (AR, 1954); 8--Unesco (1984, 40); 9--Lawton (1983, 78); 10--Gerosa (1985, 252). **144.** 1--Weaver (1972, P-30); 2--Seler (1915, P-48); 3--Robicsek (1978, 134); 4--Seler (1915); 5--Stela A, Copan, Honduras; 6--Thompson (1954, 2); 7--Seler (1908, 21); 8--Wien (1965, 32); 9--Anton (1970, 33); 10--Seler (1915, 154).

CHAPTER ELEVEN

145. 1--Schiering (1957, 6); 2--Frankfort (1955, 95); 3--Gimbutas (1974, 58); 4--Frankfort (1955, 4); 5--Moscati (1965, 79); 6--Porada (1962, 49); 7--Martha (1889, 165); 8-10--D' Alviella (1956, P-4 & 5). **146.** Frankfort (1955, 121). **147.** Higgins (1981, 163). **148.** 1--Higgins (1967, 207); 2--Mode (1973, 239); 3--Westendorf (1968); 4--Pijan (1932, 138); 5--Galanina (1970, 49); 6--Porada (1962, 86). **149.** Jettman (1964, 32); Borovka (1967, 35); **150.** Sundler (1929, 387).

COMPARATIVE CHRONOLOGIES

I

I/A-1. OA (30:2), 1984-1. 2. OA (27:3), 1981-236. 3. Rawson, 1980-31. 4. Visser, 1948-157. 5. Rawson, 1980-101. 6. AA (15:5), 1985-2. 7. Snellgrove, 1978-165. 8. Wiletts, 1965-131. 9. Siren, 1980-104. 10. Tubner, 1973-183/145. 11. Yetts, 1912-8. 12. Moscow Academy, 1960. I/M-1. Norman, 1976-10. 2. Emmerich, 1963-71. 3. Nicholson, 1967-15, and Norman, 1976-10. 4. Emmerich, 1963-87. 5. Larousse, 1963. 6. Miller, 1973-34. 7. Benson, 1967-86. 8. Ferguson, 1984-231. 9. Tablet of the Foliated Cross, Palenque. 10. Duran, 1972-334. 11. Pasztory, 1983-31. 12. Willey, 1965-47.

II

II/A-1. Tek'un, 1963-15. 2. Salmony, 1963-14.5. 3. Cryaznor, 1969-91. 4. Siren, 1929-119. 5. Pal, 1972-1. 6. Anand, 1957. 7. Pal, 1972-3 I. 8. Pal. 1972-3M. 9. Pal, 1972-3K. 10. Grosher, 1962-84. 11. Pal, 1972-3L. 12. Pal, 1972-3F. 13. Huntington, 1985-5.8. 14. Snodgrass, 1985-7. II/M-1. Bernal, 1969-71. 2. Bernal, 1969-146. 3. Emmerich, 1963-89. 4. Norman, 1976-3056. 5. Willey, 1966-3.85. 6. Norman, 1976-117a. 7. Norman, 1976-161. 8. Willey, 1966-3.85. 9. Willey 1966-3.85. 10. Robicsek, 1975-245. 11. Pijan, 1946-461. 12. Bernal, 1980-91. 13. Stierlin, 1964-124. 14. Seler, 1923-11; also Codex Nuttall. 15. Chase, 1981-25. 16. Chase, 1981-25. 17. Seler, 1904-161. 18. Aztec Calendar Stone, Museo Nacional, Mexico.

III

III/A-1. Smith, 1979-75. 2. Fogg Museum, Cambridge. 3. Laufer, 1912-145. 4. DeMorant, 1931-3. 5. Willetts, 1965-29. 6. Laufer, 1912-271. 7. Luce, 1970-414a. 8. Sri Lanka, 1979-14. 9. Zimmerman, 1923-38. 10. Sarraut, nd-127. III/M-1. Norman, 1976-3.10. 2. Coe, 1966-48. 3. Wauchope, 1965-244. 4. Weaver, 1981-210b. 5. Willey, 1966-3.896. 6. Siren, 1928-21. 7. Moser, 1973-44.

IV

IV/A-1. AR (1951, 5:20). 2. Visser, 1948-147. 3. Visser, 1948-157. 4. Ridley, 1974-49. 5. McCune, 1962-2. 6. Jinhuai, 1985-9. 7. Watson, 1962-103b. 8. Sullivan, 1976-131. 9. Sullivan, 1961-63. 10. Gong, 1984-9. 11. Society, 1560-264. 12. Hackmack, 1973-13.24. IV/M-1. Bernal, 1969-4. 2. Bernal, 1969-3. 3. Seler, 1915-7. 4. Franch, 1983-277. 5. Robicsek, 1972-86. 6. Thompson, 1954-57. 7. Dockslader, 1964-50. 8. Willey, 1965-60. 9. Seler, 1923-379. 10. Pasztory, 1983-213.

V

V/A-1. Sullivan, 1961-6. 2. Rawson, 1980-98. 3. Willetts, 1963. 4. Munsterburry, 1968-26. 5. Shotin, 1969-30. 6. Hau, 1981. 7. Visser, 1948-115. 8. Laufer, 1912-28. 9. Visser, 1948-223. 10. Reed, 1966-269. 11. Turner, 1974-238. 12. OR, 16:8, 1985-20. 13. Packer, 1985-66. 14. Newark, 1971-24. 15. Jickeng, 1984-143. V/M-1. Stone, 1972-66. 2. Stone Sculpture, Kaminaljuyu, Guatemala. 3. Pasztory, 1978-28. 4. Aveni, 1980. 5. Robicsek, 1978-132. 6. Shao, 1976-215. 7. Seller, 1915-187. 8. Spinden, 1975-34. 9. Smith, 1973-18. 10. Pasztory, 1983-54.

VI

VI/A-1. Visser, 1948-153. 2. OA, 2:2, 1949-63. 3. Covarrubias, 1954-15. 4. McCune, 1962-2, and Kim, 1948. 5. McCune, 1962-2, and Kim, 1948. 6. Snellgrove, 1978-99. 7. Boothalingam, 1969-9. 8. Snellgrove, 1978-213. 9. AA, 14:5, 1984-116. 10. Kebudayaan, NA. VI/M-1. Covarrubias, 1957-23. 2. Emmerich, 1963-72. 3. Abel, 1981-40. 4. Temple of Quetzalcoatl, Teotihuacan. 5. Adams, 1977-48. 6. Pasztory, 1978-9. 7. Codex Vaticanus, Spinden, 1975-262. 8. Covarrubias, 1954-18. 9. SeJoune, 1962-129.

VII

VII/A-1. Munsterburry, 1968-26. 2. OA, 2:11, 1949-21. 3. Wieger, 1965-383. 4. Carter, 1951-50. 5. Constern, 1952-246. 6. Constern, 1952-246. 7. Munsterberg, 1924-266. 8. Munsterberg, 1924-393. 9. Munsterberg, 1924-PL4. 10. Toynbee, 1973. 11. Plum Blossoms, Ltd. Hong Kong. VII/M-1. Norman, 1976-38. 2. Norman, 1976-38. 3. Hammond, 1982-4.13. 4. Davies, 1982-77. 5. Miller, 1986-64. 6. Lothrop, 1964. 7. Bushnell, 1965-107. 8. Seler, 1904-161. 9. Willey, 1985-17. 10. Pijan, 1946-181. 11. Sejourne, 1962-31. 12. Dockstader, 1973-112.

VIII

VIII/A-1. Silbergeld, 1982-9. 2. Visser, 1948-201. 3. Willetts, 1965-24. 4. Van Heusden, 1952. 5. Sullivan, 1961-27. 6. Chu-Lu, 1968-395. 7. AA, 5:1, 1975-48. 8. Watson, 1962-30. 9. Buddhas, 1980-121. 10. AAA (37, 1984, 25). 11. Kempers, 1959-10. 12. Kempers, 1980-92. VIII/M-1. Kidder, 1973-10d. 2. Kidder, 1973-10a. 3. Adams, 1977-10.76. 4. Hammond, 1982-4.13. 5. Stierlin, 1964-59. 6. Stierlin, 1964-59. 7. Knobl, 1975-4. 8. Robicsek, 1978-66. 9. Coe, 1967-68. 10. Thompson, 1954-20. 11. Stone, 1972-123. 12. Pasztory, 1983-296. 13. Spinden, 1957-78.

IX

IX/A-1. Stierlin, 1964-140. 2. Siren, 1928-28A. 3. Watson, 1962-37d. 4. VanHeusden, 1952-56. 5. Watson, 1962-27a. 6. Fong, 1980-96. 7. Kleykamp, 1923. 8. Tregear, 1980-72. 9. OCS, 1976-92. 10. Hay, 1973-122. 11. L'art du Champa, nd-27. 12. Smith, 1979-231. IX/M-1. Bernal, 1969-77. 2. Bernal, 1969, and Chicago Natural History Museum.

3. Seler, 1960/IV-148. 4. Stierlin, 1964-140. 5. Emmerich, 1963-125. 6. Covarrubias, 1957-104. 7. Adams, 1977-69. 8. Westheim, 1972-138. 9. Museo Nacional 1945-47.

X

X/A-1.Smith, 1979-75. 2. Shan-hsi, 1979. 3. OCS, 1976-81. 4. Jenyns, 1951-11. 5. Rawson, 1980-136. 6. Nai, 1983-30. 7. Siren, 1970-P130. 8. Loewe, 1979-P124. 9. Loewe, 1979-10. 10. Committee, 1973-102. 11. Visser, 1948-229. 12. Smithsonian, 12:5, 1986-34. 13. Bhoothalingam, 1969-17. 14. Backhafer, 1972. 15. Ions, 1967-51. 16. Reynolds, 1978-102. X/M-1. Emmerich, 1963-87. 2. Bernal, 1969-5. 3. Bernal, 1969-23. 4. Adams, 1971-103c. 5. Seler, 1915-37.5. 6. Miller, 1973-53 to 57. 7. Gallenkamp, 1985-49. 8. Pasztory, 1978-12. 9. Dockslader, 1964-82. 10. Coe, 1967. 11. Linne, 1956. 12. Pasztory, 1983-165. 13. Von-Winnig, 1968-413. 14. Seler, 1960/1-24. 15. Kircheberg, 1956-344. 16. Bernal, 1980-44. 17. Robicsek, 1978-105.

XI

XI/A-1. Kuwayama, 1983-22B. 2. AA, 7:5, 1977-27. 3. Field Museum, 1927-19. 4. Jinhuai, 1985-9. 5. Tregear, 1980-72. 6. VanDier-Nicolas, 1983-42. 7. OA, 30:1, 1984-5. 8. Munsterberry, 1924-424g. 9. Huntington, 1985-24. 10. Munsterberry, 1924-494. XI/M-1. Siren, 1928-21D. 2. Emmerich, 1963-71. 3. Emmerich, 1963-89. 4. Sejourne, 1966-30. 5. Nicholson, 1967-24. 6. Fuente, 1970. 7. Seler, 1908-4. 8. Knorozov, 1963-16. 9. Spinden, 1957-53. 10. Pasztory, 1983-260.

XII

XII/A-1. Hawly, 1949-4, and AAA, 1982:35-88. 2. Laufer, 1912-75. 3. Laufer, 1912-36. 4. Laufer, 1912-94. 5. Price, 1983-5. 5A. Salmony, 1963-16. 6. Hansford, 1968-61. 7. Tubner, 1973-89. 8. Beckert, 1984-12. 8A. Salmony, 1963-28. 9. Lee, 1982-211. 10. Waley, 1923-22. 11. Fillcozat, 1973-4. 12. Burton, 1921. 13. Herberts, 1962-230. XII/M-1. Norman, 1976-2.7f. 2. Bernal, 1969-98. 3. Norman, 1976-2.7c. 4. Willey, 1965-26. 5. Stone, 1972-123. 6. Graham, 1981-2. 7. Stierlin, 1964-73. 8. Robicsek, 1978-116. 9. Willey, 1965-18. 10. Campbell, 1974-142. 11. Eckholm, 1971-7. 12. Stierlin, 1981-210.

XIII

XIII/A-1. Watson, 1962-10a. 2. AAA, 1982 (35)-88. 3. OA, 25(3)1979-338.12. 4. Visser, 1948-59. 5. Davidson, 1950-19.3. 6. Salmony, 1963-18. 7. Watson, 1961-36. 8. Hao, 1981-61. 9. Hau, 1981-58. 10. AR, 47:3, 1986-270. 11. Salmony, 1963-28. 12. Siren, 1930-105B. 13. Kidder, 1985-128. 14. NK, 16:10, 1932-312. 15. Roberts, 1979. 16. OA, 12:1, 1975-77.2. XIII/M-1. Stone, 1972-66. 2. Norman, 1976B-3.1. 3. Bernal, 1969-299.5. 4. Norman, 1976-42. 5. Bernal 1969-27. 6. Pasztory, 1978-3. 7. Covarrubias, 1957-35. 8. Seler, 1908-679.21. 9. Robicsek, 1981-89. 10. Robicsek, 1978-137. 11. Coggins, 1984-8. 12. ARCH, 9:1, 1959-38.5. 13. Ekholm, 1971-501.9.

TABLES

TABLE TWO

A/I. Rawson (1980-101). II. Siren (1929-119). III. Willetts (1965-29). IV. Kidder (1964-3) and Hung (1987-277). V. Han (1981). VI. OA (2:2, 1949-63). VII. Carter (1951-50). VIII. Van Heusden (1952). IX. Fong (1980-96). X. Loewe (1979-10 and 24). XI. AA (7:5, 1977-27). XII. Price (1983-5). XIII. OA (25:3, 1979-338, 12). M/I. Norman (1976-10)/Nicholson (1967-15). II. Bernal (1969-71). III. Norman (1976-3.10). IV. Bernal (1969-5). V. Stone (1972-66). VI. Emmerich (1963-72). VII. Norman (1976-165). VIII. Kidder (1973-10d). IX. Bernal (1969-77). X. Bernal (1969-5). XI. Siren (1928-21D). XII. Bernal (1969-98). XIII. Norman (1976B-3.1).

MAPS

MAP-1 Neolithic sites (Flon, 1986-261); Writing sites (Keightley, 1983-381). **MAP-2** Toynbee, 1973-56, and Cheng 1963. **MAP-3** Toynbee, 1973-56, Hansford 1968-74, and Cheng 1963. **MAP-4** Drum distribution: Flon, 1985-291. **MAP-5** Gunnar Thompson, 1988. **MAP-6** Grove, 1984-1. **MAP-7** Location of Izapan archeological sites: Norman, 1976-1.1. Motagua jade source: Abel, 1981-42. **MAP-8** Archeological sites: Wauchope, 1965(2)-277, 379; Willey, 1966-3.10; and Meyer, 1970.

INDEX

Author's Sketch

photograph by Karri Simmons

The author is a brilliant scientist who has published innovative works on economics, American government, and anthropology. He is also an accomplished artist with a U.S. patent in ceramics. His numerous multi-media creations in stained glass, graphics, and ceramic sculpture have brought him public acclaim for his broad artistic talents. A Phi Beta Kappa, *magna cum laude* graduate of the University of Illinois, he has taught anthropology and rehabilitation at several universities. His two master's degrees, and a Ph.D., were earned at the University of Wisconsin--Madison during the turbulent years from 1968 to 1979.

Gunnar's first book on the subject of ancient Meso-American scroll symbols, *The Spirit Sign*, was published in 1974. He followed this with two novels dealing with contemporary society and history. *The Dreamstone* is a romance that takes place during the turbulent 1960's, when American colleges were the scene of a patriotic student revival. *Leonardo's Bed* features romance and espionage--as desperate men fight for control of Leonardo Da Vinci's ultra-secret invention: the Creativity Machine.

Nu Sun Institute

The Institute is a non-profit organization with the mission of providing educational programs, conducting research, and encouraging public participation in the growth of civilization. Civilization is threatened by war, famine, ignorance, and disease. Therefore, the Institute is dedicated to helping people overcome these impediments to the progress of humanity. In order to further this effort, the Institute seeks to build bridges of understanding among the world's people.

Future projects of the Institute include the establishment of a museum of ocean voyagers, a Pacific Peace Studies Center, and a quarterly journal. There will also be a Peace Voyage to commemorate the journey of Nu Sun across the Pacific. It will involve an expedition of Asian sailing vessels from Indo-China to Japan, Siberia, Canada, the United States, Mexico, El Salvador, Guatemala, Nicaragua, and back to China via Polynesia.

The policies of nations and the views of their people are enslaved by outdated ideologies, while even science struggles in an aura of dogma that continues to hide the truth. Much work lies ahead if we are to emerge from the darkness of ignorance to achieve the next level of the growth of civilization. Your support of this endeavor is a contribution to the positive future of our planet.

THANK YOU!

For further information, write the author:
4974 North Fresno Street, Suite 136
Fresno, California 93726